# FRENCH
# CHEESES

DORLING KINDERSLEY

# FRENCH CHEESES

Foreword by **Joël Robuchon**

Written by
**Kazuko Masui and Tomoko Yamada**

Photography **Yohei Maruyama**

Consultant **Randolph Hodgson**

**DORLING KINDERSLEY**
London • New York • Stuttgart • Moscow

A DORLING KINDERSLEY BOOK

Produced for Dorling Kindersley by PAGE*One*,
Cairn House, Elgiva Lane, Chesham, Buckinghamshire HP5 2JD
PROJECT DIRECTORS Bob Gordon, Helen Parker
EDITOR Anderley Moore

SENIOR MANAGING EDITOR Krystyna Mayer
SENIOR MANAGING ART EDITOR Lynne Brown
PRODUCTION CONTROLLER Meryl Silbert

Visit us on the World Wide Web at http://www.dk.com

First published in Great Britain in 1996
by Dorling Kindersley Limited
9 Henrietta Street, London WC2E 8PS

A CIP catalogue record for this book
is available from the British Library

ISBN 0-7513-0346-1

Printed and bound in Singapore

# Contents

Foreword  6

How to use this book  8

# Foreword

At last – and what a pleasure for me to say so!

Because among all the cheese books published to date – including that admirable work by Pierre Androuët – none as far as I know is based on so many valuable photographs for the identification and choice of a cheese ripened to perfection.

This book is for people who care for the good things in life, for amateurs with a love of cheese and serious gourmets alike. It takes you on a journey through the many regions of France, teaching you all you ought to know about cheese, and helping you in your choice. Expert knowledge is the key to an appreciation of pure and authentic flavours. Here is a reliable handbook for those who wish to share those flavours with their friends, and a clear and easy-to-follow initiation into the secrets of cheesemaking. Connoisseurs may read it with interest and pleasure. Amateurs will give it pride of place among their books and profit whenever they consult it.

Writing this preface fills me with a sense of duty, so that others may share what I know. Yes, I love cheese! It's a marvellous product, inscribed in that great trinity of the table, which it forms with bread and wine.

Cheese is part of what we have been eating from the beginning of time. A national French food for as long as people recall, it reflects nature as much as their own history. A concentrate of that life-giving liquid, namely milk, it allows us to conserve its many qualities. The extent of our range of cheese, remarked on already by

**Cheeses from every region**
*The 22 different regions of France produce more than 500 cheeses from ewe, goat, and cow's milk.*

the Roman naturalist Pliny the Elder, mirrors the diversity of our land as well as the art of dairymen and women and of social and economic developments over the ages. The example of monastic cheesemakers or that of cheese such as *tommes* or *reblochons* given in lieu of tax demonstrate the point.

To conclude then, what could be more satisfactory than to know for oneself which cheese to choose in preference to another? It's an informed choice, which shows understanding and results in joy.

JOËL ROBUCHON

# How to use this book

This book is the ideal quick-reference guide to selecting and identifying French cheeses at home, in your local cheese shop, or travelling in France. More than 350 cheeses are organized alphabetically. Similar cheeses of the same family or type are grouped. Details are given on where the cheeses are made, methods of production, appearance, smell, and taste. Special feature boxes that appear throughout the book give useful background information.

At the end of the book, useful terms are explained in a concise glossary, which is followed by a list of French shops and markets that specialize in cheese. The book concludes with a comprehensive index that also indicates where each cheese in the book was purchased.

**EXPLANATION OF TERMS USED**

**AOC** stands for Appellation d'Origine Contrôlée, which is a government body that controls the quality and production of important cheeses. Turn to p. 77 for a full explanation of AOC.

***Fermier***, ***artisanal***, ***coopérative***, and ***industriel*** refer to the method of production. Turn to p. 22 for a full explanation of these terms.

**Affinage** is a French word that means both the ripening and curing of a cheese.

**Pâte** is a French word that refers to all that is within the rind or crust of a cheese.

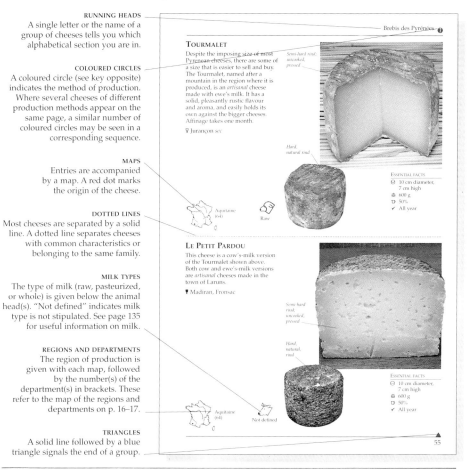

RUNNING HEADS
A single letter or the name of a group of cheeses tells you which alphabetical section you are in.

COLOURED CIRCLES
A coloured circle (see key opposite) indicates the method of production. Where several cheeses of different production methods appear on the same page, a similar number of coloured circles may be seen in a corresponding sequence.

MAPS
Entries are accompanied by a map. A red dot marks the origin of the cheese.

DOTTED LINES
Most cheeses are separated by a solid line. A dotted line separates cheeses with common characteristics or belonging to the same family.

MILK TYPES
The type of milk (raw, pasteurized, or whole) is given below the animal head(s). "Not defined" indicates milk type is not stipulated. See page 135 for useful information on milk.

REGIONS AND DEPARTMENTS
The region of production is given with each map, followed by the number(s) of the department(s) in brackets. These refer to the map of the regions and departments on p. 16–17.

TRIANGLES
A solid line followed by a blue triangle signals the end of a group.

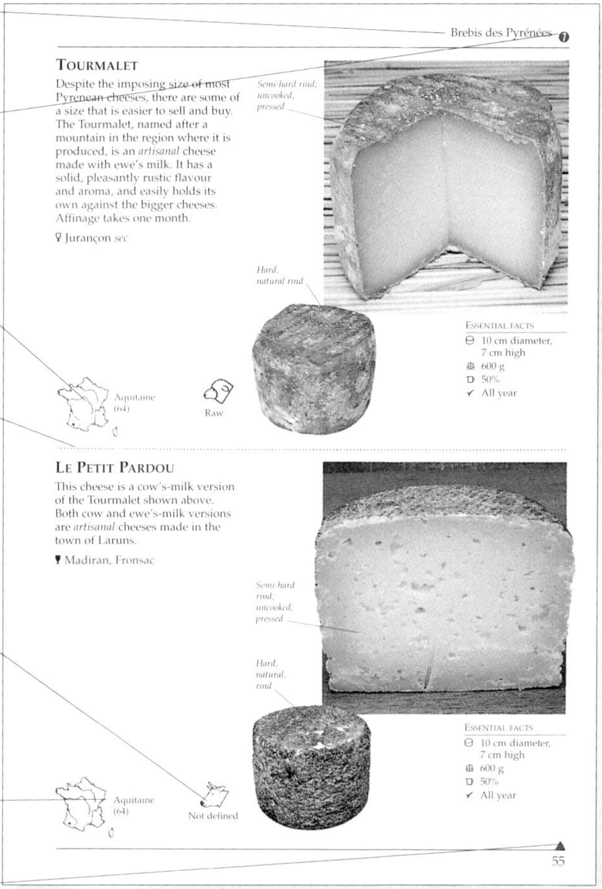
Brebis des Pyrénées

TOURMALET

Despite the imposing size of most Pyrenean cheeses, there are some of a size that is easier to sell and buy. The Tourmalet, named after a mountain in the region where it is produced, is an *artisanal* cheese made with ewe's milk. It has a solid, pleasantly rustic flavour and aroma, and easily holds its own against the bigger cheeses. Affinage takes one month.

Jurançon *sec*

Semi-hard rind; uncooked, pressed

Hard, natural rind

Aquitaine (64)

Raw

ESSENTIAL FACTS
10 cm diameter, 7 cm high
600 g
50%
All year

LE PETIT PARDOU

This cheese is a cow's-milk version of the Tourmalet shown above. Both cow and ewe's-milk versions are *artisanal* cheeses made in the town of Laruns.

Madiran, Fronsac

Semi-hard rind; uncooked, pressed

Hard, natural, rind

Aquitaine (64)

Not defined

ESSENTIAL FACTS
10 cm diameter, 7 cm high
600 g
50%
All year

55

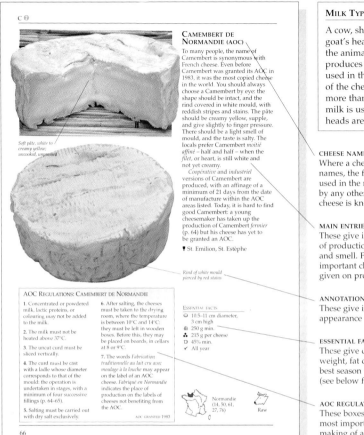

c ⓶

CAMEMBERT DE
NORMANDIE (AOC)
To many people, the name of
Camembert is synonymous with
French cheese. Even before
Camembert was granted its AOC in
1983, it was the most copied cheese
in the world. You should always
choose a Camembert by eye: the
shape should be intact, and the
rind covered in white mould, with
reddish stripes and stains. The pâte
should be creamy yellow, supple,
and give slightly to finger pressure.
There should be a light smell of
mould, and the taste is salty. The
locals prefer Camembert *moitié
affiné* – half and half – when the
*filet*, or heart, is still white and
not yet creamy.
Coopérative and industriel
versions of Camembert are
produced, with an affinage of a
minimum of 21 days from the date
of manufacture within the AOC
areas listed. Today, it is hard to find
good Camembert: a young
cheesemaker has taken up the
production of Camembert *fermier*
(p. 64) but his cheese has yet to
be granted an AOC.

Soft pâte, white to
creamy yellow;
uncooked, unpressed

❦ St. Emilion, St. Estèphe

Rind of white mould
pierced by red stains

AOC REGULATIONS: CAMEMBERT DE NORMANDIE

1. Concentrated or powdered
milk, lactic proteins, or
colouring may not be added
to the milk.

2. The milk must not be
heated above 37°C.

3. The uncut curd must be
sliced vertically.

4. The curd must be cast
with a ladle whose diameter
corresponds to that of the
mould: the operation is
undertaken in stages, with a
minimum of four successive
fillings (p. 64–65).

5. Salting must be carried out
with dry salt exclusively.

6. After salting, the cheeses
must be taken to the drying
room, where the temperature
is between 10°C and 14°C:
they must be left in wooden
boxes. Before this, they may
be placed on boards, in cellars
at 8 or 9°C.

7. The words *Fabrication
traditionnelle au lait cru avec
moulage à la louche* may appear
on the label of an AOC
cheese. *Fabriqué en Normandie*
indicates the place of
production on the labels of
cheeses not benefiting from
the AOC.

AOC GRANTED 1983

ESSENTIAL FACTS
⊖ 10.5–11 cm diameter,
   3 cm high
⚖ 250 g min.
∴ 215 g per cheese
◻ 45% min.
✓ All year

Normandie
(14, 50, 61,
27, 76)
Raw

66

---

MILK TYPE SYMBOLS

A cow, sheep, or
goat's head depicts
the animal that
produces the milk
used in the production
of the cheese. Where
more than one type of
milk is used, several
heads are shown.

CHEESE NAMES
Where a cheese is given two or more
names, the first is the local name
used in the region of origin, followed
by any other names by which the
cheese is known.

MAIN ENTRIES
These give information on place
of production, appearance, flavour,
and smell. For some AOC or more
important cheeses, details are also
given on production methods.

ANNOTATIONS
These give information on
appearance of each cheese.

ESSENTIAL FACTS
These give dimensions, shape,
weight, fat content, dry matter, and
best season to buy and eat a cheese
(see below for key to symbols).

AOC REGULATIONS BOXES
These boxes list some of the
most important guidelines in the
making of a cheese as outlined
by the AOC (p. 77).

---

ESSENTIAL FACTS SYMBOLS
⊖ Shape
⚖ Weight
∴ Dry matter – the residue after
   all the water in the cheese has
   been eliminated.
◻ Fat content – the amount of
   fat contained in the dry matter.
   "Not defined" indicates that
   the fat content is not stipulated.
✓ Season indicates when the
   cheese is usually eaten.

DRINKS SYMBOLS
Ⅱ Beer or cider
⵿ Champagne
⊔ Coffee
❦ Red wine
⵿ White, or *rosé* wine
◻ Spirits (e.g. *marc*)

---

KEY TO COLOURED CIRCLES IN RUNNING HEADS

The coloured circles in the running heads give at-a-glance information
on the methods of production used.

① Fresh, rindless cheese that is shaped and kneaded and has no affinage;
   e.g. *fromage frais* (fresh cheeses), p. 143–147

② Uncooked, unpressed, soft cheese with a white mould, e.g. Camembert, p. 66

③ Uncooked, unpressed, soft cheese with a washed rind, e.g. Munster, p. 158

④ Uncooked, unpressed, soft cheese with a natural mould sometimes covered in
   ashes, e.g. *chèvre* (goat's cheeses), p. 78–111

⑤ Uncooked, unpressed, soft cheese with veins of blue mould,
   e.g. *bleu* (blue cheeses), p. 29–35

⑦ Uncooked, pressed, semi-hard cheese, with a natural mould,
   e.g. Saint-Nectaire, p. 184

⑧ Uncooked, pressed, semi-hard cheese with a washed, rubbed, and waxed
   rind, e.g. monastery cheeses such as Port-du-Salut, p. 173

⑨ Cooked, pressed, hard cheese, e.g. Beaufort, p. 26

⑩ Cheese started with whey, e.g. Brocciu, p. 116

⑫ Product based on cheese, e.g. *fromage fort*, p. 134–136

# The origins of cheese

*"Rest with me on green foliage: we have ripe fruit,*
*soft chestnuts, and plenty of fresh cheese."* VIRGIL, 42 BC

CHEESE IS ONE OF the most ancient forms of manufactured food. The first real evidence of cheese is in ancient Sumerian writings from around 3000 BC, which refer to around 20 soft cheeses. Remains of cheesemaking equipment discovered in Europe and Egypt also appear to date back to around 3000 BC. However, we can only guess at when the craft of cheesemaking actually started. The most likely theory is that in around 10,000 BC, when sheep and goats were domesticated, early herdspeople began to take

#### Cow's-milk cheeses
*Since their domestication thousands of years ago, cattle have been bred selectively for the quantity and quality of milk they produce for cheesemaking.*

advantage of the fact that sour milk naturally separates into curds and whey. If drained off, shaped, and dried, the curds provided them with a simple and nourishing food. Cow's-milk cheeses came two or three thousand years after the sheep and goat's-milk cheeses as cattle were not domesticated until considerably later.

#### Cheese in ancient Greece and Rome
References to cheese and cheesemaking are dotted through ancient literature, including the Old Testament. Homer's *Odyssey* tells how Ulysses and his men hide in the Cyclops' cavern, while the one-eyed giant milks his ewes and goats, then curdles half the milk, drains the curds, and sets them aside in wicker baskets.

## Roman cheeses

The Romans enjoyed eating cheese both raw and cooked in little cakes called *glycinas* made from sweet white wine and olive oil. In a treatise on farming written in AD 60–65, Roman agricultural writer Columella tells how cheeses were made from fresh milk, which was curdled by the addition of *coagulum* – rennet extracted from the fourth stomach of a lamb or kid.

The curds were pressed to expel the whey, and then sprinkled with salt and left to harden in a shady place. Columella explains that, apart from enhancing the flavour, the salt helped to dry and preserve the cheese, and so the process of salting and hardening was repeated. The ripe cheeses were washed, dried, and packed for shipping, perhaps to an army depot, since cheese was included in a legionnaire's daily ration. Caesar himself is said to have eaten a blue cheese at Saint-Affrique, just to the west of Roquefort, where one of the world's most celebrated blue cheeses is still produced today.

**The *fromager***
*The makers and sellers of cheese are known in France as* fromagers. *Many of these craftspeople still make and ripen cheeses in family businesses following traditional techniques passed down the generations.*

## Cheese and language

The vast network of Roman roads set up communications that influenced language. The Latin word for cheese *caseus* became Italian *cacio,* German *Käse* and English *cheese,* as well as Spanish *queso* and *queijo* in Portuguese. The Italian *formaggio* and French *fromage* also derive from Latin, although the root of these words is in the Greek *formos* – the Cyclops' wicker basket.

## After the Romans

Soon after the collapse of the Roman Empire, Barbarian invaders overran much of Europe. Subsequent invasions by the Normans, Mongols, and Saracens, followed by successive outbreaks of the bubonic plague, devastated the continent. The ancient cheesemaking recipes and techniques, developed over thousands of years, were gradually forgotten, surviving only in the mountains and in remote monasteries. It was there that some of the oldest traditional cheesemaking methods were preserved for us to appreciate today.

**Ancient affinage**
*Many of the techniques for ripening cheese date back thousands of years. This process, known as* affinage, *hardens the cheese so that it keeps longer.*

# Cheese, wine, and bread

*"Cheese is probably the best of all foods,
as wine is the best of all beverages."* PATIENCE GRAY, 1957

IN FRANCE, cheese and wine have been considered natural allies for as long as people can remember. This view remains valid today, but we must not forget bread, which cements the union. Indeed, there can be few greater pleasures in life than a good, ripe *fermier* cheese, matched with a glass of quality wine and a chunk of freshly baked bread. The great advantage of this union is that cheese, wine, and bread are all foods that can be enjoyed in their "raw" state, with little or no preparation, making them an ideal choice for quick snacks or picnics. It is no coincidence, therefore, that generations of French farmworkers have relied on local cheeses, wines, and bread to fortify them while they work in the fields.

**Wine with cheese**
*The best wine to enjoy
with cheese is one that
you like. By tasting a
range of combinations,
you can develop your
own preferences.*

### The "Holy Trinity" of the table
Because of their close association, cheese, wine, and bread have occasionally been called the Holy Trinity of the table, an expression that may have been coined by the French humanist François Rabelais, whose writings attest to a great liking for food. Born at Chinon in around 1494, he would, of course, have tasted at least

**Crusty French bread**
*This long crusty baguette is traditionally eaten
fresh from the bakery. With a hunk of cheese and
a good wine it makes a simple, hearty meal.*

some of the outstanding goat's-milk cheeses Touraine is still famous for today.

Rabelais was a Roman Catholic monk for much of his life and was thus familiar with the concept of the Holy Trinity – inseparable God the Father, Jesus Christ the son, and the Holy Spirit – yet even he admitted that some cheeses are better served with fruit, than bread: "There is no match you could compare to Master Cheese and Mistress Pear".

### The action of yeasts and bacteria
Although bread, cheese, and wine are produced from different materials – bread is made from grain, wine from grapes, and cheese from milk – they each depend on yeasts and bacteria for their development. Without the changes brought about by fermentation, bread doughs would not rise, wines would be devoid of alcohol, and cheeses would simply not taste like cheese. In addition, it is the action of the fermentation that makes all of these products keep.

Just as the flavour, body, and bouquet of a wine depend on the grape variety, production techniques, and the technique and length of ageing, so the taste, texture, flavour, and aroma of cheeses depend on the milk from which they are produced – cow, goat, ewe, or mixed milks – and the methods used to make and ripen them.

### Accompanying breads
The combination of foods is a matter of harmony and contrasts, be it in looks, textures, temperatures, flavours, or smells, all of which are subject to

personal likes and dislikes. A simple rule of thumb might be that the more delicate the cheese, the whiter and less salted ought to be the bread to go with it, while spiced breads, which are often made with sour milk and thus already contain a dairy flavour, are most enjoyable with a powerful blue cheese.

### Which wine to choose

Although much advice is given on which wines should be selected to accompany a particular food or dish, there are no hard and fast rules. The best selections are almost always based on individual tastes because different people naturally prefer different combinations. The only way to know and develop your own preferences is to sample as many wines with as wide a variety of foods as you can.

Compared with a dish composed of a number of ingredients, cheese is a unique product that may be matched relatively easily with a wine. Matches are usually made in terms of texture and taste rather than smell, and a particular wine is often selected to accompany a particular cheese on the basis of similarities, contrasts, or complementary characteristics.

A smooth, fatty cheese may go very well with a similarly smooth, slightly oily wine, while a cheese with high acidity often contrasts very well with a sweet, alcoholic wine. Very salty cheeses may be complemented by a wine with good acidity. It is worth bearing in mind that, as a general rule, the longer a cheese is left to ripen the more it will dominate and "attack" the flavour of a wine.

Many people erroneously believe that cheese should be eaten exclusively with red wine. One of the principal reasons for this may be that cheeses are usually served at the end of a meal, when it is difficult to return to a dry white wine after a red, especially if the red is full-bodied. It is, however, true to say that white wines go better with many cheeses than reds and it is well worth sampling a few combinations for the experience.

Many of the wines recommended in this book by Robert and Isabelle Vifian come from the same region as the cheese with which they are matched. Their choice is often based on the traditional combinations of wine and cheese favoured by the local people.

Wine is not the only drink that goes well with cheese, however. In areas such as Normandie where little or no wine is produced, the cheeses are often better matched with a good local beer or cider, or sometimes even coffee. With cheeses that have been cured in *eau-de-vie* it is worth trying a good *marc*.

It is important to remember that the wine suggestions in this book are no more than pointers – it is individual taste and pleasure that count most of all.

**An alternative to meat**
*Cheese is a valuable source of protein and an appetizing alternative to meat as a main meal served with potatoes, fresh green salad, and a good wine.*

# French cheeses today

*"How can anyone be expected to govern a country with 325 cheeses?"* GENERAL CHARLES DE GAULLE

SINCE CHARLES DE GAULLE made his famous statement over 30 years ago, the number of cheeses produced in France has, according to recent estimates, increased to around 500 – a count that could be higher still if we include local, homemade cheeses that are unlikely to be found outside their region of production. We might deduce from these figures alone that French cheesemaking is prospering, an impression confirmed by official statistics as well as the wide range of cheeses on offer in many shops, restaurants, and supermarkets.

**A wide variety**
*The increased demand for a wider variety of cheeses has led to the mass-production of cheeses such as Camembert, which is now available worldwide.*

## Changing attitudes

A growing preference for vegetarian foods and a modern tendency for people to browse during the day rather than sit down to cooked meals, both favour cheese. Little could be easier, tastier, or more nourishing than a light meal of a few good pieces of cheese, with bread, salad, and fresh fruit on the side. No doubt we shall continue to see cheeses being offered at the end of a formal lunch or dinner. However, more and more people accept that unless we plan our menus in order to leave room for cheese, only the heartiest of appetites can do them justice.

## The effect of the supermarket

One of the greatest changes to the sale and production of French cheeses has been the increase in numbers of supermarkets. Even in traditionally rural areas of France, supermarkets are gradually replacing the village shops that used to sell a wide variety of household goods, food, and drink. Despite constant criticism by people who have forgotten the frustrations of not finding what they want in the village shop, supermarkets have brought down prices and offer a wider variety of fresher produce. Cheeses, however, pose a problem for supermarkets as most of them require expert care if they are to be allowed to reach maturity when their textures and flavours are at their peak. While the village grocer might have had the knowledge and patience to mature some Camembert or Brie, he also took the risk of being left with some rather smelly, old cheeses that no one would buy. Supermarkets, which rely on a quick turnover and are best at selling large quantities of uniform goods, cannot afford to take this risk and prefer to stock mainly *industriel* (factory), rather than *artisanal* (artisan) or *fermier* (farmhouse) cheeses.

## Specialist cheese shops

It is at the specialist cheesemonger – be it in a small market town or a great city – where the best cheeses can be bought. Just like people with a passion for good wines, lovers of cheese have become both better informed and more demanding in their choice. What they are looking for is character and flavour, the attributes given to a cheese by the care and attention of the artisan cheesemaker using traditional techniques rather than by the technician applying science in a factory.

The traditional cheesemaker is backed up by the careful husbandry of the farmer producing the finest milk. However, it is not only the traditional cheeses that are proving so popular. New cheeses, too, are being developed and made by hand, in limited numbers, on small farms in many areas of France.

### Into the future

Over the last 50 years, French cheese-making has been subject to a number of European regulations that are too often based on the methodology of the factory and do not take account of the advantages of the farm. They tend to be drawn up by scientists and, as a result, are unsympathetic to the needs of France's many *artisanal* and *fermier* cheesemakers,

several of whom have been producing traditional cheeses for generations. Unless people discover for themselves the superiority of a good, handmade, *fermier* cheese over one that has been mass-produced in a factory they will never understand why it is so important – and worthwhile – to protect and promote small-scale cheesemaking.

Ultimately, the future of France's many traditional cheeses depends on people being aware of what is available, knowing what to select or buy in a shop or a restaurant, and asking for it if is not already on display. This book will provide you with all the information you need to locate them.

### Cheese markets
*Some of the best regional* fermier *and* artisanal *cheeses can be found in cheese markets, where local cheesemakers often have their own stalls.*

# Map of France

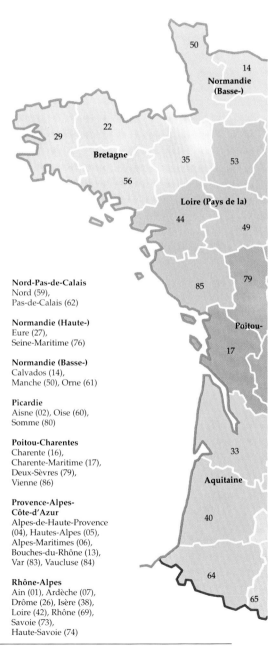

T HIS MAP shows the administrative regions (*régions*) of France, each of which is made up of a number of standard-sized departments (*départements*). In total there are 96 departments and 22 regions, all of which are listed below. To find out where a cheese is produced, first look up the minimap that accompanies the entry in the book and make a note of the name of the region and the numbers of the departments given in the text. The red spot shows you roughly where to look on the map. The list below gives the names of the departments, many of which are named after rivers.

**Alsace**
Bas-Rhin (67),
Haut-Rhin (68)

**Aquitaine**
Dordogne (24),
Gironde (33) Landes (40),
Lot-et-Garonne (47),
Pyrénées-Atlantiques (64)

**Auvergne**
Allier (03), Cantal (15),
Haute-Loire (43),
Puy-de-Dôme (63)

**Bourgogne**
Côte d'Or (21),
Nièvre (58),
Saône-et-Loire (71),
Yonne (89)

**Bretagne**
Côtes-d'Armor (22),
Finistère (29),
Ille-et-Vilaine (35),
Morbihan (56)

**Centre**
Cher (18), Eure-et-Loire
(28), Indre (36),
Indre-et-Loire (37),
Loir-et-Cher (41),
Loiret (45)

**Champagne-Ardenne**
Ardennes(08), Aube (10),
Marne (51),
Haute-Marne (52)

**Corse**
Corse-du-Sud (2A),
Haute-Corse (2B)

**Franche-Comté**
Doubs (25), Jura (39),
Haute-Saône (70),
Territoire de Belfort (90)

**Ile-de-France**
Paris (Ville de) (75),
Seine-et-Marne (77),
Yvelines (78),
Essonne (91),
Hauts-de-Seine (92),
Seine-Saint-Denis (93),
Val-de-Marne (94),
Val-d'Oise (95)

**Languedoc-Roussillon**
Aude (11), Gard (30),
Hérault (34), Lozère (48),
Pyrénées-Orientales (66)

**Limousin**
Corrèze (19), Creuse (23),
Haute-Vienne (87)

**Loire (Pays de la)**
Loire-Atlantique (44),
Maine-et-Loire (49),
Mayenne (53), Sarthe (72),
Vendée (85)

**Lorraine**
Meurthe-et-Moselle (54),
Meuse (55), Moselle (57),
Vosges (88)

**Midi-Pyrénées**
Ariège (09), Aveyron (12),
Haute-Garonne (31),
Gers (32), Lot (46),
Hautes-Pyrénées (65),
Tarn (81),
Tarn-et-Garonne (82)

**Nord-Pas-de-Calais**
Nord (59),
Pas-de-Calais (62)

**Normandie (Haute-)**
Eure (27),
Seine-Maritime (76)

**Normandie (Basse-)**
Calvados (14),
Manche (50), Orne (61)

**Picardie**
Aisne (02), Oise (60),
Somme (80)

**Poitou-Charentes**
Charente (16),
Charente-Maritime (17),
Deux-Sèvres (79),
Vienne (86)

**Provence-Alpes-
Côte-d'Azur**
Alpes-de-Haute-Provence
(04), Hautes-Alpes (05),
Alpes-Maritimes (06),
Bouches-du-Rhône (13),
Var (83), Vaucluse (84)

**Rhône-Alpes**
Ain (01), Ardèche (07),
Drôme (26), Isère (38),
Loire (42), Rhône (69),
Savoie (73),
Haute-Savoie (74)

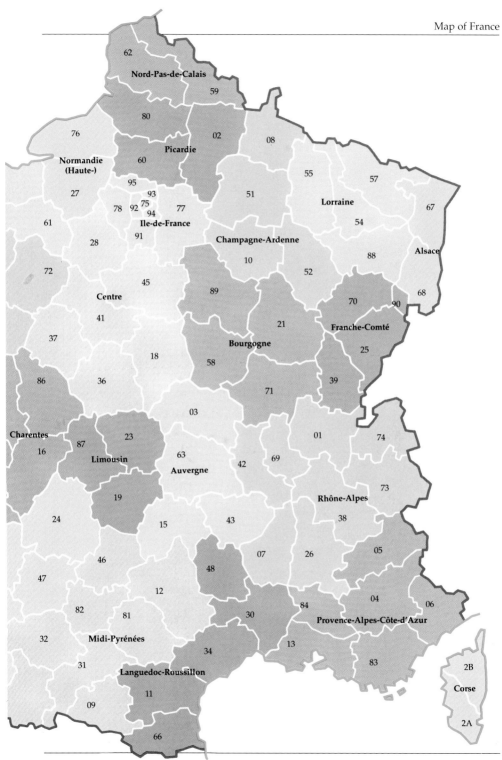

## ABBAYE DE CÎTEAUX

Although the Abbey of Saint-Nicholas-des-Cîteaux dates back some 900 years, production of this *fermier* cheese began as recently as 1925. It is as soft to the eye as it is to the palate, and rather milder than the majority of washed-crust cheeses. Sixty tons are made every year from the milk of 70 Montbéliard cows. Most of the cheeses are eaten locally.

❦ Beaujolais or Bourgogne, young and fruity, chilled

*Semi-hard pâte; uncooked, unpressed*

ESSENTIAL FACTS
- ◎ 18 cm diameter, 3.5 cm high
- ⚖ 700 g
- ▯ 45%
- ✓ All year

*Smooth, washed, greyish-yellow rind*

 Bourgogne (21)

 Raw

## ABBAYE DE LA JOIE NÔTRE-DAME

This *fermier* cheese has been produced by the nuns of the Abbaye de la Joie Nôtre-Dame since 1953. The recipe was passed on to the convent when it became independent from the Abbaye de la Coudre (p. 210). This fine and elegant cheese is one of the numerous descendants of Port-du-Salut (p. 173), the very first French monastery cheese, which it resembles both in appearance and taste. During affinage it is washed with brine for four to six weeks.

❦ Bordeaux, young and fruity

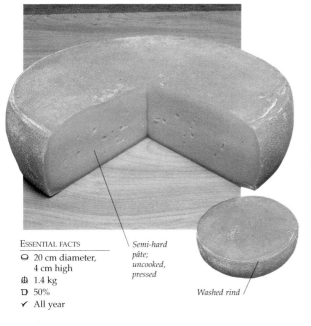

ESSENTIAL FACTS
- ◎ 20 cm diameter, 4 cm high
- ⚖ 1.4 kg
- ▯ 50%
- ✓ All year

*Semi-hard pâte; uncooked, pressed*

*Washed rind*

 Bretagne (56)

Raw

## ABBAYE DU MONT DES CATS

The monks of the abbey, near the town of Godewaersvelde (Plain of God) in Flanders, started production of this *artisanal* cheese in 1890 using the Port-du-Salut recipe (p. 173). It is made in a small independent dairy from milk that has been bought in from neighbouring farms. The cheese shown has been cured using modern methods and is not yet ripe. The small holes are characteristic of this cheese. Locally, it is often served as a breakfast cheese with coffee. Affinage takes a minimum of one month, during which time the cheese is regularly washed with brine dyed with *rocou*, a reddish extract of annatto seeds.

❦ Graves

Nord-Pas-de-Calais (59)

Raw

*Washed rind*

ESSENTIAL FACTS
- ⊖ 25 cm diameter, 4 cm high
- ⚖ 2 kg
- ☋ 45–50%
- ✓ All year

*Hard pâte; uncooked, pressed*

---

## ABBAYE DE LA PIERRE-QUI-VIRE

Both this cheese and the Boule des Moines (below) are *fermier* cheeses made by 12 of the 85 monks at the Abbaye de la Pierre-qui-Vire from the milk of 40 cows. Since the monks use neither chemical fertilizers nor pesticides, both cheeses are organic. During the affinage of two weeks the cheese is washed with brine. It should be eaten when young.

❦ Beaune

## BOULE DES MOINES

This soft, fresh version of the above cheese was launched to boost sales. The flavoured pâte has a strong smell of garlic.

❦ Irancy, young and fruity

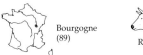

Bourgogne (89)

Raw

*Soft pâte, smooth and supple; uncooked, unpressed*

*Washed rind*

ESSENTIAL FACTS
- ⊖ 10 cm diameter, 2.5 cm high
- ⚖ 200 g
- ✓ All year; best in summer and autumn

**Abbaye de la Pierre-qui-Vire**

ESSENTIAL FACTS
- ⊖ 5–7 cm diameter
- ⚖ 100–150 g
- ✓ All year, especially summer and autumn

*Soft pâte, mixed with garlic, chives, and pepper*

**Boule des Moines**

Creamy to pale yellow pâte, supple without elasticity, with small, even holes; half-cooked at 45–50°C, pressed

Dark yellow to brown rind, with cloth traces and a blue casein label on the side

Abondance d'alpage fermier, affinage of ten months

Abondance d'hiver fermier, affinage of seven months

ESSENTIAL FACTS

- ⊝ 38–43 cm diameter, 7–8 cm high
- ⚖ 7–12 kg
- ⸪ 58 g min. per 100 g cheese
- ⚲ 48% or 27.84 g min. per 100 g cheese
- ✔ Autumn onwards for cheeses made at a chalet d'alpage

# ABONDANCE (AOC)

This medium-sized mountain cheese from Haute Savoie in the Rhône-Alpes is produced using milk from cows of the Abondance, Montbéliard, and Tarine breeds. The animals must not be fed any silage or other fermented fodder. The *fromage d'alpage* (p. 54) shown here was made in September at an alpine *chalet*. It has a strong smell and a distinct and complex flavour, with a balance of acidity and sweetness and a long aftertaste. The crust, including the grey layer beneath, should be removed before eating.

*Artisanale, coopérative,* and *industriel* versions of Abondance are produced, but around 40% of the 348 tonnes made each year are *fermier* cheeses, and production is increasing. *Fermier* cheeses have an oval, blue *casein* label on the side, while all other versions have a square label. Affinage takes at least 90 days, during which time a maximum of three samples are taken from the core of the cheese with a cheese iron.

❦ Vin de Savoie, Côtes de Nuits Villages, Morey St. Denis, Fixin

---

AOC REGULATIONS:
ABONDANCE

1. The milk may be heated once to a maximum of 40°C, but only at the renneting. Systems or machinery that would allow the rapid heating to above 40°C before renneting may not be kept on the premises.

2. Salt is applied to the surface of the cheese either directly or with brine.

3. A *casein* label must bear the following information: France; Abondance; the ID number of the place of production: *fermier* for the farm category.

AOC GRANTED 1990

Rhône-Alpes (74)

Raw, whole

# How Abondance is Made

It takes 100 litres of milk from cattle grazing in the mountain pastures to make a single Abondance of 9.5 kg.

### Renneting and coagulation
When the rennet is added, the milk is heated to 32–35°C. Coagulation (**2**) takes 35 minutes.

### Cutting the curd (*le décaillage*)
The curd (*caillé*) is carefully cut into small pieces and stirred vigorously to separate out the whey. As it separates, the curd turns grainy (**3**). The whey, which is usually thrown away, contains proteins and sugars.

### Scalding
The curd is heated to 30°C and on to 50°C, over 45 minutes. The whey continues to separate, while the curd turns into grains the size of wheat, with a milky colour, rubbery consistency, and slightly sugary taste. Scalding dries the curd and cooks it. If the curd is heated too quickly or too much the pâte may break or swell during affinage.

### Drawing off (*le soutirage*)
The curd is gathered, or "drawn off" in a linen gauze (**4**).

### First pressing
The curd is pressed (**5**) into a wooden hoop mould lined with gauze (**1**). A rope can be tightened to adjust the diameter of the cheese, which expands above and below the hoop (**6**). Seven or eight filled hoops are stacked (**7** and **8**) and pressed in the *pressoir* for 20 minutes. The curd grains begin to stick to each other.

### Second pressing and labelling
The moulds are turned immediately and casein labels slipped in on the side. After the fourth turning, in the evening, when the wet gauze is changed for a dry one, the moulds are pressed at maximum force. The curd grains fuse, and the cheese takes its final shape. The cheese is taken out of the mould and left for a day in a room at 13–16°C to let the pâte cool without drying the crust.

### Salting
The cheese is soaked in brine for 12 hours to speed up the formation of the crust, improve its appearance, and reduce the risk of mould. The cheese is allowed to dry naturally for 24 hours in a room at 12–14°C.

### Affinage
The affinage takes place over a minimum of 90 days in a well-ventilated cellar at 12°C and 95% humidity. On alternate days the surface of the cheese is rubbed with coarse salt and wiped with a cloth soaked in *morge*. (This is made by mixing brine with the sticky, light-brown substance found on the crusts of old cheeses.) The abrasive action of the salt limits the growth of mould and helps build up the strong crust (**9**) that conserves these large cheeses for a long time.

## AISY CENDRÉ

This *artisanal* cheese from Bourgogne is made by burying a young cheese in ashes for a month. A number of cheeses can be used as a base for Aisy Cendré but the one shown here is a young Epoisses de Bourgogne (p. 133), a strong, washed cheese. It is not yet matured and would be perfect for people who prefer an unripe centre. The heart is white, with a texture of plaster, and is surrounded by a more creamy pâte. The salty taste indicates that it is still young.

❢ Hautes Côtes de Nuits Villages

*Soft to slightly hard pâte; uncooked, unpressed*

*Rind covered with ashes*

ESSENTIAL FACTS

- ⊖ 10 cm diameter, 3 cm high
- ⚖ 200–250 g
- ⛿ 50%
- ✓ All year

Bourgogne (21)

Raw, whole

---

# Categories and conditions of production

The four main categories of production permitted by the AOC (see page 77) are *fermier*, *artisanal*, *coopérative*, and *industriel*.

The category of *fermier* is not a guarantee of quality – it merely implies that a cheese is made according to traditional methods.

| CATEGORY | CONDITIONS OF PRODUCTION | QUANTITIES PRODUCED | WHERE THE CHEESES ARE SOLD |
|---|---|---|---|
| *Fermier* (made in a farmhouse, *chalet d'alpage*, *buron* or other mountain hut) | An individual producer uses the milk of animals (cows, goats, sheep) raised on his or her farm to make cheese following traditional methods. Milk from neighbouring farms is not allowed. Only raw milk may be used. | Small | Regional markets and a few *fromageries* in large towns. Some are exported to other countries. |
| *Artisanal* | An individual producer uses the milk of animals raised on his or her farm, or buys in milk to make cheese. (The producer is the owner of the dairy but all the milk may be bought elsewhere.) | Small to medium | Regional markets, and *fromageries* in towns and suburbs. |
| *Coopératives* (also *fruitières*) | The cheese is made in a single dairy with milk provided by members of the cooperative. | Medium to large | All of France. |
| *Industriel* | The milk is bought from a number of producers, sometimes from distant regions. Production is industrial. | Large | All of France; sometimes exported to other countries. |

## Arômes au Gène de Marc

This is a seasonal *artisanal* cheese that is ready to eat at the end of autumn. It is produced following a traditional method of curing cheeses in the wine-growing region of Lyons. Ripe cheeses such as Rigotte (p. 176), Saint-Marcellin (p. 182), Pélardon (p. 167), and Picodon (p. 170) are placed in a barrel or large jar of *marc* for a minimum of one month. The *marc*, which consists of the damp skins, pips, and stalks left after the grapes have been pressed, permeates the cheese and flavours it. This cheese needs to be eaten with wine.

❑ Marc de Côtes du Rhône;
♀ Muscat de Beaumes de Venise

*Soft to hard pâte*

*Natural rind, covered with marc de raisins*

**ESSENTIAL FACTS**
- ⊖ 6-7 cm diameter, 2–3 cm high
- ⚖ 80–120 g
- ✓ End of autumn, winter

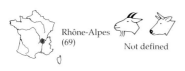

Rhône-Alpes (69)

Not defined

---

## Arômes au Vin Blanc

This cheese is made by filling the bottom of a large jar with white wine and placing a goat's-milk cheese, for example Saint-Marcellin (p. 182), on a wire rack just above the wine's surface. The jar is then sealed tightly and left for two to three weeks. As the wine evaporates, the cheese absorbs its aroma, while the pâte grows soft and moist. This is a refined and sought-after cheese, worthy of Lyons, the city of gourmets. It should not be eaten on its own.

♀ Bourgogne, St. Romain

*Soft, moist pâte*

*No rind*

**ESSENTIAL FACTS**
- ⊖ 6-7 cm diameter, 2–3 cm high
- ⚖ 80–120 g
- ✓ End of autumn, winter

Rhône-Alpes (69)

Not defined

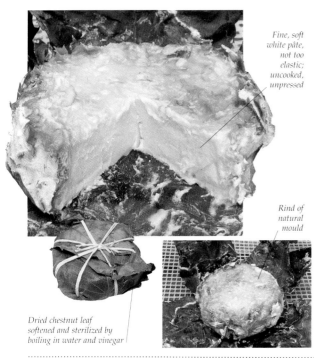

Fine, soft white pâte, not too elastic; uncooked, unpressed

Rind of natural mould

Dried chestnut leaf softened and sterilized by boiling in water and vinegar

## Banon à la Feuille

This small mountain cheese was made by a couple from the village of Puimichel near the town of Banon in Provence. *Fermier, artisanal*, and *industriel* versions are produced. After an affinage of two weeks, the cheese is dipped in *eau-de-vie* and wrapped in a chestnut leaf. The alcohol protects the cheese against bad mould. The cheese shown has been made with goat's milk only. The pâte has a milky smell when young. As it ripens, the surface takes on the colour and aroma of the leaf.

❑ *Marc* of the region,
♀ Vin de Cassis

Essential facts

◔ 6–7 cm diameter,
  2.5–3 cm high
⚖ 90–120 g
◻ 45%
✔ All year (cow's); spring
  to autumn (goat's)

## Poivre d'Âne / Pèvre d'Aï

The cheese used as a base for Poivre d'Âne is the same as for Banon à la Feuille and may be made solely with either goat's or cow's milk, or a mixture of the two. Affinage, in dried savory, takes one month and *fermier, artisanal*, and *industriel* versions are produced. Pèvre d'Aï is the old Provençal name given to *Satureia hortensis* or summer savory, a southern European herb similar to thyme and mint, with a peppery bite that is used to flavour this cheese.

♀ Coteaux d'Aix *rosé*

Rind covered in dried savory

Soft pâte; uncooked, unpressed

Essential facts

◔ 6–7 cm diameter,
  3 cm high
⚖ 100–120 g
◻ 45%
✔ All year (cow's); spring
  to autumn (goat's)

Provence-Alpes-Côte-d'Azur (04)

Raw

## BARGKASS

Le Thillot, where this *fermier* cheese is produced, is a little village in the Vosges mountains of northeast France, famous for its cheeses, the best-known being Munster (p. 158). In the local dialect, *barg* means mountain, *kass* cheese. Bargkass has a soft but firm pâte, which is slightly elastic, with a few small holes. It has a light, soft smell and a rounded, relaxed taste with a slightly acid aftertaste. The cheese is best eaten with black sourdough bread. Affinage takes between six and eight weeks, during which time the cheese is brushed and turned once a week.

🍷 Pinot Noir

*Light brown or brown rind, marked by the cloth during pressing*

*Slightly elastic pâte; uncooked, pressed*

Lorraine (88)

Raw

ESSENTIAL FACTS

- 30 cm diameter, 6 cm high
- 7–8 kg
- Not defined
- May to October

## BEAUMONT

This *industriel* cheese was first made in 1881 at Beaumont, near Geneva in Switzerland, using the same method as for Tamié (p. 187). It is one of the first mass-produced cheeses to use raw milk. Affinage takes four to six weeks, during which time the cheese is washed.

🍷 Vin de Savoie, Hautes Côtes de Beaune

*Semi-hard pâte, elastic to touch; uncooked, pressed*

*Pinkish-yellow, washed rind*

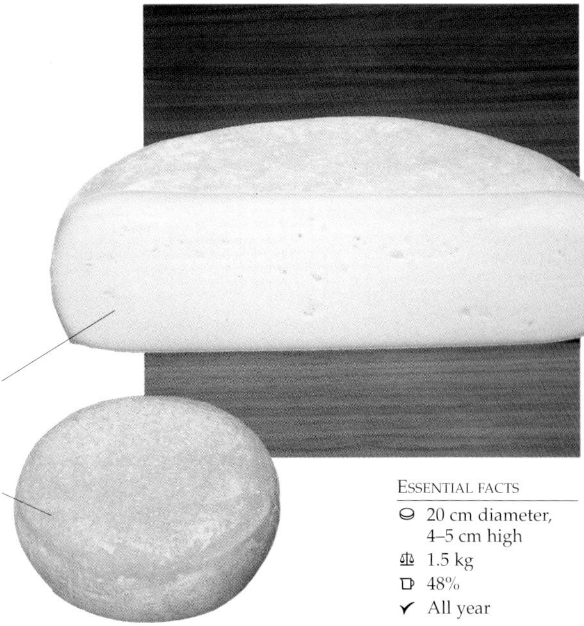

Rhône-Alpes (74)

Raw

ESSENTIAL FACTS

- 20 cm diameter, 4–5 cm high
- 1.5 kg
- 48%
- All year

*Slightly concave circumference*

ESSENTIAL FACTS

- ◎ 35–75 cm diameter, 11–16 cm high
- ⚖ 20–70 kg
- ♣ 62 g min. per 100 g cheese
- ⌂ 48%
- ✓ All year; autumn if made in a *chalet d'alpage*

*Hard, yellowish rind forms during affinage*

**Beaufort, affinage of five to six months**

## BEAUFORT (AOC)

Beaufort is a large, round mountain cheese produced in the province of Savoie in the French Alps. Large cheeses with cooked and pressed pâtes are commonly called *gruyères* in France (not to be confused with Swiss Gruyère).

The average weight of a Beaufort is 45 kg, or all the milk produced by a herd of 45 cows in a day. Around 12 litres of milk make 1 kg of Beaufort. A good cheese should have a moist, sticky crust and a concave surface due to the *cercle de Beaufort* used to shape it (p. 20).

### Types of Beaufort

Three versions of Beaufort are produced: Beaufort, Beaufort *d'été* (summer Beaufort) and Beaufort

Rhône-Alpes (73, 74)

Raw, whole

d'*alpage*, which is made in *chalets* in the mountains. The pâte of a winter cheese is white, that of a summer cheese, pale yellow. It is said that the chlorophyll from the grass and carotene from the alpine flowers give the summer cheeses both colour and flavour.

**Production and affinage**
*Fermier, chalet d'alpage, coopérative,* and *industriel* versions of Beaufort are made. Affinage takes at least four months from the date of production, within areas specified by the AOC at below 15°C with at least 92% humidity, during which time the cheese is constantly wiped and rubbed with brine.

In November, five- or six-month-old Beauforts (shown top right) appear at the Parisian markets and are the first of the *fromages d'alpage*. They have a soft, clear scent of milk, butter, flowers, and honey. The supple pâte has a flowery aroma, as well as a hidden acidity and salt. The taste lingers on the palate. Beaufort of this age goes well with white wine.

Some Beauforts are allowed an affinage of one year in a dark, cool cellar at 8–9°C and 98% humidity. Twice a week, the cheese is washed with brine and turned. A year-old cheese has a moist crust, under which there is a thin, grey layer that gradually melts into the pâte. The flavour is complex, with a stronger aroma than the younger cheeses and a more subtle taste of salt.

**Beaufort cows**
The mahogany-coloured Beaufort cows, the Tarines or Tarentaises are indispensable in the making of Beaufort cheese. This ancient mountain breed, originally from the Indo-Asian continent, crossed Central Europe before reaching France. The cows were named Tarines in 1863 and were entered in the *Herd Book* in 1888. During the winter they are kept in sheds to protect them from the heavy winter snow, and according to AOC regulations, they are not allowed to

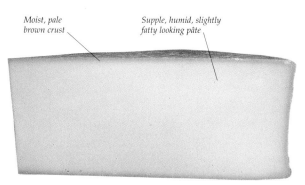

*Moist, pale brown crust*

*Supple, humid, slightly fatty looking pâte*

Beaufort *d'alpage*, **affinage of five to six months**

Beaufort *d'alpage*, **affinage of approximately one year**

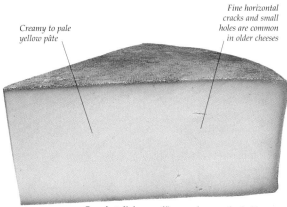

*Creamy to pale yellow pâte*

*Fine horizontal cracks and small holes are common in older cheeses*

Beaufort *d'alpage*, **affinage of one-and-a-half years**

be fed any silage or other fermented fodder. In spring, they are taken high into the mountains to graze on the lush grass and flowers of the alpine meadows. In autumn they descend to the lower meadows, returning to the villages before the winter snows settle. Tarine cows are strong, hardy animals that adapt well. Their milk is of excellent quality, with a fat content of 36.3% and protein content of 31.8%. They calve once a year, and in the 10 years of its working life, each cow produces an average of 4,338 kg of milk. Some of this milk is used to make several other great mountain cheeses such as Tomme de Savoie (p. 188) and Emmental (p. 132).

♀ Seyssel, Chablis

---

AOC REGULATIONS: BEAUFORT

**1.** The milk must be taken into the dairy immediately after milking. Only where refrigeration tanks are in use on the farm may it be transported once a day. If the milk is refrigerated, the rennet must be added within 24 hours of milking, or 36 hours in winter.

**2.** No system or machinery that would allow the milk to be heated above 40°C before renneting is allowed on the premises.

**3.** The name of the cheese must be shown in blue *casein* letters that must always remain legible.

**4.** The terms *été* and *alpage* may be used only as follows: *été* for dairy products from June to October, including those made at a *chalet d'alpage*; *alpage* for summer products made twice a day at an alpine *chalet* with the milk from a single herd (no other milk may be mixed with it).

**5.** The salt must be applied to the surface of the cheese either directly or with brine.

**6.** If the cheese is sold cut and prepacked, the pieces must show a portion of the crust that is characteristic of Beaufort AOC.

AOC GRANTED 1976

CUTTING A BEAUFORT (*above*)
The double-handled knife, called a guillotine is lightly moistened. It is then pushed towards the centre of the cheese in a see-sawing fashion.

CHEESE IRON (*top*)
This is used for taking samples from the inside of a cheese. The pâte of young Beaufort is elastic and yields easily to the knife.

CHEESE CELLAR (*above*)
A fromager's cellar in Chambèry where as many as 1,000 cheeses may be stored in November. The temperature is 8–9°C, with a humidity of 98%.

# Bleu

## ✓ BLEU D'AUVERGNE (AOC)

There are two different sizes of
Bleu d'Auvergne. The larger size
has a diameter of 20 cm, with a
height of 8–10 cm and weight of
2–3 kg. The smaller size is 10 cm
in diameter, varies in height, and
weighs anything from 350 g to
1 kg. Although these cheeses are
traditionally round, a rectangular
version is produced for export and
prepack sale. This is 29 cm long,
8.5 cm wide, 11 cm high, and
weighs 2.5 kg. The cheeses shown
here are part of the 122 tonnes that
were made with raw milk, out of
a total 8,295 tonnes produced in
1991. The pâte is sticky, moist, and
crumbly, with an even spread of
veins, and its taste is tart and gluey.
The spice of the mould blends
perfectly with the well-integrated
salt. This cheese is delicious in
salad dressings, with chicory, nuts,
or raw mushrooms. It also makes
an excellent seasoning for piping-
hot, fresh pasta.

Both *coopérative* and *industriel*
versions of Bleu d'Auvergne are
made within the areas specified
by the AOC. Affinage takes a
minimum of four weeks from the
date of production for cheeses
weighing over 1 kg, and two weeks
for those weighing below 1 kg.

The AOC was granted in 1975.

♆ Sauternes, Maury (VDN)

*Natural rind /*

*Pâte evenly veined
with blue mould;
uncooked, unpressed*

Auvergne (63,
15, 43); Midi-
Pyrénées (12, 46);
Limousin (19);
Languedoc-
Roussillon (48)

Raw,
pasteurized

ESSENTIAL FACTS

◯ 20 cm diameter, 8–10 cm high (large);
10 cm diameter, variable height (small)

⚖ 2–3 kg (large); 1 kg (small)

∴ 52 g min. per 100 g

꒙ 50%

✔ All year

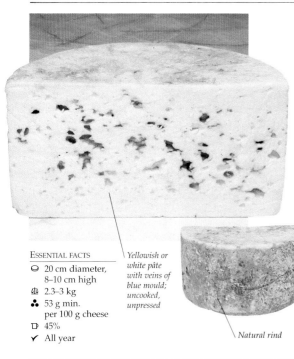

## BLEU DES CAUSSES (AOC)

This commercially produced *coopérative* or *industriel* cheese is a mild cow's-milk version of Roquefort (p. 178). The solid flavour is a result of the affinage, which lasts at least 70 days, and usually three to six months, and takes place in natural caves called *fleurines* (p. 178) in the limestone plateaux of the Causses. The pâte of the summer cheeses is moist and ivory-yellow; winter cheeses are white and have a strong taste. They are best when matched with a naturally sweet white wine of good acidity, especially at the end of a meal.

The AOC was granted in 1975.

Ŷ Barsac *moelleux*,
Banyuls Grand Cru (VDN)

ESSENTIAL FACTS
- ⊖ 20 cm diameter, 8–10 cm high
- ⚖ 2.3–3 kg
- ∴ 53 g min. per 100 g cheese
- ⏚ 45%
- ✔ All year

*Yellowish or white pâte with veins of blue mould; uncooked, unpressed*

*Natural rind*

Midi-Pyrénées (12, 46); Languedoc-Roussillon (48, 30, 34)

Raw

## BLEU DE COSTAROS

This traditional *fermier* cheese from the village of Costaros in the Auvergne is known locally as *fromage à vers*, meaning cheese eaten by worms – a reference to the cheese mite (*le ciron*) that lives in it. The slightly hard, elastic pâte is irregularly punctured by small holes and is sticky, with a faint smell and flavour of mould. A local cheesemaker says that she eats the crust: "Oh, yes, all of it, even the worms."

Ŷ Loupiac, Rivesaltes (VDN)

*Uncooked, unpressed pâte*

*Hard natural rind forms during affinage*

ESSENTIAL FACTS
- ⊖ 10 cm diameter, 7–8 cm high
- ⚖ 550–600 g
- ⏚ Not defined
- ✔ All year

*Veins of natural concentrated mould*

Auvergne (43)

Raw

## BLEU DU HAUT JURA (AOC)

This mild blue cheese is also known as Bleu de Gex or Bleu de Septmoncel, but its official name is Bleu du Haut Jura. The rind is covered with a layer of white, powder-like mould that should be gently wiped off before eating. The pâte's aroma evokes the milk of rich pastures. Locally, it is often eaten with boiled potatoes.

The cows that are milked to make this cheese graze in the mountains of the Jura. It is said that the mould of the mountain grass and flowers passes into their milk, where it flourishes. Today, spores of the blue mould *Penicillium glaucum* are introduced into the milk. During affinage, air is inserted with a syringe into the pâte to allow the mould to grow internally.

During the affinage of around one month within AOC specified areas, the cheeses are dried and ripened naturally in the cellars of a *coopérative* at a humidity of 80%.

The AOC was granted in 1977.

♀ Sainte Croix du Mont (VDN),
♀ Port

*Soft, ivory pâte, evenly marbled with pale green mould; uncooked, unpressed*

*Rind forms naturally; thin yellowish with a dry powdery mould, may show red spots*

*Gex is stamped on surface*

*Holes where air is inserted with syringe*

### BLEU FONDU À LA POÊLE

To make this tasty recipe, simply cut the cheese into slices and melt them slowly in a frying pan. They make an excellent topping for chicken breasts, or are equally delicious spread on slices of country bread and accompanied by a glass of Vin jaune d'Arbois.

### ESSENTIAL FACTS

- ⊖ 36 cm diameter, height not specified
- ⚖ 7.5 kg
- ● 52 g min. per 100 g
- ▯ 50%
- ✔ All year; best in summer

Rhône-Alpes (01); Franche-Comté (39)

Raw

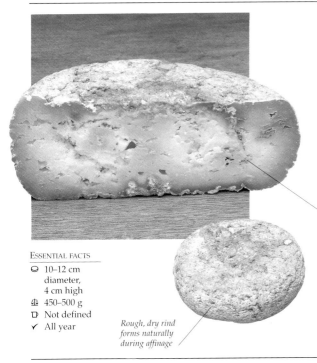

## BLEU DE LANGEAC

Locally, this *fermier* cheese from the town of Langeac in the Auvergne goes by the simple name of *fromage de la région*, meaning cheese of the region. It has a completely dry crust and a slight aroma. The pâte is firm and has a definite taste of mould. This is a salty and solid cheese, made from good, strong milk. Affinage takes two months.

♀ Cérons *moelleux*, Sauternes *meilleur marché*, Banyuls (VDN)

*Yellowish pâte, veined with natural mould; uncooked, unpressed*

ESSENTIAL FACTS

- ◯ 10–12 cm diameter, 4 cm high
- ⬛ 450–500 g
- ◻ Not defined
- ✓ All year

*Rough, dry rind forms naturally during affinage*

Auvergne (43)

Raw

## BLEU DE LAQUEUILLE

Antoine Roussel from the village of Laqueuille first made this cheese in 1850 with mould grown on rye bread (his statue can be seen in the village). The pâte has a slight smell of the cellar and tastes of blue mould. Bleu de Laqueuille belongs to the same family as Fourme d'Ambert (p. 138). Today, production is limited to an *industriel* version. Affinage takes three months.

♀ Monbazillac *moelleux*, Rivesaltes (VDN)

*Rind forms naturally during affinage*

ESSENTIAL FACTS

- ◇ 49 cm diameter, 9.5 cm high
- ⬛ 2.5 kg
- ◻ 45%
- ✓ Summer, autumn

*Soft pâte with blue mould; uncooked, unpressed*

Auvergne (63)

Pasteurized

## BLEU DE LOUDES

The pâte of this *fermier* cheese from the town of Loudes in the Auvergne is firm and elastic, sticky, and slightly sour, with no particular smell. The presence of the mould is not immediately obvious. The cheese shown has been cut and exposed to the air for 24 hours. Affinage takes six weeks.

♈ Sainte Croix du Mont *moelleux*, Rivesaltes (VDN)

*Firm pâte with traces of natural blue mould and a few holes; uncooked, unpressed*

*Hard, dry rind forms naturally during affinage*

Auvergne (43)

Raw

ESSENTIAL FACTS

⊖ 11 cm diameter, 6 cm high
⚖ 600–650 g
🜄 Not defined
✓ All year

## BLEU DU QUERCY

A mild, commercially produced *bleu industriel* from the Quercy region suitable for the uninitiated who have yet to acquire a taste for blue cheeses. Affinage takes three months.

♈ Cérons *moelleux*, Maury (VDN)

*Pâte regularly veined, with natural green mould; uncooked, unpressed*

*Rind appears naturally during affinage*

Midi-Pyrénées (46)

Pasteurized

ESSENTIAL FACTS

⊖ 18 cm diameter, 9–10 cm high
⚖ 2.5 kg
🜄 45%
✓ All year

## BLEU DE SASSENAGE

This traditional mountain cheese, a sweet *bleu*, was first made by monks, and the recipe spread to the surrounding villages. In a charter of 1338, Baron Albert of Sassenage allowed the free sale of the cheese made by people on his land. Today, production is principally *industriel*. The summer version has a simple flavour of the milk produced by cows grazing in the mountains, and is characterized by a comforting roundness and the faint perfume of the mould. Affinage takes two to three months.

♀ Barsac *moelleux*, Banyuls

ESSENTIAL FACTS

Soft pâte;
uncooked,
unpressed

◯ 30 cm diameter, 8–9 cm high
⚖ 5–6 kg
🍶 45%
✓ Summer, autumn

*Natural white and reddish rind*

Rhône-Alpes (38)

Pasteurized

## BRESSE BLEU

This commercially produced *industriel* cheese was first made after World War II in the province of Bresse in southern France. The soft pâte is peppered with small patches of blue mould. Three different sizes are produced. The large size is around 10 cm in diameter, 6.5 cm high, and weighs 500 g. The medium size is 8 cm in diameter, 4.5 cm high, and weighs 225 g. The small size is just 6 cm in diameter, 4.5 cm high, and weighs 125 g. Affinage takes two to four weeks.

♀ Monbazillac *moelleux*, Rivesaltes (VDN)

ESSENTIAL FACTS

Soft, supple
pâte;
uncooked,
unpressed

◯ 6–10 cm diameter, 4.5–6.4 cm high
⚖ 125–500 g
🍶 55%
✓ All year

*Rind of white mould*

Rhône Alpes (01)

Pasteurized

## BLEU DE TERMIGNON

Termignon is the name of the village in which this cheese is produced, at an altitude of 1,300 m in the French Alps. This is an outstanding cheese of great quality, a little fatty, natural and down-to-earth, made by just one woman, in very limited quantities, in a *chalet d'alpage*. She keeps her nine cows high up in the National Park of Vanoise, where the animals feed on grass and flowers. It is here that the source of the mould may be found. The mould passes into the milk to create a refined flavour that permeates the cheese. The blue mould is natural and is not artificially induced as in most other blue cheeses. It develops and expands much more slowly and less evenly. The crust of this cheese is white, brown, hard, and looks like a rock, and the pâte is crumbly. During affinage, the cheeses are regularly turned and wiped for four to five months.

♀ Tokay Selection de Grains Nobles *moelleux*, Rivesaltes Grand Cru (VDN)

**Bleu de Termignon after an affinage of five months**

*Rind forms naturally during affinage*

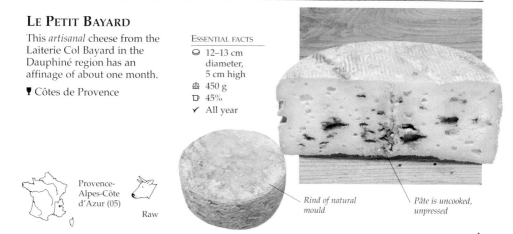

ESSENTIAL FACTS

◈ 28 cm diameter, 10 cm high
⊕ 7 kg
▯ 50%
✓ All year

Rhône-Alpes (73)

Raw

**Dry cheese**

## LE PETIT BAYARD

This *artisanal* cheese from the Laiterie Col Bayard in the Dauphiné region has an affinage of about one month.

❢ Côtes de Provence

ESSENTIAL FACTS

⊖ 12–13 cm diameter, 5 cm high
⊕ 450 g
▯ 45%
✓ All year

Provence-Alpes-Côte d'Azur (05)

Raw

*Rind of natural mould*

*Pâte is uncooked, unpressed*

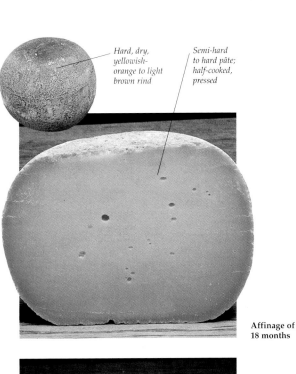

Hard, dry, yellowish-orange to light brown rind

Semi-hard to hard pâte; half-cooked, pressed

Affinage of 18 months

Affinage of 24 months

Pâte varies in colour from yellowish-orange to red, with a few small holes

## BOULE DE LILLE / MIMOLETTE FRANÇAISE

The name Boule de Lille allegedly derives from the *cave d'affinage,* or ripening cellar, in the city of Lille where affinage originally took place. The name Mimolette derives from *mi-mou* or half-soft. Some say this cheese originated in Holland, while others maintain that it has always existed in France. The true story behind its origins is probably that during the 17th century, the French minister Colbert forbade the import of foreign goods, including cheese, and the French began making Mimolette themselves. The method of production is the same as for the Dutch cheese Edam.

This is a northern *coopérative* or *industriel* cheese, about the size of a baby's head, flattened at top and bottom, with no distinct aroma. The pâte is semi-soft at the beginning, then slowly hardens and dries as the cheese ripens and finally cracks. Results of ripening vary, depending on the level of humidity in the cellar. The minimum affinage takes about six weeks; three months for a young Mimolette; six months for a *demi-étuvée* or *demi-vieille* (half-old); twelve months for a *vieille en étuvée* (old); and two years for a *très vieille* (very old) cheese. The colour of the pâte changes from carrot to orange brown, and with it the taste. The dry cheese can be grated and used for cooking.

♀ Banyuls (VDN)

ESSENTIAL FACTS

⊘ 20 cm diameter, 15 cm high

⚖ 2–4 kg

⁛ 54 g per 100 g cheese

𝄐 40%

✔ All year

Nord-Pas-de-Calais (62)

Pasteurized

# Brebis de Pays

## BREBIS DE PAYS DE GRASSE

This *fermier* cheese is made in the area around the town of Grasse. The ewes whose milk is used to make the cheese feed on the grass and lavender of the arid mountain plateaux, exposed to the pure air of the Alps and the Mediterranean breezes. The taste is light, and slightly acid for a sheep's-milk cheese made with quality milk. Brebis de Pays de Grasse is a perfect accompaniment to a baguette hot out of the oven. Affinage takes about six weeks.

♀ Cassis

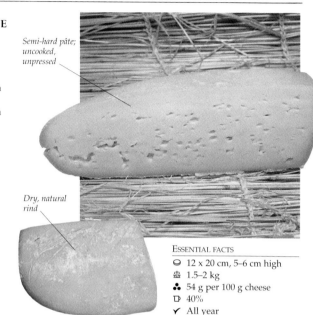

*Semi-hard pâte; uncooked, unpressed*

*Dry, natural rind*

Provence-Alpes-Côte-d'Azur (06)

Raw

**ESSENTIAL FACTS**

- 🗢 12 x 20 cm, 5–6 cm high
- ⚖ 1.5–2 kg
- ❖ 54 g per 100 g cheese
- ◻ 40%
- ✔ All year

## BERGER PLAT

This *fermier* cheese is produced on a farm called Le Berger des Dombes in the province of Lyon. It was first made as a result of the introduction of Lacaune sheep into the region, the same breed as the ewes of Roquefort (p. 178). The rind is white or beige with a pale blue mould. Berger Plat is a cheese of gentle scent and taste. During affinage, the cheeses are left to rest on a bed of straw for 15–21 days.

❢ Coteaux de Lyonnais, Beaujolais

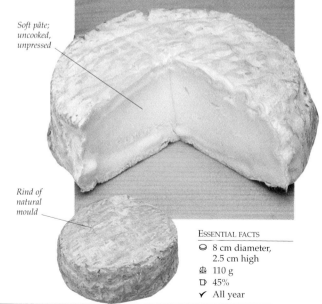

*Soft pâte; uncooked, unpressed*

*Rind of natural mould*

Rhône-Alpes (01)

Raw, whole

**ESSENTIAL FACTS**

- 🗢 8 cm diameter, 2.5 cm high
- ⚖ 110 g
- ◻ 45%
- ✔ All year

## BREBIS DU BERSEND

This *fermier* cheese from the village of Bersend is one of the few sheep's-milk cheeses produced in the province of Savoie. Until the 19th century, many ewes were reared in this mountainous area, close to the Swiss and Italian borders. Their numbers fell but at last appear to be on the increase again. Affinage takes a minimum of two months in a natural cellar.

♀ Roussette de Savoie

_Rind of natural white, brown, or grey mould_

ESSENTIAL FACTS
- ◎ 12 cm diameter, 5 cm high
- ⚖ 580 g
- ◻ 45%
- ✓ Best in summer

*Semi-hard pâte, slightly elastic under pressure; uncooked, unpressed*

Rhône-Alpes (73)

Raw

---

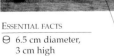

## BREBIS DU LOCHOIS (PUR)

This *fermier* cheese is a recently introduced sheep's-milk cheese in an area dominated by goat's-milk cheeses. There are only two producers in the whole of the Touraine. The cheese shown here was made in the village of Perrusson near the town of Loches. Affinage takes at least two weeks.

♀ Menetou Salon

_Rind of natural mould_

ESSENTIAL FACTS
- ◎ 6.5 cm diameter, 3 cm high
- ⚖ 120–130 g
- ◻ 45%
- ✓ Best from end of winter to summer

*Soft pâte; uncooked, unpressed*

Centre (37)

Raw

## LE CAUSSEDOU

This mild, gentle *fermier* cheese is produced by La Ferme Poux-del-Mas in the Quercy region. In French a *causse* is a limestone plateaux, for which the Quercy is famous, and *doux* means soft, describing the nature of the Caussedou. A natural blue mould appears on the rind after a few days. Affinage takes a minimum of 15 days at 13°C.

❣ Cahors

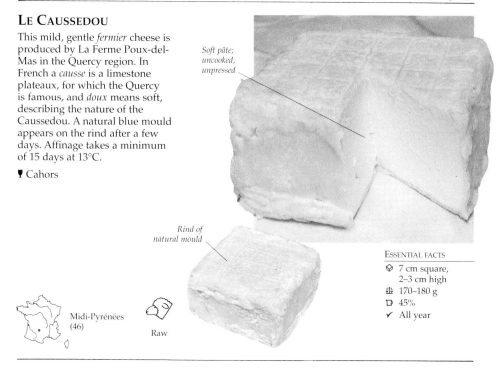

*Soft pâte; uncooked, unpressed*

*Rind of natural mould*

Midi-Pyrénées (46)

Raw

## FROMAGE DE BREBIS

This is a rich *fermier* cheese produced by GAEC Saint-Pierre in the village of Meyrueis. It is thick, with a robust flavour. In a cheese weighing 95 g, 25 g are fat, which accounts for a lot of calories! Affinage takes five to ten days.

❣ Minervois

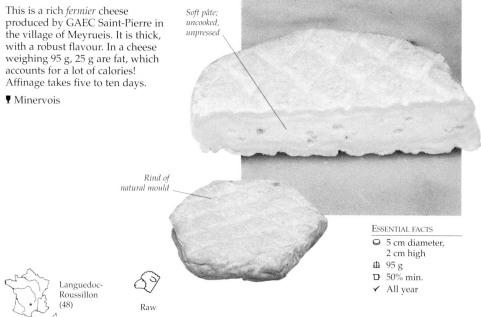

*Soft pâte; uncooked, unpressed*

*Rind of natural mould*

Languedoc-Roussillon (48)

Raw

ESSENTIAL FACTS

⬭ 5 cm diameter, 2 cm high
⚖ 95 g
D 50% min.
✓ All year

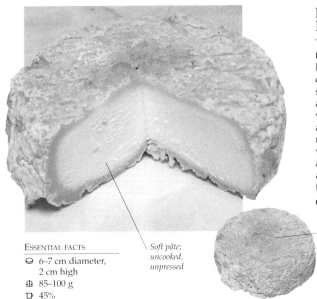

## FROMAGE FERMIER PUR BREBIS

This *fermier* cheese is produced by the GAEC La Bourgeade near Saint-Hilaire Foissac on the western edge of the Massif Central. The cheese shown here looks soft at the centre and harder at the edges because it was bought at the beginning of its affinage from the farm where it was made. The flavour is slightly sour, with a well-balanced saltiness and a subtle sweetness that leaves a pleasant aftertaste. Affinage takes one to four weeks.

🍷 St. Pourçain

*Rind of natural mould*

**ESSENTIAL FACTS**

*Soft pâte; uncooked, unpressed*

- ☺ 6–7 cm diameter, 2 cm high
- ⚖ 85–100 g
- ☋ 45%
- ✓ March to December

Limousin (19)

Raw

## FROMAGEON FERMIER AU LAIT CRU DE BREBIS

Although it is made from the same ewe's milk as Roquefort (p. 178), the Fromageon is a very different cheese, with a mild flavour. It is produced according to traditional *fermier* methods on a farm belonging to J. Massebiau at La Cavalerie in Rouergue. Affinage takes a minimum of 10 days.

🍷 Côtes du Roussillon

*Rind of natural mould*

**ESSENTIAL FACTS**

*Soft pâte; uncooked, unpressed*

- ☺ 6–7 cm diameter, 2 cm high
- ⚖ 85 g
- ☋ Not defined
- ✓ End of winter to summer

Midi-Pyrénées (12)

Raw

## Le Lacandou

In the northern part of the Aveyron, where the mountains stretch as far as the eye can see, M. Lacan makes the Lacandou following traditional *artisanal* methods. The farmer who produces the milk does not feed any silage to his ewes, allowing them to graze on the mountainside. Affinage takes three weeks.

❢ Côtes du Roussillon, Crozes Hermitage

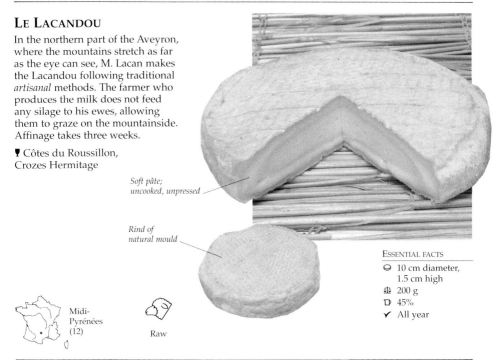

*Soft pâte; uncooked, unpressed*

*Rind of natural mould*

 Midi-Pyrénées (12)

Raw

### Essential facts
- ◔ 10 cm diameter, 1.5 cm high
- ⚖ 200 g
- 🌡 45%
- ✔ All year

## Moularen

Two women make this *fermier* cheese in the village of Montlaux, at an altitude of 600 m, where it snows occasionally. The ewes stay outdoors for eight months of the year and lamb in both October and March, enabling them to produce milk all year round. As with many washed-rind cheeses, the surface of Moularen cheese is pale orange. The pâte is creamy and thick and pleasant in the mouth. Affinage takes three weeks.

❢ Bandol or Bandol *rosé*

*Soft pâte; uncooked, unpressed*

*Orange rind washed with brine*

 Provence-Alpes-Côte-d'Azur (04)

 Raw

### Essential facts
- ◔ 11 cm diameter, 2.5 cm high
- ⚖ 240 g
- 🌡 50%
- ✔ Best from end of winter to summer

## Pérail

This *fermier* or *artisanal* cheese is made according to traditional methods on the limestone plateaux of the Causse du Larzac in the province of Rouergue. It has a smell of ewe's milk and a smooth texture like very thick cream. The flavour is soft and velvety. Affinage takes at least one week.

❢ St. Chinian

*Soft pâte; uncooked, unpressed*

*Rind of natural mould*

ESSENTIAL FACTS
- ◔ 8–10 cm diameter, 1.5–2 cm high
- ⚖ 80–120 g
- ▯ 45–50%
- ✓ Winter to summer

 Midi-Pyrénées (12)

 Raw

## Tricorne de Marans

The Tricorne was extinct for many years, but in 1984 production was started up again at the coastal town of Marans. The cheese shown was produced by two women using milk produced by their 150 ewes. The flavour is rich and slightly sweet and sour. The quality of the milk results in a high fat content. Cow and goat's milk may be used if the ewe's milk is in short supply. For a goat's-milk cheese, 1.5 litres of milk are needed, but for a sheep's-milk cheese of the same size just 0.7 litres of ewe's milk are sufficient. This *fermier* cheese is usually eaten fresh, although it may be ripened for two or three weeks to three months.

❢ Haut Poitou

*Fresh or soft pâte; uncooked, unpressed*

ESSENTIAL FACTS
- △ 8 cm sides, 3 cm high
- ⚖ 250 g
- ▯ 48%
- ✓ All year; best at end of winter for ewe's-milk cheese

*Rind: none when fresh; depends on the ripening*

 Poitou-Charentes (17)

 Raw

# Brebis des Pyrénées

The cheeses shown here are from the rugged Béarn and Basque regions in the western Pyrénées, where there is a long tradition of making sheep's-milk cheeses. Most are *fermier* cheeses made from whole raw milk, with an undefined proportion of fat. A long affinage makes them hard.

The AOC Ossau-Iraty-Brebis Pyrénées was granted in 1980. These white *fermier* cheeses are usually simply called "mountain cheeses" or "sheep's cheeses". Due to the limited amounts of ewe's milk available and short period of production, almost all these cheeses are sold and eaten locally.

It is a good idea to cut this cheese a while before eating to allow it to breathe. Brebis des Pyrénées goes well with white wines such as Jurançon *sec*, Irouléguy, Pacherenc du Vic-Bilh, and Bordeaux *sec*.

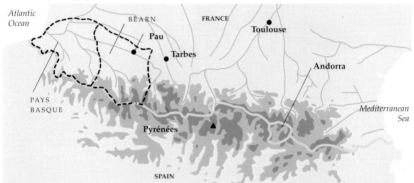

## Ossau-Iraty-Brebis Pyrénées (AOC)

These cheeses are made with the milk of Manech ewes, and *fermier*, *artisanal*, *cooperative*, and *industriel* versions are produced. There are three main sizes: small (Petit-Ossau-Iraty-Brebis Pyrénées); intermediate (non-*fermier*); large (*fermier*). Affinage takes at least 90 days; 60 days for the small version. The temperature of the cellar must be below 12°C.

♀ Irouléguy, Graves *sec*

- ◔ 18–28 cm diameter, 7–15 cm high (sizes vary according to production)
- ⬤ 2–7 kg (depending on size)
- ⦂ 58 g min. for 100 g cheese
- ⛝ 50% min.
- ✓ All year, depending on affinage; autumn for mountain cheeses

### AOC Regulations: Ossau-Iraty-Brebis Pyrénées

**1.** No ewe's milk may be made into cheese until 20 days after lambing.

**2.** Renneting must take place within 48 hours.

**3.** Coagulation must be obtained by renneting. Any other enzyme, especially of fungal or microbial origin, is forbidden.

**4.** The term *montagne* may be used only for cheeses made from the milk of ewes grazing on summer pastures between 10 May and 15 September.

**5.** Any cheese not conforming to the regulations must be sold as *fromage de brebis*, or sheep's-milk cheese.

AOC GRANTED 1980

Aquitaine (64, 65)

Whole

**STAMP OF QUALITY**
The producer imprints his initials into the rind of the cheese using special metal stamps.

## ABBAYE DE BELLOC

*Semi-hard pâte; uncooked, lightly pressed*

*Grey layer beneath rind*

This *fermier* cheese is made from the milk of red-nosed Manech ewes. The milk is bought in from neighbouring farms and taken to the Abbaye de Nôtre-Dame de Belloc in the Pays Basque, where it is made into cheese. The cheese shown has a fine, dense pâte that is rich in fat. The strong, lingering flavour, like caramelized brown sugar, is the result of a long affinage of six months, a similar effect to a stew that has been simmering for a long time. It is hard to believe that the only additive is salt. Bread and wine go well with this cheese, which is one of the few Pyrenean sheep's-milk cheeses to be found in Paris.

𝖸 Pacherenc du Vic-Bilh, Bordeaux *sec*

### ESSENTIAL FACTS

- ⊖ 25 cm diameter, 11 cm high
- ⚖ 5 kg
- ▯ 60% minimum
- ✔ All year

*Grey, light brown, mahogany, or beige natural rind*

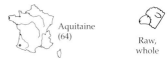

Aquitaine (64)

Raw, whole

## ARDI-GASNA (1)

*Semi-hard pâte; uncooked, pressed*

In the Basque language, *ardi* means ewe and *gasna* is cheese. When asked who produces Ardi-Gasna, the owner of the cheese shop where it was bought in Saint-Jean-Pied-de-Port said, "My shepherd made it". The shepherd tends 200 to 250 sheep and in May he moves up to the mountains, where he milks the ewes and makes the cheese. The end product is the result of a long-standing agreement between the shepherd and the shop owner, who ripens each cheese with great care. The rind is yellow, orange, beige, and slightly moist. The pâte under the rind is greyish, the taste refined. This is a *fermier* cheese with an affinage of at least three months.

❦ Margaux, Madiran

### ESSENTIAL FACTS

- ⊖ 19 cm diameter, 7 cm high
- ⚖ 3 kg
- ▯ 50%
- ✔ All year, depending on affinage

*Natural rind*

Aquitaine (64)

Raw, whole

## ARDI-GASNA (2)

This *fermier* cheese is made at the farm of Aire-Ona high in the Pyrénées, where 250 ewes and 60 cows are reared. In the Basque language, *aire* means air and *ona* pure or good. In spring, the animals are taken up to graze on the lush alpine pastures over the summer. The spring cheese, made from ewe's milk, is highly recommended. In November the animals come down from the mountains and the calves and lambs are born. During winter they are fed on corn and hay. Affinage may last up to two years, but the young cheese, ripened for two to three months only, has a pleasant aroma.

❦ Irouléguy,
Côtes de Bordeaux (young)

*Semi-hard pâte; uncooked, lightly pressed*

*Natural rind*

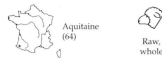

Aquitaine
(64)

Raw, whole

ESSENTIAL FACTS
- ⊝ 27 cm diameter, 8–9 cm high
- ⚖ 4 kg
- ⊅ Not defined
- ✓ Best in spring

## FROMAGE DE VACHE BRÛLÉ

These two *fermier* cheeses are also made in the Pays Basque from cow's milk. The Fromage de Vache Brûlé is scented with charred oak wood. The pâte is fine and sour.

❦ Bergerac, light and fruity

*Pâte is semi-hard; uncooked, slightly pressed*

*Rind of charred oak*

## CAILLÉ DE LAIT DE VACHE

This speciality is made by mixing fresh cheese with sugar or honey It is eaten with coffee, or mixed with sugar and Armagnac for dessert.

☕ Coffee

Raw, whole

Aquitaine
(64)

ESSENTIAL FACTS
- ⊝ 13–15 cm diameter, 5–6 cm high
- ⚖ 1–1.3 kg
- ⊅ Not defined
- ✓ Best in spring

Semi-hard pâte; uncooked, pressed

## AUBISQUE PYRÉNÉES

The letter "F" stamped on this young *fermier* cheese is the initial of one of three shepherds, who, according to local people, are the only producers of this cheese in the Vallée d'Ossau in the province of Béarn. It is made from a mixture of ewe and cow's milk, the proportions of which vary according to season and availability. The flavour is mild and smooth. Generally, the higher the percentage of cow's milk, the softer the flavour. The mixture of the two milks requires a shorter affinage of two months than that required by a pure ewe's-milk cheese.

❢ Madiran (young), Côte de Blaye

ESSENTIAL FACTS

- ◒ 26–30 cm diameter, 10 cm high
- ⚖ 5 kg
- ▯ Not defined
- ✓ Spring to autumn

Natural rind

Aquitaine (64)
Raw

---

## BREBIS PAYS BASQUE LE CAYOLAR

A young *fromager* goes to market in the morning in a van. On arrival, he opens one side of the van, disclosing a mobile cheese shop. His *fermier* cheese has a brown rind, a viscous grey and shiny pâte, and holes due to the pressure applied in the manufacturing process and during the affinage of seven months. The proportion of fat is probably very high. The name could not be more straightforward: Brebis, Pays Basque, le Cayolar, in other words a ewe's-milk cheese made in a *cayolar*, or mountain hut of the Basque Country. This one was bought in Saint-Jean-Pied-de-Port.

♀ Pacherenc du Vic-Bilh

ESSENTIAL FACTS

Semi-hard pâte; uncooked, pressed

- ◒ 19 cm diameter, 7.5 cm high
- ⚖ 2.5 kg
- ▯ Not defined
- ✓ Best at the end of summer

Hard, natural rind

Aquitaine (64)

Raw, whole

## BREBIS

This *fermier* cheese, which was bought in the little mountain village of Izeste in the Vallée d'Ossau, is made in a *cayolar*, or mountain hut. It is surprisingly strong given the smooth, mild flavour of the milk. The letters "C" and "D" stamped in the rind are the initials of the shepherd and owner – M. Daniel Casau. Affinage takes three months.

♀ Irouléguy, Graves *sec*

*Semi-hard pâte; uncooked, slightly pressed*

*Natural rind*

Aquitaine (64)

Raw, whole

ESSENTIAL FACTS

- ⊖ 26 cm diameter, 8 cm high
- ⚖ 4.05 kg
- ⅅ Not defined
- ✓ Best at the end of summer

## MIXTE

A stream, the Gave d'Ossau, passes through the village of Izeste from its source on the Pic du Midi d'Ossau, which reaches a height of 2,887 m. In the village there is a little house, at the entrance of which a small sign reads: "cow, goat, ewe". The locals come here with their churns to buy milk. Just inside the door two or three cheeses are displayed, which the owner of the house cuts on a wooden board. The flavour of these cheeses is compact, with an aroma that fills the mouth. The strength of this cheese is surprising considering that the milk is so mild and smooth. Affinage takes three months.

♀ Irouléguy, Graves *sec*

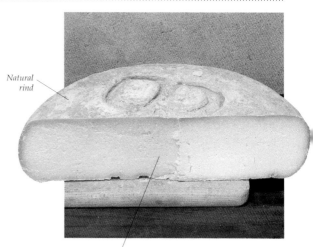

*Natural rind*

*Semi-hard pâte; uncooked, slightly pressed*

Aquitaine (64)

Raw, whole, 50% of each

ESSENTIAL FACTS

- ⊖ 27–31 cm diameter, 8 cm high
- ⚖ 5.1 kg
- ⅅ Not defined
- ✓ Best at the end of summer

## Brebis Pyrénées

At the market in the town of Saint-Jean-de-Luz a *fromager* and his daughter, who is also his apprentice, sell large, hard *fermier* cheeses that no one is allowed to touch. They have been produced on a farm near Arudy, a town in the Vallée d'Ossau. Affinage takes six to ten months.

♀ Pacherenc du Vic-Bilh

*Semi-hard pâte; uncooked, pressed*

ESSENTIAL FACTS

- ◯ 26–28 cm diameter, 9–10 cm high
- ⚖ 5–6 kg
- ⏲ Not defined
- ✓ All year, depending on affinage

*Hard, dry natural rind*

Aquitaine (64)

Raw, whole

---

## Fromage de Brebis

The region where this *fermier* mountain cheese is produced is often snowbound in the winter, with limited means of transport. Cheese is an important food since it can be made with the plentiful summer milk and stored for months. Fromage de Brebis is made for six to seven months of each year, and has an affinage of eight months. It is a large and heavy cheese, with a reddish-brown rind. The yellow pâte is compact, and the rind, which preserves it, quite solid. This is a tasty cheese that should be chewed for a while to allow all the flavours to develop. Most of the production is consumed in the region.

♀ Pacherenc du Vic-Bilh, Côtes de Blaye

*Semi-hard pâte; uncooked, pressed*

ESSENTIAL FACTS

- ◯ 25 cm diameter, 9 cm high
- ⚖ 5 kg
- ⏲ Not defined
- ✓ Best in autumn

*Natural rind*

Aquitaine (64)

Raw

## FROMAGE DE BREBIS ET VACHE FERMIER

This *fermier* cheese is made from a mixture of cow and ewe's milk. The "S" stamped on the rind is the initial of the cheesemaker, M. Sanche, who makes only 200 cheeses in a year and sells them wholesale to M. J-C. Chourre when they are still *blanc*, or fresh. M. Chourre, who has ten farms under contract to produce these cheeses, ripens and sells them. There are always some 1,500 cheeses ripening in his cellar, which has been in his family for generations. The quality of the cheeses depends on the milk – the ewes that give the best milk are two to three years old. Affinage takes around three months.

**❢** Irouléguy

*Hard pâte with small holes; uncooked, slightly pressed*

*Natural, reddish-yellow rind*

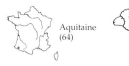

Aquitaine (64)

Raw

ESSENTIAL FACTS

  ◎ 24–26 cm diameter, 8 cm high
  ⚖ 3.5 kg
  ⴅ Not defined
  ✔ All year, best in summer

## FROMAGE DE BREBIS VALLÉE D'OSSAU (AOC)

A superb *fromagerie*, or cheese shop, can be found at Saint-Jean-de-Luz, a port near the French-Spanish border and a base for tuna fishing boats. Here you can buy sheep's-milk cheeses from the two main cheese-producing regions of the Pyrénées: the Béarn and the Pays Basque. The owner, M. C. Dupin, is a *maître affineur*, a master cheese ripener. His cheeses are refined and elegant, a perfect union of mountains and soil, ewe, shepherd, and *affineur*, with all the balanced flavours this imparts to the palate. Affinage lasts five months. Match this cheese with an Irouléguy, the red wine of the Pays Basque.

The AOC was granted in 1980.

**❢** Irouléguy, Entre Deux Mers *sec*

*Semi-hard pâte; uncooked, slightly pressed*

*Natural, hard rind*

Aquitaine (64)

Raw, whole

ESSENTIAL FACTS

  ◎ 26 cm diameter, 9 cm high
  ⚖ 5 kg
  ⴅ 50%
  ✔ Spring to autumn

*Semi-hard pâte;
uncooked,
pressed*

*Natural rind*

ESSENTIAL FACTS

- ⊖ 9–26 cm diameter,
  5–11 cm high
- ⚖ 0.5–6 kg
- ⛉ Not defined
- ✔ Summer to winter

## FROMAGE FERMIER AU LAIT DE BREBIS

This sweet, salty *fermier* cheese, from the province of Béarn in the Pyrénées, is produced at the Penen farm in three different sizes: large, medium, and small. The owner of the farm milks the ewes, makes the cheese, and sells it at the town market. Of her cheeses she says, "People now prefer young cheeses, not too salty. I make them to be eaten immediately. It is better to sell them quickly, especially the heavy cheeses. But a minimum of salt is necessary. It's really best to leave them a while, but then they get smaller and more expensive." At the start of affinage the cheese are wiped, then brushed over a period of four months.

♀ Jurançon *sec*

Aquitaine
(64)

Raw,
whole

---

ESSENTIAL FACTS

- ⊖ 11–20 cm diameter,
  5–6 cm high
- ⚖ 1–2 kg
- ⛉ Not defined
- ✔ All year; best
  in spring

*Velvety,
natural rind*

*Semi-hard pâte;
uncooked, pressed*

## FROMAGE FERMIER AU LAIT DE VACHE

This cow's-milk cheese, like the ewe's-milk cheese shown above, is another *fermier* cheese produced by the Penen farm in the province of Béarn. It comes in three different sizes: large, medium, and small. During affinage it is wiped and brushed, sometimes with salt, and then left for at least two months.

❢ Madiran

Aquitaine
(64)

Raw

## FROMAGE D'OSSAU, LARUNS

This *fermier* cheese is made in the Hameau de Bagès, in the department of Laruns, one of the cheesemaking centres of the Ossau Valley. It has a robust flavour and is traditionally eaten at the end of a meal consisting of a nourishing local soup called *garbure* (made from leeks, cabbage, celery, white beans, bacon, goose confit, and goose fat simmered together for three to four hours) followed by roast lamb. Affinage takes five months.

♀ Jurançon *sec*

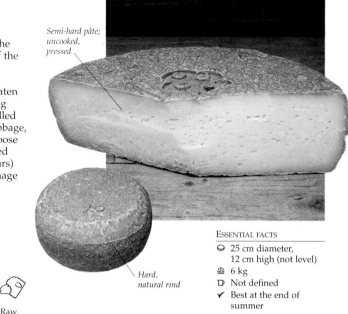

Semi-hard pâte; uncooked, pressed

Hard, natural rind

Aquitaine (64)

Raw, whole

### ESSENTIAL FACTS

- ◯ 25 cm diameter, 12 cm high (not level)
- ⚖ 6 kg
- ↴ Not defined
- ✓ Best at the end of summer

## FROMAGE DE VACHE

This is a *fermier* cheese made in Hameau de Bagès, in the department of Laruns in the Ossau Valley. Surrounded by mountains and just 29 km from the Spanish border, the town perches high in the Pyrénées at an altitude of 531 m, where the air is pure and cold. The cheese has a rich, complex flavour. Affinage takes at least two months.

♥ Madiran

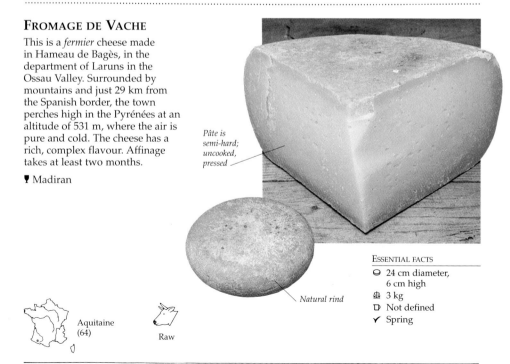

Pâte is semi-hard; uncooked, pressed

Natural rind

Aquitaine (64)

Raw

### ESSENTIAL FACTS

- ◯ 24 cm diameter, 6 cm high
- ⚖ 3 kg
- ↴ Not defined
- ✓ Spring

## FROMAGE DE PAYS, MIXTE

A sign in the shop in the area of the Col d'Aubisque where this cheese was bought says simply Fromage de Pays, or regional cheese. Most of the farms in the area raise cows and ewes. When there is not enough ewe's milk for making cheese, cow's milk is added. The pâte is sweeter, closer to butter, yellower, and less dry when the two milks are mixed. The usual affinage of this fermier cheese is eight months.

♀ Jurançon *sec*

*Semi-hard pâte, yellowish; uncooked, pressed*

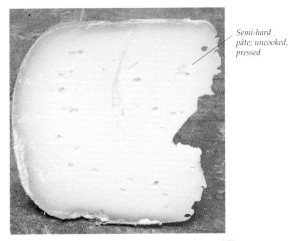

*Natural rind*

ESSENTIAL FACTS

- ◌ 25 cm diameter, 9 cm high
- ⚖ 4.6 kg
- ⊡ Not defined
- ✓ All year, depending on affinage

 Aquitaine (64)

 Raw

---

*Semi-hard pâte; uncooked, pressed*

## LARUNS

Every year, a cheese fair is held in Laruns, where shepherds from all over the region come to show and sell their products, and price levels are fixed for the next year. Because ewe's milk is more concentrated than cow's milk, only 5.5 litres are needed to make 5.8 quarts of cheese, compared with 10 litres of cow's milk. The rind of the *fermier* cheese shown here is dry, while the pâte is grey, very crumbly, with the colour of a ripe ewe's-milk cheese. The affinage of six months has given the cheese a balanced blend of acidity, salt, and fat. The strong animal smell of sheep adds flavour to the cheese. A total lack of softness is one of the characteristics of the cheeses from the Ossau Valley.

♀ Jurançon *sec*

ESSENTIAL FACTS

- ◌ 28 cm diameter, 9 cm high
- ⚖ 5 kg
- ⊡ Not defined
- ✓ All year, Laruns; October, Montagne d'été

*Hard, dry, natural rind*

Aquitaine (64)

Raw

## MATOCQ (AOC)

This *artisanal* cheese is named after its maker, M. C. Matocq, who produces it from sheep's milk in the town of Asson in the Béarn. It is a solid, well-structured cheese with a salty flavour. Affinage takes four months.

Matocq is one of the few cheeses to have a label and an AOC. It falls into the AOC category of Ossau-Iraty-Brebis Pyrénées, which was granted in 1980.

♀ Jurançon *sec*

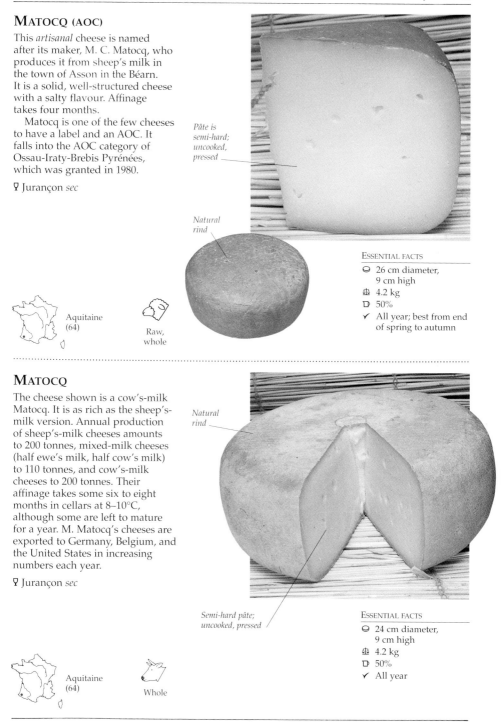

*Pâte is semi-hard; uncooked, pressed*

*Natural rind*

Aquitaine (64)

Raw, whole

ESSENTIAL FACTS

◒ 26 cm diameter, 9 cm high

⚖ 4.2 kg

Ⅾ 50%

✔ All year; best from end of spring to autumn

## MATOCQ

The cheese shown is a cow's-milk Matocq. It is as rich as the sheep's-milk version. Annual production of sheep's-milk cheeses amounts to 200 tonnes, mixed-milk cheeses (half ewe's milk, half cow's milk) to 110 tonnes, and cow's-milk cheeses to 200 tonnes. Their affinage takes some six to eight months in cellars at 8–10°C, although some are left to mature for a year. M. Matocq's cheeses are exported to Germany, Belgium, and the United States in increasing numbers each year.

♀ Jurançon *sec*

*Natural rind*

*Semi-hard pâte; uncooked, pressed*

Aquitaine (64)

Whole

ESSENTIAL FACTS

◒ 24 cm diameter, 9 cm high

⚖ 4.2 kg

Ⅾ 50%

✔ All year

Semi-hard pâte; uncooked, slightly pressed

## Ossau Fermier

This *fermier* cheese has an affinage of four-and-a-half months. Cheeses from the Pyrénées are never ripened in a hurry. The one shown here is a little young but perfect, with small holes spread evenly throughout the pâte. In the mouth, this cheese seems dry and salted. It has a good scent of well-integrated fat. As it is chewed, the sour-sweet flavour and aroma are released. This is a strong cheese with nothing soft or flamboyant about it.

❦ Madiran (type Château Montus), Pauillac

ESSENTIAL FACTS

- ◎ 26 cm diameter, 9 cm high
- ⚖ 4 kg
- ⟱ Not defined
- ✔ All year, depending on affinage

Natural rind

Aquitaine (64)

Raw, whole

---

# Making cheese in the mountains

Summer arrives late in the French Alps, but each year, as soon as the last of the winter snow has disappeared from the summits, the *alpage*, or summer migration of herds, begins. In mid to late June, herds of cattle, often owned by more than one farmer, are entrusted to herdsmen or women, known as *alpagistes*, who accompany them to the upper slopes. The animals move along at their own pace, grazing and browsing on flowers. The *alpagistes* stay in *chalets*, where they milk the cows twice a day and make cheese. The *chalets* are scattered all over the mountains and provide a kind of cheesemaking relay since the animals do not stop at a single place but keep on climbing. When all the grass in one area is eaten, the herd moves on upwards in search of new pastures. By the middle of August, the herd will have reached almost 3,000 m, just below the snowline. The first snows give the signal for the descent; stage by

MOUNTAIN MILK
The rich and creamy milk produced by cattle grazing on the upper alpine slopes is used by the *alpagiste* to make cheese in *chalets* on the way up the mountain.

stage, the *alpagiste* takes the animals back down over the same slopes, which are rich and grassy again. On Saint-Michael's Day, 29 September, the herd returns to the village. The cows go back to their sheds to calve, and the production of winter cheeses begins.

In the Pyrénées a similar summer migration, known as *transhumance*, takes place, but here, the animals are sheep and goats tended by shepherds.

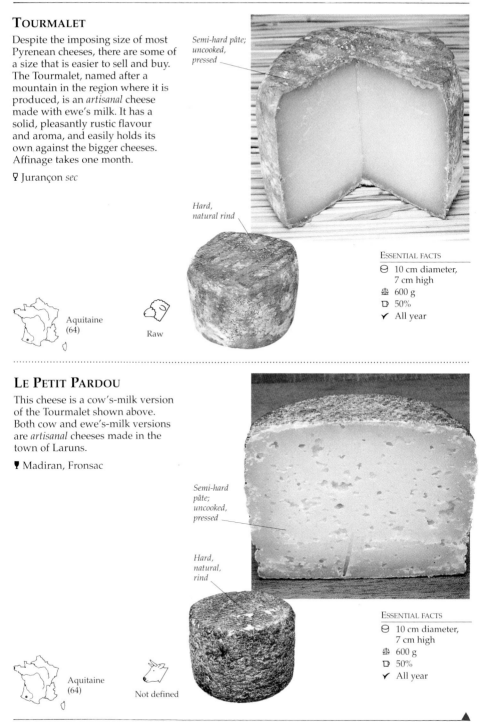

## Tourmalet

Despite the imposing size of most Pyrenean cheeses, there are some of a size that is easier to sell and buy. The Tourmalet, named after a mountain in the region where it is produced, is an *artisanal* cheese made with ewe's milk. It has a solid, pleasantly rustic flavour and aroma, and easily holds its own against the bigger cheeses. Affinage takes one month.

♀ Jurançon *sec*

*Semi-hard pâte; uncooked, pressed*

*Hard, natural rind*

Aquitaine (64)

Raw

ESSENTIAL FACTS

⊖ 10 cm diameter, 7 cm high

⚖ 600 g

🜩 50%

✔ All year

## Le Petit Pardou

This cheese is a cow's-milk version of the Tourmalet shown above. Both cow and ewe's-milk versions are *artisanal* cheeses made in the town of Laruns.

❢ Madiran, Fronsac

*Semi-hard pâte; uncooked, pressed*

*Hard, natural, rind*

Aquitaine (64)

Not defined

ESSENTIAL FACTS

⊖ 10 cm diameter, 7 cm high

⚖ 600 g

🜩 50%

✔ All year

# Brie

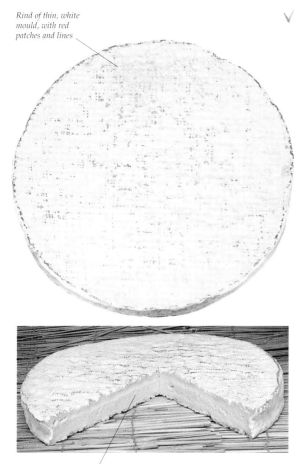

*Rind of thin, white mould, with red patches and lines*

*Soft, even-textured, creamy pâte; unpressed, uncooked*

ESSENTIAL FACTS

- ⊖ 36–37 cm diameter, 3–3.5 cm high
- ⚖ 2.5–3 kg
- ∴ 44 g min. per 100 g cheese
- ⅅ 45%
- ✓ All year

---

AOC REGULATIONS:
BRIE DE MEAUX

**1**. The milk must be heated to a maximum of 37°C once and only at the renneting.

**2**. The cheese must be cast manually into its mould with a special *pelle à Brie* (Brie shovel).

**3**. The cheese must be salted with dry salt exclusively.

AOC GRANTED 1980

---

## ✓ BRIE DE MEAUX (AOC)

Situated some 50 km east of Paris, the green region of Brie has a long history of cheesemaking. One reason for the rise in importance of the cheese was the proximity of the region to Paris, which was a great centre of consumption. The geographical separation between the places of production and affinage is a Brie tradition.

When a Brie de Meaux is sold, at least half the thickness of the cheese should be ripe. This is a refined cheese with a balanced appearance and smell, and the sweetness one would expect from a first-class dairy product. The cheese shown here is well-ripened, with a slight smell of mould. Its rind looks like white velvet and when the cheese is very ripe, the top and sides will redden. The pâte is compact, even-textured, and the colour of straw. It has a a slight scent of mould, and is full of sweet as well as smoky aromas, with a rich, condensed flavour.

Brie de Meaux is an *artisanal* or *industriel* cheese, and it must be cured within the AOC regions shown beside the map at the foot of this page, as well as in parts of Haute-Seine (92), Seine-Saint-Denis (93), Val-de-Marne (94), and Paris (75).

During production of the cheese the curd is barely cut. Drainage is spontaneous and liquid evaporates from the large surface. If drainage is too quick, the cheese may split. Affinage normally takes eight weeks.

🍷 St. Julien, Vosne Romanée, Hermitage

Île-de-France (77, 10,  51, 52, 45, 55), Bourgogne (89)

Raw

## Brie Fermier

The workshop in the Laiterie Ganot, the dairy where this *fermier* Brie is made, stands next to a cowshed. The hot, ammonia-laden air that flows from the shed is said to encourage the development of mould. Using traditional methods, Mme Clein makes the cheese, and her partner Mme Ganot cures it and then sells it at the markets of Meaux and Melun. She says: "It's good with green apples and walnuts and perhaps a glass of champagne". Since it is not the right size it cannot be called a Brie de Meaux AOC. The colour of the rind, with red marks from lying on straw, is that of a ripe Brie that is full of flavour and aroma. Affinage takes two months.

❦ St. Julien, Vosne Romanée, Hermitage

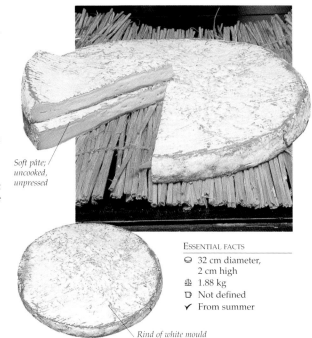

*Soft pâte; uncooked, unpressed*

*Rind of white mould*

| Essential facts | |
| --- | --- |
| ◒ | 32 cm diameter, 2 cm high |
| ⚖ | 1.88 kg |
| ◨ | Not defined |
| ✔ | From summer |

Île-de-France (77)

Raw

## Brie Noir

The aged Brie shown on the right has had an affinage of about a year. It is thick and velvety. The locals soak it in their *café au lait* for breakfast.

♀ Château Chalon *jaune*, Arbois *jaune*

*Rind is crumbly*

*Dry pâte needs to be chewed*

| Essential facts | |
| --- | --- |
| ◒ | 30 cm diameter, 2 cm high |
| ⚖ | 1.45 kg |
| ◨ | Not defined |
| ✔ | All year |

Île-de-France (77)

Raw

*Rind of thin, white mould, with brown or red stains and lines*

*Soft, even-textured pâte of uniform cream colour; uncooked, unpressed*

**Affinage of ten weeks**

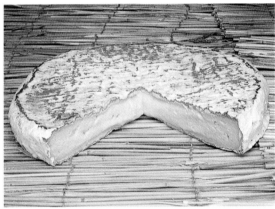

**Affinage of ten weeks**

**Fresh cheese**

# BRIE DE MELUN (AOC)

Brie de Melun and Brie de Meaux are both from the same region, but whereas the Meaux is refined and relaxed, Melun is strong, robust, and salty. This difference derives from the varying methods of production. Coagulation for Meaux takes less than 30 minutes thanks to renneting, while Melun depends on lactic fermentation, which takes at least 18 hours. The affinage also takes longer and cheeses are left to mature for a minimum of four weeks, but usually seven to ten.

The *artisanal* cheese shown has a musty smell, and the pâte is creamy, sweet, and slightly salty.

Most Brie de Melun is eaten in the region and sold fresh or ripe at local markets. The fresh cheese is sour due to the lactic fermentation, and sweet, like good thick milk.

🍷 Bourgogne

ESSENTIAL FACTS

- ⬭ 27–28 cm diameter, 3.5–4 cm high
- ⚖ 1.5–1.8 kg
- ⁛ 40 g for 100 g cheese
- ◖ 45%
- ✔ All year

### AOC REGULATIONS: BRIE DE MELUN

**1.** The milk must be heated once only to a maximum of 30°C, but only at the renneting.

**2.** Coagulation must be caused mainly by lactic fermentation but also by renneting.

**3.** Coagulation must take at least 18 hours.

**4.** Drainage must be slow.

**5.** The curd must be cast manually.

**6.** The cheese must be salted exclusively with dry salt.

AOC GRANTED 1980

 Ile-de-France (77); Aube (10); Bourgogne (89)

Raw

## BRIE DE COULOMMIERS

It is said that Coulommiers is the ancestor of all Brie cheeses. Until 1984, this *fermier* version of the Brie de Coulommiers was produced by Mme Storme, who used to rear 50 cows. The cheeses were then taken to be ripened for four weeks by a family firm in the region, the *Société Fromagère de la Brie*.

The local people prefer the cheese when it is firm, not runny. Its sweet aroma and smell of mould spread in the mouth. Today, the *fermier* version is no longer made, and only an *artisanal* version is produced.

❢ Bourgogne, Bordeaux, Côtes du Rhône

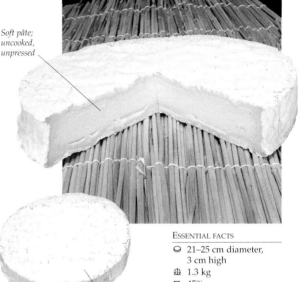

*Soft pâte; uncooked, unpressed*

*Rind of white mould*

ESSENTIAL FACTS
- ◒ 21–25 cm diameter, 3 cm high
- ⚖ 1.3 kg
- ▯ 45%
- ✔ Autumn to winter

Ile-de-France (77)

Raw

---

## BRIE DE MONTEREAU

This *artisanal* cheese is close to Brie de Meaux in taste. Its aftertaste and smell are strong for a Brie. The cheese shown is still quite young. Affinage takes five to six weeks.

❢ Bourgogne, Bordeaux, Côtes du Rhône

ESSENTIAL FACTS
- ◒ 18–20 cm diameter, 3 cm high
- ⚖ 0.81 kg
- ▯ 40–45%
- ✔ Summer to winter

*Soft pâte, no elasticity; uncooked, unpressed*

*Rind of white mould, sometimes with red stains*

Ile-de-France (77)

Raw

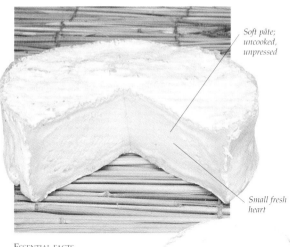

*Soft pâte; uncooked, unpressed*

*Small fresh heart*

## COULOMMIERS

Brie cheeses come in three sizes: large, medium, and small. The Coulommiers is small but quite thick. The one shown here is at the point of affinage, which is how the local people prefer it. It has a small heart with the sourness of a fresh cheese, set in a pâte of pale yellow that has a sweet and melting taste. In this one single cheese, it is possible to see the different stages of affinage. Production may be *fermier*, *artisanal*, or *industriel*, with an affinage of eight weeks for the raw milk version and at least four weeks for the pasteurized version.

❢ Bourgogne, Bordeaux, Côtes du Rhône

*Rind of white mould, with some red stains*

ESSENTIAL FACTS

- ⊖ 12.5–15 cm diameter, 3–4 cm high
- ⚖ 400–500 g
- ♣ 140 g min. per cheese
- ⊡ 40% min.
- ✓ End of summer (*fermier*); all year (pasteurized)

 Ile-de-France (77)

Raw or pasteurized

---

## LE FOUGERUS

This *artisanal* cheese belonging to the Brie group is slightly larger than a Coulommiers. Originally, it was made on a farm for family consumption, with the fern leaf serving as decoration and flavouring. It was commercially produced for the first time at the beginning of the 20th century. The scent of the fern blends with the smell of the mould. The pâte is supple and sweet and has a salty taste. Affinage takes four weeks.

*Rind of white mould*

❢ Bourgogne, Bordeaux, Côtes du Rhône

ESSENTIAL FACTS

*Soft pâte; uncooked, unpressed*

- ⊖ 16 cm diameter, 4 cm high
- ⚖ 650 g
- ⊡ 45–50%
- ✓ Spring to autumn

 Ile-de-France (77)

 Raw

## Brie de Nangis

This *artisanal* cheese was ousted by the Brie de Melun (p. 58) and disappeared from the market for some time. It was revived by a single maker but is no longer produced in the town of Nangis. The heart of the cheese shown here is barely ripe and would suit those who prefer their Brie young. Affinage takes four to five weeks.

❢ Bourgogne, Bordeaux, Côtes du Rhône

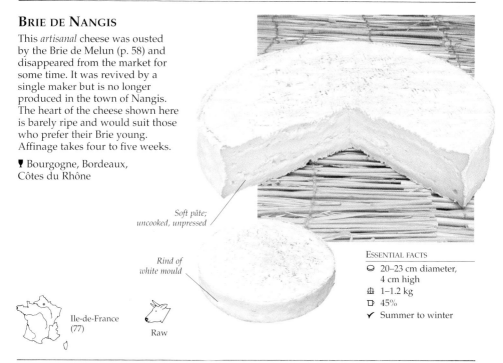

*Soft pâte; uncooked, unpressed*

*Rind of white mould*

Ile-de-France (77)

Raw

ESSENTIAL FACTS

◒ 20–23 cm diameter, 4 cm high
⚖ 1–1.2 kg
ᴅ 45%
✔ Summer to winter

---

## Brie le Provins

After a total, but happily short disappearance, the Provins has made a modest re-entry, although production is limited to just one cheesemaker. The heart of the medium-sized Brie shown here is on the point of turning into a creamy pâte. It no longer rasps on the tongue nor the bottom of the mouth. Some people like young Brie, but it is best when ripened, as here, because the bouquet of the milk, a lingering aroma, and a clear and refined smell of mould are fully developed. This is an *artisanal* cheese with an affinage of four to five weeks.

❢ Bourgogne, Bordeaux, Côtes du Rhône

*Soft pâte; uncooked, unpressed*

Ile-de-France (77)

Raw

*Rind of white mould*

ESSENTIAL FACTS

◒ 27 cm diameter, 4 cm high
⚖ 1.5–1.8 kg
ᴅ 45%
✔ Summer to winter

# Cabécou / Rocamadour (AOC)

Made with raw goat's milk from the plains, these tiny but highly pleasing cheeses mature well, acquiring body and presence. Each year some 490 tonnes are produced in the triangle between Rocamadour, Gramat, and Carlucet. In the *langue d'Oc*, the old language of the south, a *cabécou* is a small goat. The fresh, young spring cheeses, smelling of grass and milk, are well worth trying. Under the name of Rocamadour, this group of cheeses was granted AOC status on 16 March, 1996.

Soft pâte; uncooked, unpressed

**①** Cabécou de Gramat

Rind of natural mould

Rind of natural mould

**②** Cabécou

### CABÉCOU DE GRAMAT

This *fermier* cheese has an affinage of a minimum of ten days

♈ Jurançon *sec*, Vouvray *sec*, Tursan

### CABÉCOU

This is a *fermier* Cabécou from the region of Quercy.

♈ Jurançon *sec*, Vouvray *sec*, Tursan

### PICADOU

This cheese is produced by wrapping a ripe Cabécou in walnut or plane leaves. It is then sprayed with *marc* of plums and preserved in an airtight container. The aroma of the *marc* permeates the cheese. The crushed pepper causes an almost crispy, pleasant sensation in the mouth, adding spice to an already piquant cheese, hence its name.

❑ *Marc, Eau de vie* of plums

ESSENTIAL FACTS

◎ 4–5 cm diameter, 1–1.5 cm high

⚖ 30–40 g

▯ 45%

✓ Spring to autumn

Soft pâte; uncooked, unpressed

Midi-Pyrénées (46)

Raw

**③** Picadou

## Cabécou de Rocamadour (AOC)

These small *fermier* and *artisanal* cheeses are small and mature rapidly. They have a thin rind, and a tender, creamy pâte with a subtle scent reminiscent of milk and mould. The aftertaste is equally light, of sugar and hazelnuts. Affinage takes anything up to four weeks. The cheeses shown here have all had different periods of affinage.

The AOC was granted in 1996.

Gaillac, Bergerac *sec*

Midi-Pyrénées
(46)

Raw

Essential facts

- 4–5 cm diameter, 1–1.5 cm high
- 30–40 g
- 45%
- Spring to autumn

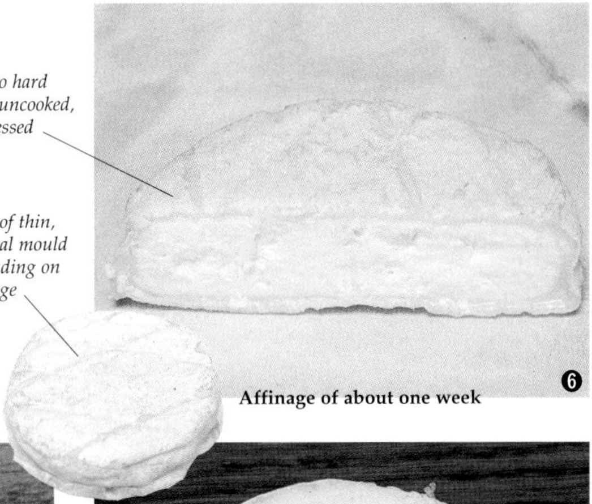
*Soft to hard pâte; uncooked, unpressed*
*Rind of thin, natural mould depending on affinage*
6

**Affinage of about one week**

4

**Affinage of about six weeks**

7

**Affinage of about two weeks**

5

**Affiange of about two weeks**

8

**Affinage of about four weeks**

# HOW CAMEMBERT IS MADE

Normandie is a mild region in northern France where it tends to rain a lot. The gentle sun and humidity produce lush green grass on which the typical black-and-white Normande cows can feed. Their milk is of excellent quality, and has made Normandie famous for its butter and cream, as well as its noble cheeses such as Pont l'Evêque, Livarot, and Camembert.

**CAMEMBERT *FERMIER***
This colourful sign advertising farmhouse Camembert marks the entrance to the farm where François Durand has made cheeses since 1981.

Since 1981, François Durand, who was born in Paris in 1961, has produced Camembert *fermier* just outside the village of Camembert in Normandie. He makes at least 650 cheeses a week with the milk of 45 cows. Some 2.3 litres of milk are required in order to make just one Camembert of 250 g. Total production of the cheeses takes two days. Although it is of an excellent quality, his cheese has not been granted an AOC, which recognizes Camembert de Normandie only.

**MILK FROM NORMANDE COWS**
The cows are milked twice a day, once in the morning and once in the evening.

**MILKINGS**
The milk is transported from the milking place in refrigeration tanks (12°C).

**THE STARTER**
The day before production, the starter is added.

**SKIMMING**
Fat (20%) is skimmed off. The milk is heated to 32°C.

**WARMING THE MILK**
The warm milk is poured into 100-litre buckets. The air temperature is 30°C, with near 100% humidity.

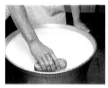

**RENNETING**
Liquid rennet from the fourth stomach of a calf is mixed in at a rate of 17 cc per 100 litres of milk.

**COAGULATION**
Coagulation occurs over a period of 90 minutes to 2 hours.

**PREPARING THE SURFACE**
A grooved, stainless-steel table is covered by a mat of boiled poplar wood.

**PLASTIC MOULDS**
The moulds are 13 cm high and 11.5 cm in diameter. The sides are perforated.

**CLEANING THE CURD**
A brush is used to remove any impurities that gather on the surface of the curd.

**CUTTING THE CURD**
The curd is cut four times vertically and horizontally with a 60-cm knife.

**LADLING OUT THE CURD**
The curd is ladled out of the bucket and into the moulds.

**FILLING THE MOULDS**
The ladle used has the same diameter as the moulds themselves.

**FOUR LAYERS OF CURD**
Each mould is given one ladle full of curds, four times round.

**THE FIFTH LAYER OF CURD**
One hour later, a fifth ladle of curds is added to the moulds.

**DRAINING OFF THE WHEY**
The whey drains naturally with the weight of the curd. It is fed to pigs.

**TURNING**
Seven hours later, each mould is carefully turned by hand.

**COVERING**
A metal plate (95 g) is laid on the white cheese which is left to rest for the night.

**REMOVING THE MOULD**
The next day, the moulds are removed. The metal plate helps the cheeses drain.

**REMOVING THE PLATES**
The metal plates are removed from each of the cheeses.

**ADDING THE MOULD**
Three sorts of *Penicillium candidum* diluted in water are sprayed on the cheeses.

**SALTING THE TOP AND SIDES**
After five days, fine dry salt is applied directly to the top and sides.

**SALTING THE UNDERSIDES**
The cheeses are lined up, flipped over and the undersides lightly salted.

**ADDING MOULD TO THE TOPS**
The new top of each cheese is sprayed with diluted mould.

**RESTING**
The cheeses are left to rest for a night before going to the drying room.

**DRYING ROOM**
This room is set at 13°C, 85% humidity. The cheeses stay here for two weeks.

**FIFTH DAY**
After five days, the cheeses are still quite deep and are developing a crust.

**EIGHTH DAY**
After eight days, the cheeses have shrunk. They are turned during drying.

**TWO WEEKS**
After two weeks the white mould characteristic of Camembert has developed.

**WRAPPING**
The cheeses are wrapped in wax paper ready for packing.

**PACKING**
The cheeses are put in wooden boxes and sent to the *fromager* or cheese shop.

**READY TO EAT**
After 2 weeks ripening at a *fromager* the Camemberts are ready to eat.

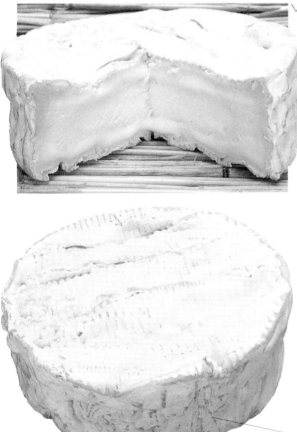

## CAMEMBERT DE NORMANDIE (AOC)

To many people, the name of Camembert is synonymous with French cheese. Even before Camembert was granted its AOC in 1983, it was the most copied cheese in the world. You should always choose a Camembert by eye: the shape should be intact, and the rind covered in white mould, with reddish stripes and stains. The pâte should be creamy yellow, supple, and give slightly to finger pressure. There should be a light smell of mould, and the taste is salty. The locals prefer Camembert *moitié affiné* – half and half – when the *filet*, or heart, is still white and not yet creamy.

*Coopérative* and *industriel* versions of Camembert are produced, with an affinage of a minimum of 21 days from the date of manufacture within the AOC areas listed. Today, it is hard to find good Camembert: a young cheesemaker has taken up the production of Camembert *fermier* (p. 64) but his cheese has yet to be granted an AOC.

🍷 St. Emilion, St. Estèphe

*Rind of white mould pierced by red stains*

---

### AOC REGULATIONS: CAMEMBERT DE NORMANDIE

1. Concentrated or powdered milk, lactic proteins, or colouring may not be added to the milk.

2. The milk must not be heated above 37°C.

3. The uncut curd must be sliced vertically.

4. The curd must be cast with a ladle whose diameter corresponds to that of the mould: the operation is undertaken in stages, with a minimum of four successive fillings (p. 64–65).

5. Salting must be carried out with dry salt exclusively.

6. After salting, the cheeses must be taken to the drying room, where the temperature is between 10°C and 14°C: they must be left in wooden boxes. Before this, they may be placed on boards, in cellars at 8 or 9°C.

7. The words *Fabrication traditionnelle au lait cru avec moulage à la louche* may appear on the label of an AOC cheese. *Fabriqué en Normandie* indicates the place of production on the labels of cheeses not benefiting from the AOC.

AOC GRANTED 1983

ESSENTIAL FACTS

- ⬯ 10.5–11 cm diameter, 3 cm high
- ⚖ 250 g min.
- ⁘ 215 g per cheese
- ⧖ 45% min.
- ⌇ All year

Normandie (14, 50, 61, 27, 76)

Raw

## CAMEMBERT AFFINÉ AU CIDRE DE LA MAISON

This cheese is a speciality of the *fromager* who makes it by soaking a young Camembert with its white rind on in cider for about 15 days. The cheese absorbs the taste of the cider and the aroma of the apple. Its smell stings the nose a little.

❢ Beaujolais, Ⅱ Cider

*Marks from cloth used during affinage*

## CŒUR DE CAMEMBERT AU CALVADOS

This is a peeled Camembert, soaked in Calvados, a spirit distilled from cider; both the cheese and the Calvados are specialities of the region of Normandie.

Ⅱ Cidre-Jasnières, Calvados,

*Decorated with a walnut*

## CANCOILLOTTE / METTON

A cheese called Metton, of which both *artisanal* and *industriel* versions are produced, is used to make Cancoillotte. The Metton is made from skimmed milk, which is coagulated, thinly cut, and heated to a maximum of 60°C, pressed, pounded, and then ripened for a few days. Cancoillotte is made by melting the Metton in a little water or milk over a low heat and adding salt and butter. Hot or cold, the Cancoillotte is spread on bread and eaten for breakfast or as a snack, sometimes with vegetables or meat. It is sold in containers, plain, or with butter, garlic, or wine. The taste is simple. La Cancoillotte is a popular food in the Franch Comté.

❢ Côtes du Jura
Bourgogne Passetoutgrains

*Metton comes in grains*

Metton

*Pale yellow, lightly salted, and creamy, with the consistency of liquid honey*

Cancoillotte

Franche-Comté (25)

Skimmed

# Cantal, Salers, Laguiole, and Aligot

**Affinage of six months**

*Ivory, semi-hard, compact pâte; uncooked, pressed twice*

## CANTAL / FOURME DE CANTAL (AOC)

*Fermier, coopérative,* and *industriel* versions of Cantal are produced. A piece of Cantal feels heavy and moist, and the pâte will melt in the hand when kneaded. The salt that is added to it brings out the full flavour of this cheese. A well-ripened Cantal has a strong taste, while a young cheese has the sweetness of raw milk.

The AOC was granted in 1980.

❢ Côtes d'Auvergne, Chateaugay, Moulin à Vent Calvados

ESSENTIAL FACTS

⊖ 36–42 cm diameter, 35–40 cm high

⚖ 35–45 kg

♣ 57 g min. per 100 g matured cheese; 56 g min. for *fromage blanc* just after pressing

Ð 45%

✔ All year

Auvergne (15, 43, 63, 12); Midi-Pyrénées (19)

Raw, pasteurized

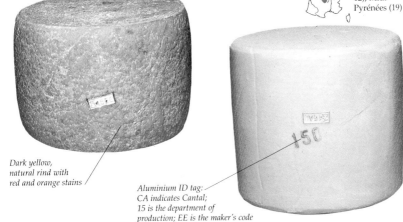

*Dark yellow, natural rind with red and orange stains*

*Aluminium ID tag: CA indicates Cantal; 15 is the department of production; EE is the maker's code*

**Affinage of eight days**

## How Cantal is Made

Three different sizes of Cantal are produced: a regular sized cheese at about 40 kg; small at c.20 kg; and Cantalet at about 10 kg.

### Renneting
The milk is heated to 32°C. The curd forms approximately one hour after renneting.

### Cutting the curd
The curd is cut into cubes of 1 cm, then brewed; the whey is removed.

### First pressing
The curd is gathered in a compact mass and quantities of 80–100 kg at a time are wrapped in a cloth and passed through the press (**1**). This results in a thick slice called a *tome* (**2**), which is cut and pressed several times to expel the whey.

### Maturing of the shape
After pressing, the *tome* is allowed to rest for eight hours at 12–15°C. This encourages the natural development of lactic acids that protect and modify the physical structure of the *tome*, necessary for its affinage. The matured *tome* is broken into small pieces with the help of a grinding machine. This process is commonly used in other countries, but in France it is unique to Cantal.

### Curing with salt
The *tome*, reduced to nut-sized pieces, is salted, with a minimum of 24 g salt per 1 kg of volume in summer, 21 g in winter, and then brewed. The salt dissolves and mixes evenly with the *tome*. The next day, when the *tome* has gathered, it is rapidly crumbled; a handful is squeezed tightly and then thrown. If the pieces come away from the hand easily, curing is complete.

### Casting and pressing
A cloth-lined mould is filled with ground *tome* (**3**), closed with a metal lid, and then passed through the press (**4**). Over the next 48 hours, the cheese will be passed through the press three or four times. The cloth is changed each time.

### Affinage
Once the cheese is the shape of Cantal, it is removed from the mould and transferred to the *cave d'affinage*, a cool (10°C), damp (90% humidity), dark, and lightly ventilated room. For at least 30 days from the date of production, the cheese is rubbed and turned twice a week. There are three stages of affinage: 30 days gives a young, white, sweet cheese; two to six months gives a golden, medium cheese (*entre-deux* or *doré*) cheese; six months gives a yellow old (*vieux*) cheese.

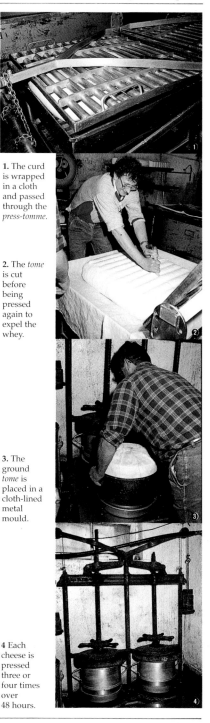

**1.** The curd is wrapped in a cloth and passed through the *press-tomme.*

**2.** The *tome* is cut before being pressed again to expel the whey.

**3.** The ground *tome* is placed in a cloth-lined metal mould.

**4** Each cheese is pressed three or four times over 48 hours.

*Firm, yellow, semi-hard pâte; uncooked, pressed twice*

**Affinage of ten months**

*Dry, natural rind*

## SALERS (AOC)

For 2,000 years, Salers and Cantal have been produced in the mountains of the Auvergne following traditional methods that have remained fundamentally the same. Salers is the *fermier* version of Cantal, and the AOC regulations stipulate that it must be made with milk from cows that grazed on mountain pastures in summer; Cantal is made from the milk of the other seasons. Of the 32 AOC cheeses currently registered in France, Salers is the only entirely *fermier* cheese: its red aluminium tag states this. Affinage in the areas defined by the AOC is for a minimum of three months from the date of production. The cheese is ripened and preserved at a temperature below or equal to 12°C.

### How dry matter affects the flavour

Salers and Cantal are not cooked-pâte cheeses, but they are pressed twice and the *tome* is ground between pressings, which is why they contain more than 57 g dry matter; a cooked and pressed cheese such as Beaufort (p. 26) contains even more. Usually, half of a cheese is composed of water, and it is rare that the percentage of dry matter should exceed 50 g per 100 g cheese. The high percentage of dry matter in Salers shows that it is a compact cheese with a firm pâte. As a result, it has volume, complexity, and an unequalled quality of flavour.

### Period of production

The mountains of Cantal are snowbound for half the year. In April or May, the cows and herdspeople leave for the mountains. Huts of stone, called *burons*, serve as living quarters, as well as dairies and ripening cellars. In the Savoie region of the Alps, these are called *chalets*. In 1948, there were 1,000 *burons* in the region and the cheeses made there were called Salers *haute montagne*. Now there are only 20 *burons* left. In 1961, a law decreed that Salers *haute montagne* must be made between 20 May and 30 September but this period was extended to 1 May to 30 October.

| DRY MATTER PER 100 G CHEESE | | | | |
|---|---|---|---|---|
| CANTAL | SALERS | LAGUIOLE | BEAUFORT | BRIE |
| 57 g min. | 57 g min. | 57 g min. | 62 g min. | 44 g min. |

| FAT CONTENT PER 100 G CHEESE | | | | |
|---|---|---|---|---|
| CANTAL | SALERS | LAGUIOLE | BEAUFORT | BRIE |
| 25.6 g min. | 26.1 g min. | 26.1 g min. | 29.7 g min. | 19.8 g min. |

## Production

Salers is produced by 92 farms. Each farm raises 35 to 50 cows. Every herd produces one Salers of approximately 40 kg per day, the equivalent of 350 to 400 litres of milk. The number of Salers made by all of the farms during the six months of the permitted season in 1991 amounted to some 18,000 cheeses, or 720 tonnes (compared with 16,146 tonnes of Cantal).

## The Salers cows

Salers cows calve about once a year and give between 6.9 and 8.9 litres of milk per day or 3.3 tons milk per year. It is of high quality and has a 34% protein content and 38% fat content. Equally appreciated for its meat, this breed of cow originates from the Massif Central. It is robust, and even-tempered, with a reddish-brown coat and lyre-shaped horns.

## Affinage of 10 months

The cheese shown opposite has had an affinage of ten months. The letters and numerals SA 15 HK on the red tag refer to the department and the maker. The brown crust resembles the surface of a dry rock. It is created by being repeatedly rubbed and left in a cool cellar at a temperature of 12°C. Its thickness protects the pâte, which is the colour of egg yolk and gives off a strong, meaty smell. The pâte is firm yet surprisingly soft, and leaves a moist, fatty feeling on the tongue. In the mouth, the flavour opens up and has a full, sweet, nutty aroma of arnica, anemones, dandelions, gentians, and other mountain flowers that blossom in summer, as well as the tang and sourness of old salt. Salers is a strong cheese.

## Affinage of 18 months

The rind of the cheese shown below is fissured and a bloom has formed after 18 months. This is caused by cheese mites that eat the rind and invade the pâte. Some people wait for this stage of the affinage: they scrape the powder from the rind and eat the cheese.

❡ St. Pourçain, Touraine

Affinage of 18 months

Midi-Pyrénées, Limousin (15, 43, 63)

Raw, whole summer milk

*Firm, yellow, semi-hard pâte; uncooked, pressed twice*

*Natural, dry, light, orange and white rind, which darkens with affinage*

ESSENTIAL FACTS

⊖ 40 cm diameter,
   30–40 cm high
⚖ 30–50 kg
∴ 58 g min. per 100 g cheese
ᗡ 45% min., 26.1 g min.
   per 100 g cheese
✓ All year, depending on
   affinage

# LAGUIOLE (AOC)

Laguiole derives its name from the village on the plateau of Aubrac. The name is pronounced laïyole – without the g. The cheese has a firm, golden pâte and a thick rind. Cantal (p. 68), Salers (p. 70), and Laguiole share the same method of production, their shapes are almost identical, and they all contain a high percentage of dry matter. Affinage takes at least four months from the date of production in the listed areas. The temperature of affinage and conservation must be below 14°C.

The AOC was granted in 1976.

**The history of Laguiole**

According to local history, Laguiole was first made at a monastery in the mountains of Aubrac during the 19th century. The monks taught their method of production to the *buronniers,* who still make cheese in their *burons,* or mountain huts.

Production reached its peak at the beginning of the 20th century. At that time, the summer migration of herds and herdspeople lasted just 142 days, from 25 May to 13 October. A cow then produced only 50 kg cheese – not only did the cows of the Aubrac breed give no more than a maximum of 3 to 4 litres of milk per day, but cheese production too was limited to the period of migration. Despite this, 1,200 *buronniers* produced 770 tonnes of high-quality Laguiole each summer.

**An association is established**

Towards the end of the 19th century, an association was formed to boost sales and the village of Laguiole became the centre of production for this cheese.

In 1939, the association changed its role to protection of the cheese. Despite this, a sharp decrease in the workforce reduced the number of *burons* to 55. During the 1960s, annual production decreased to 33 tonnes. To put an end to this, the Coopérative Fromagère Jeune Montagne was created in 1960. In 1976, production was finally allowed throughout the year.

## The Laguiole cows

Sadly, there has been a marked decline in the quality of Laguiole cheeses since 1981, due to the introduction of Holstein cows. These cows, originally from Holland, produce a lot of milk but the protein content is inferior to that of the Aubrac breed. The Holsteins did not adapt well to their new environment, so studies were carried out to find a better breed that could adapt to the climate and soil of Aubrac. A Swiss breed, the Pie-Rouge-de-l'Est, was selected: these cows give 4,800 litres of milk in 300 days, with a protein content of 32.5%. Further studies are underway to reach a goal of 5,000 litres per year of milk, with a minimum of 32% protein.

## Production

Laguiole is made in three different departments. With 47 villages producing 649 tonnes (1991), there is no comparison in terms of quantity with the Salers nor the Cantal.

Although most of the production is *coopérative*, there are currently three *burons* that make Laguiole from raw milk produced on the plateau of Aubrac, but this cheese is sold to tourists without being ripened for the minimum of four months stipulated by the AOC.

❢ Côtes du Frontonnais

# HOW A LARGE, ROUND CHEESE IS CUT

When cutting a large, round cheese, some of which, like Laguiole, can weigh as much as 50 kg, great care must be taken to make straight, clean cuts through the pâte.

**1.** The first step is to stand the cheese firmly on one end ready to make the first vertical cut.

**2.** Using a strong cheese wire, the cheese is first cut from top to bottom in two equal halves.

**3.** Each half is then cut horizontally into two halves.

**4.** Each piece is then cut into triangles of various sizes which can vary in size.

**KNIVES OF LAGUIOLE**
In the past, the people of Laguiole worked in Spain over the winter. While there, they came across jackknives. When they returned to France, they began to make similar knives. These were so successful that they became known as knives of Laguiole.

Midi-Pyrénées (12); Auvergne (15); Languedoc-Roussillon (48)

Raw, whole

*No rind*

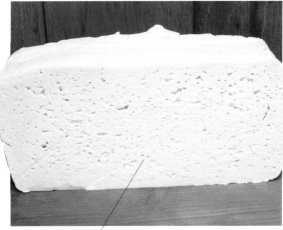

*Fresh, white, spongy, elastic, non-salted pâte*

**COOKING CHEESE**
Melted Aligot
can stretch two
or three metres
when pulled
with a spatula
and must be
eaten piping hot.

## ALIGOT / TOMME FRAÎCHE

There are two possible origins for the name of this cheese. One theory says that *aligot* is a corruption in the local language of the Latin *aliquid*, meaning "something", which was the word used by pilgrims begging for money in the medieval monasteries. Monks gave them soup with bread and fresh *tomme*, meaning a lump of cheese. The second possible origin comes from the ancient French verb *alicoter*, which meant "to cut". In due course this was shortened to *aligot*.

*Fermier*, *coopérative*, and *industriel* versions of Aligot are produced. This cheese is used in many dishes and is often eaten with potatoes. A speciality of the region is Aligot with mashed potatoes. Pieces of Aligot are mixed swiftly and melted in hot mashed potatoes, then seasoned with garlic, the juice of grilled sausages, salt, and pepper. Another local dish is Aligot with *tripoux*, or chestnut purée, accompanied by the favourite local red wine, St. Pourçain.

🍷 St. Pourçain

ESSENTIAL FACTS

⊗ Large hexagonal block
⚖ 20 kg, also vacuum packs
   of 2.5 kg
🍼 45%
✔ All year; especially spring
   to summer

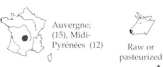

Auvergne;
(15), Midi-
Pyrénées (12)

Raw or
pasteurized

## CARRÉ DE L'EST

This cheese has a moist rind that sticks to the fingers and feels elastic. The pâte is evenly perforated and is soft, sticky, salty, and melts in the mouth. The cheese is easiest to eat when covered with mould. *Coopérative* and *industriel* versions are produced, with an affinage of three to four weeks.

❢ Coteaux Champenois, Pinot Noir d'Alsace, Sancerre

ESSENTIAL FACTS
◈ 11 cm square, 3 cm high
⚖ 300 g
◷ 45%
✔ All year

Alsace, Champagne-Ardenne, Lorraine

Pasteurized

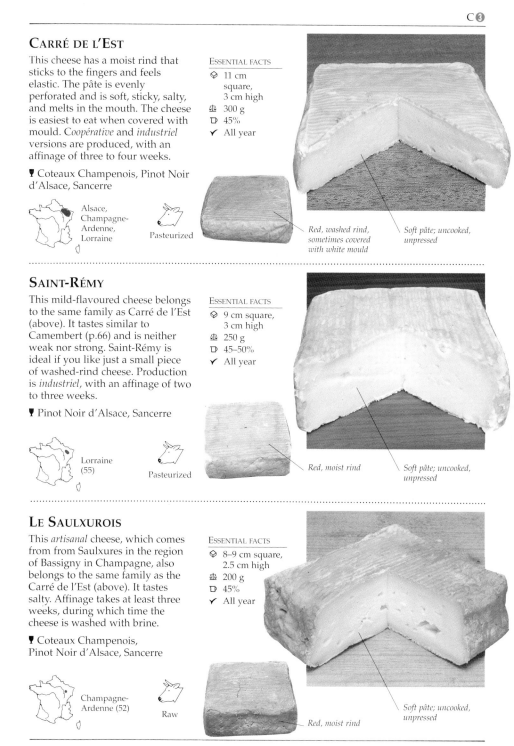

*Red, washed rind, sometimes covered with white mould*

*Soft pâte; uncooked, unpressed*

## SAINT-RÉMY

This mild-flavoured cheese belongs to the same family as Carré de l'Est (above). It tastes similar to Camembert (p.66) and is neither weak nor strong. Saint-Rémy is ideal if you like just a small piece of washed-rind cheese. Production is *industriel*, with an affinage of two to three weeks.

❢ Pinot Noir d'Alsace, Sancerre

ESSENTIAL FACTS
◈ 9 cm square, 3 cm high
⚖ 250 g
◷ 45–50%
✔ All year

Lorraine (55)

Pasteurized

*Red, moist rind*

*Soft pâte; uncooked, unpressed*

## LE SAULXUROIS

This *artisanal* cheese, which comes from from Saulxures in the region of Bassigny in Champagne, also belongs to the same family as the Carré de l'Est (above). It tastes salty. Affinage takes at least three weeks, during which time the cheese is washed with brine.

❢ Coteaux Champenois, Pinot Noir d'Alsace, Sancerre

ESSENTIAL FACTS
◈ 8–9 cm square, 2.5 cm high
⚖ 200 g
◷ 45%
✔ All year

Champagne-Ardenne (52)

Raw

*Soft pâte; uncooked, unpressed*

*Red, moist rind*

Soft pâte; uncooked, unpressed

White rind of Penicillium candidum mould

## AOC Regulations: Chaorce

**1.** Coagulation must be mainly lactic and lasts for a minimum of 12 hours.

**2.** Drainage must be both spontaneous and slow.

AOC GRANTED 1977

## CHAOURCE (AOC)

Not all cheeses need to mature. The cheese shown is very young and melts in the mouth like light snow. Production is *artisanal* and *industriel* within specified areas of Bourgogne and Champagne. Affinage takes a minimum of two weeks, and usually at least one month.

🍷 Champagne *rosé*,
🍷 Coteaux Champenois, Irancy, Sancerre

### Essential facts

- ⊖ 9 cm diameter, 6–7 cm high (small); 11 cm diameter, 5–6 cm high (large)
- ⚖ 250 g min. (small); 450 g min. (large)
- ⅅ 50% min.
- ✓ All year; best summer to autumn

Champagne-Ardenne (10); Bourgogne (89)

Not defined

## CHAUMES

This *industriel* cheese is produced in Jurançon by the Fromageries des Chaumes, one of the biggest cheesemaking companies in France producing cheeses from cow and ewe's milk, low-fat cheeses, and blue cheeses. It is easy to eat, with practically no smell at first; some people may find it a little bland. Affinage takes four weeks.

🍷 Madiran, Côtes de Bourg

Semi-hard pâte; uncooked, unpressed

### Essential facts

- ⊖ 20–23 cm diameter, 4 cm high
- ⚖ 2 kg
- ⅅ 50%
- ✓ All year

Washed rind

Aquitaine (64)

Pasteurized

# The Appellation d'Origine Contrôlée (AOC)

The Appellation d'Origine Contrôlée, or AOC, applies to wines, *eaux-de-vie*, dairy, and farmhouse products. It guarantees that a product of quality has been produced within a specified region following established methods of production. The AOC is regulated by laws, the first of which was the Law for the Protection of the Place of Origin of 6 May, 1919. This law specified the place of origin of a product, including province, region, and commune. Since then, there have been numerous revisions, until the present day, when the (INAO) Institut National Appellation d'Origine was put in control. This branch of the Ministry of Agriculture represents the triangle of manufacturers, consumers, and the government.

The INAO has established precise definitions for the cheeses themselves, such as their milk, regions, methods of production, and the length of affinage. Any violation is liable to prosecution, and penalties consist of imprisonment of three months to one year, and a fine. Some of the most important points of current AOC regulations are given in this book.

There are 34 AOC cheeses. AOC status for two other cheeses has been applied for: Tomme de Savoie (p. 188) and Valençay (p. 84).

Production of AOC cheeses is increasing, with 134,864 tonnes in 1985; 135,846 tonnes in 1986; 136,371 tonnes in 1987; 139,435 tonnes in 1988; 148,297 tonnes in 1989; 149,382 tonnes in 1990; and 151,179 tonnes in 1991. In 1991, the production of Abondance (p. 20) increased by 52.6%; that of Mont d'Or (p. 228), by 46.4%.

Prices of cheese vary depending on the shop and the degree of affinage. Large, hard cheeses are sold by weight; smaller, soft cheeses are often sold by the piece.

In the table (right) the left-hand column gives the year when the AOC was granted; the column on the far right tells you where to find details of the cheese in this book.

Obligatory mark for all AOC cheeses

| YEAR | CHEESE | PAGE |
|------|--------|------|
|  | | |
| 1975 | Bleu d'Auvergne | 29 |
| 1975 | Livarot | 152 |
| 1976 | Beaufort | 26 |
| 1976 | Comté | 112 |
| 1976 | Fourme d'Ambert | 134 |
| 1976 | Laguiole | 72 |
| 1976 | Maroilles | 154 |
| 1976 | Pont-l'Evêque | 172 |
| 1976 | Reblochon | 175 |
| 1979 | Saint-Nectaire | 184 |
| 1977 | Bleu du Haut Jura | 31 |
| 1977 | Chaource | 76 |
| 1977 | Neufchâtel | 162 |
| 1978 | Munster | 158 |
| 1979 | Bleu des Causses | 30 |
| 1979 | Salers | 70 |
| 1980 | Brie de Meaux | 56 |
| 1980 | Brie de Melun | 58 |
| 1980 | Cantal | 68 |
| 1981 | Mont d'Or | 228 |
| 1983 | Camembert de Normandie | 66 |
| 1990 | Abondance | 20 |
| 1991 | Epoisses de Bourgogne | 133 |
| 1991 | Langres | 151 |
| | | |
| | | |
| 1975 | Selles-sur-Cher | 83 |
| 1976 | Crottin de Chavignol | 80 |
| 1976 | Pouligny-Saint-Pierre | 81 |
| 1983 | Picodon | 170 |
| 1988 | Cabécou/Rocamadour | 63 |
| 1990 | Chabichou du Poitou | 79 |
| 1990 | Sainte-Maure de Touraine | 82 |
|  | | |
| 1979 | Roquefort | 178 |
| 1980 | Ossau-Iraty-Brebis Pyrénées | 43 |
| | | |
| 1988 | Brocciu | 116 |

# Chèvre de la Loire (AOC)

The River Loire, the longest river in France at 1,012 km long, rises in the Massif Central from where it flows into the Atlantic Ocean. It flows first to the north, then west. The soft plains flanking this giant curve form a region justly called the Garden of France, sprinkled with Renaissance castles and an abundance of wines and cheeses.

In the 8th century, the Saracens were repelled at Poitiers. These people, of Arab descent, had been settled in the south of Spain for centuries and gradually moved north into France. When they were expelled from France, they left behind not only goats, but also the recipes for making cheese from their milk. The Loire Valley is therefore the starting point in the history of goat's-milk cheeses in France, and remains the most important area of production.

Villages on either side of the river produce goat's-milk cheeses of different sizes and shapes. These cheeses have delicately varied flavours and include five AOCs: in the eastern part of the area, there is Crottin de Chavignol (p. 80), shaped like a drum; to the west, Sainte-Maure de Touraine (p. 82), a thick stick covered with powdered charcoal; to the north of the central region, Selles-sur-Cher (p. 83), also covered with charcoal; and to the south, a small black pyramid, Valençay (p. 84), which is a candidate for an AOC of its own; to the west is Pouligny-Saint-Pierre (p. 81), a slightly more slender pyramid; and southwest, Chabichou du Poitou (opposite).

The goat's-milk cheeses of the Loire go well with white wines such as Sancerre.

## How goat's-milk cheeses are made

According to French tradition, goat's-milk cheeses should be on the table from Easter to All Saints' Day in November. Coagulation of goat's milk is usually caused by lactic fermentation. The ferment (also called starter) is mixed into the milk. The milk rests for a night and turns sour. It is then heated to 18–20°C. A very small amount of rennet is introduced and the milk rests for another 24 hours. The curd is neither cut nor heated, mixed nor pressed: drainage is instant as the curd is ladled into the moulds, and the whey runs off through the fine holes in the sides and base. The cheese is cured dry – *affiné à sec* – in a cool and well-ventilated room at 11°C and 80% humidity, which is relatively dry compared with cellars at 90 to 100%. The drying process of both rind and pâte must be balanced, otherwise the rind will wrinkle and the whey left in the pâte will stick to it from the inside. Although blue mould will appear naturally on the rind, a covering of oak ash and charcoal powder helps to create an environment that encourages its development.

PERFORATED MOULDS
The holes in the moulds used to make Valençay (left), and Selles-Sur Cher (right) allow the whey to drain off quickly.

ADDING ASH
Covering the rind of this cheese with ash encourages the blue mould to appear.

## CHABICHOU DU POITOU (AOC)

Poitou is the most important goat-breeding region in France and consequently produces many goat's-milk cheeses. This cheese, has a delicate and slightly sweet flavour with little salt and a faint acidity. Production can be *fermier*, *coopérative*, or *industriel*.

The AOC was granted in 1990.

♀ Sancerre, Pouilly Fumé

ESSENTIAL FACTS

⊖ 6 cm diameter base, 5 cm top, 6 cm high
⚖ 100–150 g
♣ 40 g min. per cheese
◻ 45% min.
✓ All year; spring to autumn (*fermier*)

Poitou-Charentes (16, 79, 86)

Whole

*Thin rind of white, yellow, or blue mould*

*Soft, even-textured pâte becomes hard and brittle when mature; uncooked, unpressed*

Chabis  Chabichou

## CHABICHOU / CHABIS

This *fermier*, *artisanal*, or *industriel* produced cheese has an affinage of ten to 20 days. The cheeses shown here are all versions of Chabichou that were bought and photographed before the AOC was granted in 1990. The variety of sizes and shapes is interesting.

♀ Sancerre, Menetou Salon

ESSENTIAL FACTS

⊖ 6.5 cm diameter base, 5 cm top, 5–7 cm high
⚖ 120 g
♣ 40 g min. per cheese
◻ 45%,
✓ All year; spring to autumn (*fermier*)

Poitou-Charentes (16)

Raw, whole

Chabichou *fermier*  Chabichou

# CROTTIN DE CHAVIGNOL (AOC)

This cheese is also known as Chavignol and should be hard, black, and knobbly on the surface.

A fresh, white Crottin weighs about 140 g and does not yet look like a true Crottin de Chavignol. After two weeks, it weighs only about 110 g. The rind begins to take on a bluish hue and the pâte becomes glossy. It is a little salty and the balance of sourness, sweetness, and the smell of milk enhance the taste. At this point, the cheese is ready to eat. After five weeks, the cheese is dry and has shrunk. The smell is strong and the pâte has a meaty texture, with a robust flavour. This is a ripe Crottin. After four months, it weighs only 40 g. The rind is rough and hard and should be removed by grating.

Annual production amounts to some 16 million cheeses, which may be *fermier*, *artisanal*, or *industriel*. Affinage must take place within AOC specified areas. It must last at least ten days from the date of production, but usually two to four weeks is allowed. The temperatures must be kept low and the room well ventilated.

Hot Crottin on salad with wine vinegar makes a good starter.

♀ Sancerre de Chavignol

*Soft white or ivory-coloured pâte; uncooked, unpressed*

*Thin rind of blue or white mould; sometimes no mould*

**Affinage of two weeks**

**Affinage of four months**

**Affinage of one month**

ESSENTIAL FACTS

⊖ 4–5 cm diameter, 3–4 cm high
⚖ 60–110 g
◨ 45% min.
⁛ 37 g min. per cheese
✔ All year; spring to autumn (*fermier*)

---

AOC REGULATIONS:
CROTIN DE CHAVIGNOL

**1.** Coagulation must be mainly lactic with a small amount of rennet.

**2.** The curd must be drained in advance.

**3.** The words *fabrication fermière* or *fromage fermier* are forbidden for cheese made with frozen curd.

AOC GRANTED 1976

Bourgogne (58), Centre (45, 18)

Whole; frozen curd may be used

# POULIGNY-SAINT-PIERRE (AOC)

This cheese is nicknamed the Pyramid or the Eiffel Tower because of its cone shape. The cheese shown was ripened for four weeks until it was ready to be eaten. The rind is dry with a good, natural, blue mould. The pâte shows an amazing whiteness and is fine-textured, moist, soft, and crumbly. It smells of goat's milk and straw. On tasting, an exquisite sourness spreads in the mouth, followed by a salty taste, and then sweetness. A softer sourness dissolves at the end, although it leaves an aftertaste. After another six or seven days the rind is even more beautiful and complex: the colours are richer, the rind becomes knobbly, and the mould spreads.

Production may be *fermier* or *industriel*, and affinage takes two weeks from the date of production, usually four or five weeks. There are two labels: green for the Pouligny *fermier*; red for the *industriel* Pouligny *laitier* (dairy).

♀ Reuilly, Sancerre

*Rind of natural mould*

*Soft pâte; uncooked, unpressed*

ESSENTIAL FACTS

◈ 6.5 cm square base, 8–9 cm high

⚖ 250 g

♣ 90 g min. per cheese

Ɒ 45% min. per cheese

✓ All year; spring to autumn (*fermier*)

---

AOC REGULATIONS: POULIGNY-SAINT-PIERRE

**1.** Coagulation must be mainly lactic with a small amount of rennet.

**2.** The words *fabrication fermière* or *fromage fermier* are forbidden for cheeses made with frozen curd.

AOC GRANTED 1976

Centre (36)

Whole

White or ivory, fine-
textured pâte;
uncooked, unpressed

Dried for 24 hours

Affinage
of three weeks

Rind of natural
mould, sometimes
covered with ashes

Affinage
of six weeks

Long,
truncated log

## SAINTE-MAURE DE TOURAINE (AOC)

The method of production for this cheese is faithful to tradition (p. 78). The milk is heated to 18–20°C, then coagulated for 24 hours, cast in a long mould, and drained spontaneously. The cheese is then taken out of its mould and a long straw is inserted, the purpose of which is to hold the fragile cheese together and ventilate its interior. The cheese is then covered with salted charcoal ashes and laid on a board to complete drainage.

Production of this cheese may be *fermier, coopérative*, or *artisanal*. Affinage takes a minimum of ten days (usually, two to four weeks) after renneting, within AOC specified areas. The cheese is turned every day in a well-ventilated, cool cellar at 10–15°C with 90% humidity. On the tenth day, the rind is pale yellow, and has no mould. The pâte is still soft and has a sour smell. During the third week, a blue mould forms on the rind, which now appears dry. The pâte, too, changes from being moist to a dry, smooth, robust texture. After the fifth or sixth week, the surface of the cheese is dry and has shrunk. The mould is blue-grey and the pâte is fine-textured, smooth and firm. This cheese is mature, balanced, round, with salt, sourness, and an aroma of walnut.

🍷 Chinon, 🍷 Vouvray

ESSENTIAL FACTS

◇ 3–4 cm diameter at one end, 4–5 cm diameter at other end, 14–16 cm long

⚖ 250 g

♣ 100 g min. per cheese

🌡 45% min., 45 g min. per cheese

✓ All year; spring to autumn (*fermier*)

Centre (37, 41, 36); Poitou-Charentes (86)

Frozen curd forbidden

## AOC REGULATIONS: SAINTE-MAURE DE TOURAINE

**1.** Coagulation must be mainly lactic with a small amount of rennet.

**2.** The fresh undrained curd (p. 78) is cast with a ladle or curd distributor.

**3.** Drainage must be natural.

AOC GRANTED 1990

## SELLES-SUR-CHER (AOC)

A good goat's-milk cheese is defined by its lingering scent and aftertaste. The local people eat the rind: they are the ones who cultivate its mould and they consider that it contains the true taste of the cheese. About 1.3 litres of milk are needed to make a single cheese. The cheese shown here was made by the Moreau family, who run a goat farm called l'Elevage Caprin de Bellevue.

After an affinage of four weeks, the surface of the cheese is very knobbly and the rind is dry. It is covered completely with a blue-grey mould, under which is a layer of powdered charcoal. The pâte is characteristic of a true goat's-milk cheese. It is slightly hard at first, then moist, heavy, and clay-like as it blends and melts in the mouth. The taste is slightly sour and salty, with some sweetness. The aroma created by the goat's milk and the mould of a dark cellar remains.

Production of this cheese may be *fermier*, *coopérative*, or *industriel*. Affinage takes place within AOC stated areas over a period of at least ten days, usually three weeks.

Ɏ Sancerre, Pouilly Fumé

*Soft pâte; uncooked, unpressed*

*Rind of natural mould, covered with salted charcoal ash*

---

**AOC REGULATIONS:**
**SELLES-SUR-CHER**

**1.** Coagulation must be mainly lactic with a small amount of rennet.

**2.** The curd must be cast with a ladle

AOC GRANTED 1975

---

**Affinage
of four weeks**

ESSENTIAL FACTS

- ⊝ 8 cm diameter base,
  7 cm diameter top,
  2–3 cm high
- ⚖ 200 g min. when fresh,
  otherwise 150 g
- ⦂ 55 g min. per cheese
- ᗡ 45% min.
- ⌄ All year; spring to autumn
  (*fermier*)

Centre
(41, 36, 18)

Whole

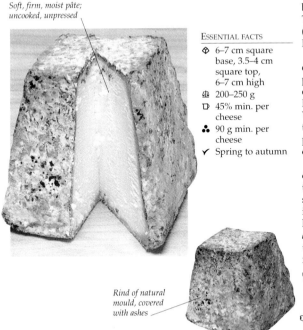

Soft, firm, moist pâte; uncooked, unpressed

Rind of natural mould, covered with ashes

### ESSENTIAL FACTS
◈ 6–7 cm square base, 3.5–4 cm square top, 6–7 cm high
⚖ 200–250 g
🝠 45% min. per cheese
∴ 90 g min. per cheese
✔ Spring to autumn

## VALENÇAY

The province of Berry has long been the source of famous cheeses. These include Crottin de Chavignol (p. 80), Selles-sur-Cher (p. 83), and Pouligny-Saint-Pierre (p. 81).

It is said that Valençay was originally shaped like a perfect pyramid. On his return from the disastrous campaign in Egypt, Napoléon stopped at the castle of Valençay and seeing the cheese that reminded him of the Egyptian pyramids, he drew his sword and chopped the top off.

When making a Valençay the drained curd is cast in a mould, then it is removed, covered with salted charcoal ashes, and ripened in a well-ventilated room at 80% humidity. Production may be *fermier*, *artisanal*, or *industriel*. Affinage takes three weeks, after which a natural mould covers the surface.

Ⴒ Quincy, Reuilly, Sancerre

Centre (36)

Raw or pasteurized

# Chèvre de Coin

Soft pâte; uncooked, unpressed

Rind of natural mould

### ESSENTIAL FACTS
⊖ 6 cm diameter, 3–3.5 cm high
⚖ 130 g
🝠 Not defined
✔ April to November

## AMBERT / CROTTIN D'AMBERT

Goat's-milk cheeses are rare in the Auvergne. The village of Saint-Just, in the suburbs of Ambert where this cheese is made, lies at an altitude of 840 m above sea-level. This is a *fermier* cheese with an affinage of ten days.

Ⴒ Côte du Forez, Beaujolais *primeur*

Auvergne (63)

Raw

## ANNEAU DU VIC-BILH

This *fermier* cheese looks hand-made and its flavour has just the right balance of sourness and salt. The cheesemaker says, "We southern people like it young." Affinage takes at least ten days.

♀ Pacherenc du Vic-Bilh

**ESSENTIAL FACTS**

☺ 10 cm diameter, 3 cm hole, 2 cm high
⚖ 200–250 g
🏷 45%
✔ Spring to autumn

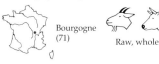

Midi-Pyrénées (65)

Raw

*Rind of natural mould powdered with charcoal*

*Soft, perfectly white pâte; uncooked, unpressed*

## APÉROBIC

The word *bic* derives from *bicot*, a small goat. This tiny *fermier* cheese is made with goat's milk in spring and summer, a mixture of goat and cow's milk in autumn, and cow's milk only in winter. It has a mild flavour, with a pleasant tang of the mould. Although Apérobic may be the smallest cheese in the world, it is ripened with care for 15 days.

♀ Bourgogne Aligoté

**ESSENTIAL FACTS**

◈ 1.5 cm diameter base, 2 cm high
⚖ 3 g
🏷 Not defined
✔ All year; spring to autumn for goat's-milk cheeses

*Rind of natural mould*

*Soft pâte; uncooked, unpressed*

Bourgogne (71)

Raw, whole

## AUTUN

This *fermier* cheese has a fine texture. The flavour is rich, refined, and rounded, with a hint of acidity. Affinage takes at least three weeks.

♀ Mercurey, Rully

**ESSENTIAL FACTS**

☻ 5-6 cm diameter, 8 cm high
⚖ 270–300 g
🏷 Not defined
✔ Spring to autumn

Bourgogne (71)

Raw

*Rind of natural mould*

*Even-textured and compact soft, white pâte; uncooked, unpressed*

## BEAUJOLAIS PUR CHÈVRE (PETIT)

This *artisanal* cheese comes from the village of Saint-Georges-de-Reneins, in the Beaujolais region. Affinage usually takes four to five weeks until the pâte hardens. The cheese shown was ripened for six weeks by a *fromager* in the city of Lyon and is completely mature. It has a slightly sour taste.

❢ Beaujolais, young and fruity

ESSENTIAL FACTS
- 5 cm diameter, 2 cm high
- 45 g
- 45%
- April to October

Rhône-Alpes (69)

Not defined

*Soft to hard pâte; uncooked, unpressed*

*Light brown rind, grey-blue natural mould*

## BESACE DE PUR CHÈVRE

This *fermier* cheese is made by a woman on her small farm at the foot of Mont Tournier, in Savoie, at an altitude of 876 m. She shapes the cheeses by hand, squeezing each one in a cloth. The cheese is at its best after two weeks of affinage.

♀ Crépy, Seyssel

ESSENTIAL FACTS
- 8 cm diameter, 4 cm high
- 170 g; 260 g fresh
- 45%
- Spring to autumn

Rhône-Alpes (73)

Raw

**Affinage of two weeks**

*Soft pâte; uncooked, unpressed*

*Rind of natural mould*

**Fresh cheese**

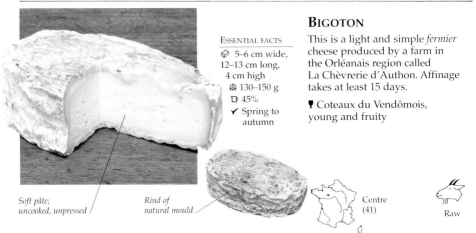

## BIGOTON

This is a light and simple *fermier* cheese produced by a farm in the Orléanais region called La Chèvrerie d'Authon. Affinage takes at least 15 days.

❢ Coteaux du Vendômois, young and fruity

ESSENTIAL FACTS
- 5–6 cm wide, 12–13 cm long, 4 cm high
- 130–150 g
- 45%
- Spring to autumn

Centre (41)

Raw

*Soft pâte; uncooked, unpressed*

*Rind of natural mould*

## BILOU DU JURA (LE PETIT)

This goat's-milk cheese comes from the Franche-Comté region, where goat's-milk cheeses are generally quite scarce. It is made with high-quality milk, and is as good as the goat's-milk cheeses of the Loire. Affinage takes at least ten days.

Ⴒ Côtes du Jura

ESSENTIAL FACTS
- ⊖ 6–7 cm diameter, 3 cm high
- ⚖ 100–150 g
- ▯ 45%
- ✓ Spring to autumn

Franche-Comté (39)    Raw

*Rind of natural mould*

*Soft pâte; uncooked, unpressed*

## BONDE DE GÂTINE

This high-quality *fermier* cheese produced by the GAEC de la Fragnée comes from the marshy Gâtine area of Poitou. Affinage usually takes from four to ten weeks, but the cheese is almost ready after just six weeks. The pâte has a pronounced acidity and saltiness and melts in the mouth, leaving a light but rich aroma.

Ⴒ Haut Poitou

ESSENTIAL FACTS
- ⊖ 5–6 cm diameter, 5–6 cm high
- ⚖ 140–160 g
- ▯ 45%
- ✓ Spring to autumn

Poitou-Charentes (79)    Raw

*Rind of natural mould*

*Soft white pâte; uncooked, unpressed*

## LE BOUCA

In the local dialect, a *bouc* is a billy-goat. This *fermier* cheese has a strong, milky aroma and a perfect balance of acidity and saltiness. The cut pâte of the cheese shown here looks good and shows the right degree of firmness. Affinage takes at least ten days.

Ⴒ Touraine

ESSENTIAL FACTS
- ⊖ 7 cm diameter, 4 cm high
- ⚖ 200 g
- ▯ 40–45%
- ✓ All year, especially spring to autumn

Centre (37)    Raw

*Rind of natural mould, covered with charcoal powder*

*Soft pâte; uncooked, unpressed*

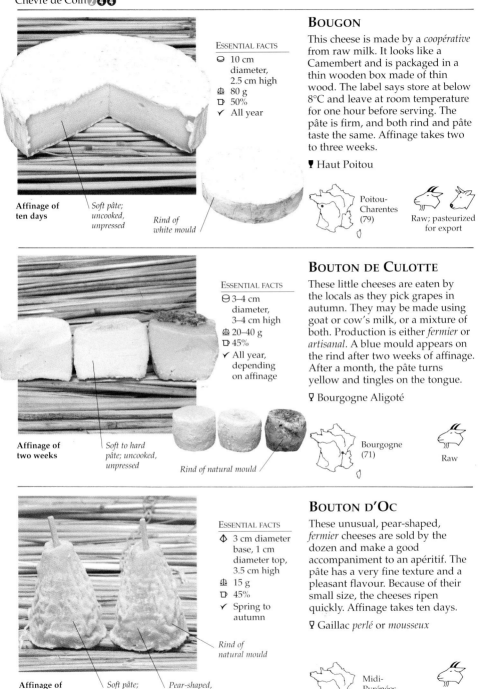

**Affinage of ten days** — *Soft pâte; uncooked, unpressed* — *Rind of white mould*

ESSENTIAL FACTS
- ☺ 10 cm diameter, 2.5 cm high
- ⚖ 80 g
- 🗋 50%
- ✓ All year

## BOUGON

This cheese is made by a *coopérative* from raw milk. It looks like a Camembert and is packaged in a thin wooden box made of thin wood. The label says store at below 8°C and leave at room temperature for one hour before serving. The pâte is firm, and both rind and pâte taste the same. Affinage takes two to three weeks.

❢ Haut Poitou

Poitou-Charentes (79)

Raw; pasteurized for export

---

**Affinage of two weeks** — *Soft to hard pâte; uncooked, unpressed* — *Rind of natural mould*

ESSENTIAL FACTS
- ☺ 3–4 cm diameter, 3–4 cm high
- ⚖ 20–40 g
- 🗋 45%
- ✓ All year, depending on affinage

## BOUTON DE CULOTTE

These little cheeses are eaten by the locals as they pick grapes in autumn. They may be made using goat or cow's milk, or a mixture of both. Production is either *fermier* or *artisanal*. A blue mould appears on the rind after two weeks of affinage. After a month, the pâte turns yellow and tingles on the tongue.

♀ Bourgogne Aligoté

Bourgogne (71)

Raw

---

**Affinage of one month** — *Soft pâte; uncooked, unpressed* — *Pear-shaped, pierced by a straw* — *Rind of natural mould*

ESSENTIAL FACTS
- ◊ 3 cm diameter base, 1 cm diameter top, 3.5 cm high
- ⚖ 15 g
- 🗋 45%
- ✓ Spring to autumn

## BOUTON D'OC

These unusual, pear-shaped, *fermier* cheeses are sold by the dozen and make a good accompaniment to an apéritif. The pâte has a very fine texture and a pleasant flavour. Because of their small size, the cheeses ripen quickly. Affinage takes ten days.

♀ Gaillac *perlé* or *mousseux*

Midi-Pyrénées (81)

Raw

## BRESSAN

Although this *fermier* cheese is made with goat's milk, cow's milk may be added depending on the season and maker. After a week of affinage, the cheese shown here has a good, balanced flavour, both sweet and sour, that will strengthen with age. In the province of Bresse it is eaten for breakfast with jam. Affinage takes at least one week.

Ⴘ Bugey, Seyssel, Roussette de Savoie

Rhône-Alpes (01), Bourgogne (71)  Raw

ESSENTIAL FACTS
- ⊖ 5 cm diameter base, 4 cm diameter top, 4 cm high
- ⚖ 100 g
- ⊡ 45%
- ✓ Spring to autumn

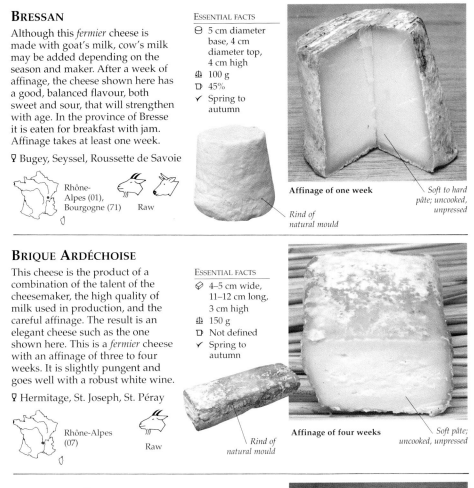

**Affinage of one week**  *Soft to hard pâte; uncooked, unpressed*

*Rind of natural mould*

## BRIQUE ARDÉCHOISE

This cheese is the product of a combination of the talent of the cheesemaker, the high quality of milk used in production, and the careful affinage. The result is an elegant cheese such as the one shown here. This is a *fermier* cheese with an affinage of three to four weeks. It is slightly pungent and goes well with a robust white wine.

Ⴘ Hermitage, St. Joseph, St. Péray

Rhône-Alpes (07)  Raw

ESSENTIAL FACTS
- ⬦ 4–5 cm wide, 11–12 cm long, 3 cm high
- ⚖ 150 g
- ⊡ Not defined
- ✓ Spring to autumn

**Affinage of four weeks**  *Soft pâte; uncooked, unpressed*

*Rind of natural mould*

## BRIQUE DU FOREZ

The cheese shown here was made from a mixture of goat and cow's milk. Since there is no smell or flavour of goat's milk, it probably contains a higher percentage of cow's milk. Production may be *fermier* or *artisanal*, with an affinage of two to three weeks.

❢ Beaujolais, Côtes Roannaises

Auvergne (63); Rhône-Alpes (42)  Raw, whole

ESSENTIAL FACTS
- ⬦ 5–6 cm wide, 13 cm long, 3.5 cm high
- ⚖ 350–400 g
- ⊡ 40–45%
- ✓ All year; spring to autumn for pure goat's-milk cheeses

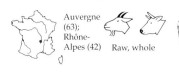

**Affinage of three weeks**  *Soft pâte; uncooked, unpressed*

*Rind of natural white mould*

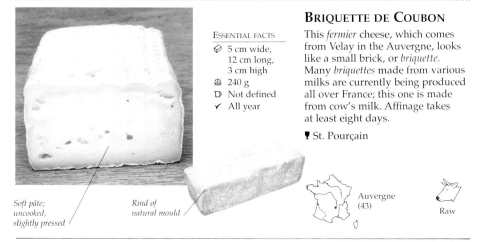

## BRIQUETTE DE COUBON

This *fermier* cheese, which comes from Velay in the Auvergne, looks like a small brick, or *briquette*. Many *briquettes* made from various milks are currently being produced all over France; this one is made from cow's milk. Affinage takes at least eight days.

❦ St. Pourçain

*Soft pâte; uncooked, slightly pressed*

*Rind of natural mould*

Auvergne (43)

Raw

---

## BÛCHETTE D'ANJOU

This *artisanal* cheese from Anjou was modelled on Sainte-Maure (p. 82) and was first made after World War II. It is a young, almost fresh cheese, with a faint smell of milk and slightly acid taste. The rind, which is covered in charcoal powder, may be eaten, but the cheese tastes better without it. Affinage takes two weeks.

❦ Saumur, Anjou Villages

*Rind of natural mould*

*Soft pâte, uncooked and unpressed*

Pays de la Loire (49)

Raw

---

## BÛCHETTE DE BANON

The light sourness of this fresh *fermier* cheese blends with the aroma of the savory, giving it the typical taste and smell of Provence. This is a cheese to eat under a shady tree on a warm summer's day, preferably at the beginning rather than at the end of a meal. Bûchette de Banon can be eaten fresh or allowed to ripen for a maximum of a week.

❦ Coteaux d'Aix *rosé*

*Smooth, soft, perfectly white pâte; uncooked, unpressed*

*No rind*

*Sprig of savory for decoration*

Provence-Alpes-Côte-d'Azur (04)

Raw

## CAPRI LEZÉEN

Each of these *fermier* cheeses produced by the GAEC du Capri Lezéen is wrapped in a chestnut leaf and packaged in a thin wooden box. The sticky, pale gold rind has a very light blue mould. The distinctive flavour comes from the creamy, slightly runny pâte. Affinage takes eight to 15 days at 100% humidity, which is high for a goat's cheese.

♀ Haut Poitou

### ESSENTIAL FACTS
- ⊖ 8–9 cm diameter, 1.5 cm high
- ⬚ 120 g
- ▯ 50%
- ✔ All year

Poitou-Charentes (79)

Raw

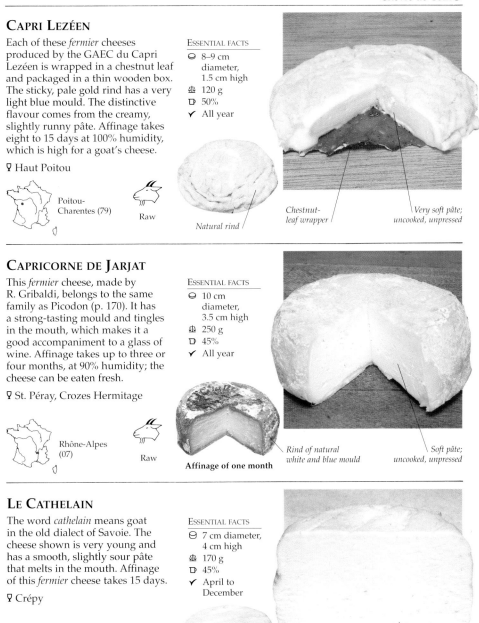

*Natural rind*

*Chestnut-leaf wrapper*

*Very soft pâte; uncooked, unpressed*

## CAPRICORNE DE JARJAT

This *fermier* cheese, made by R. Gribaldi, belongs to the same family as Picodon (p. 170). It has a strong-tasting mould and tingles in the mouth, which makes it a good accompaniment to a glass of wine. Affinage takes up to three or four months, at 90% humidity; the cheese can be eaten fresh.

♀ St. Péray, Crozes Hermitage

### ESSENTIAL FACTS
- ⊖ 10 cm diameter, 3.5 cm high
- ⬚ 250 g
- ▯ 45%
- ✔ All year

Rhône-Alpes (07)

Raw

**Affinage of one month**

*Rind of natural white and blue mould*

*Soft pâte; uncooked, unpressed*

## LE CATHELAIN

The word *cathelain* means goat in the old dialect of Savoie. The cheese shown is very young and has a smooth, slightly sour pâte that melts in the mouth. Affinage of this *fermier* cheese takes 15 days.

♀ Crépy

### ESSENTIAL FACTS
- ⊖ 7 cm diameter, 4 cm high
- ⬚ 170 g
- ▯ 45%
- ✔ April to December

Rhône-Alpes (73)

Raw

*Natural rind*

*Soft pâte; uncooked, unpressed*

Soft, refined pâte; / uncooked, unpressed

Rind of blue or white, natural mould

### ESSENTIAL FACTS

- ⊖ 5–6 cm diameter, 7–8 cm high
- ⚖ 200 g
- ⅁ 45%
- ✔ Spring to autumn

# CHAROLAIS / CHAROLLES

This *fermier* or *artisanal* cheese comes from the granite plains of the Charolais region of Bourgogne. It enhances all the best flavours of the milk, and the saltiness, acidity, and sweetness of its aroma open up in the mouth. The colours and texture of the mould are pleasing, and give a lingering aftertaste. Affinage lasts two to six weeks.

♈ Mercurey, Rully, Montagny

Bourgogne (71)

Raw

---

Soft pâte; / uncooked, unpressed

Rind of natural mould /

### ESSENTIAL FACTS

- ◈ 7–8 cm square base, 4 cm square top, 6–7 cm high
- ⚖ 250 g
- ⅁ 45%
- ✔ Spring to autumn

# CHEF-BOUTONNE

This cheese should suit modern tastes for young cheeses that are light and simple, without strong flavours. In addition to this flat-topped pyramid, there are round and square versions of Chef-Boutonne. This is a *fermier* or *coopérative* cheese with an affinage of two weeks.

♈ Haut Poitou

Poitou-Charentes (79)

Raw

---

Soft pâte; / uncooked, unpressed

Rind of natural mould /

### ESSENTIAL FACTS

- ⊖ 6 cm diameter, 3–4 cm high
- ⚖ 100–130 g
- ⅁ 45%
- ✔ Spring to end of autumn

# CHÈVRE FERMIER

This *fermier* goat's-milk cheese is produced by the Marchal farm near the town of Le Thillot in Lorraine. The cheese shown here is still slightly moist, with a blue and brown mould, and the beginnings of a dry rind. It has a good, balanced flavour of salt and acidity. Affinage takes two to four weeks.

♈ Vin gris des Côtes de Toul (*rosé*)

Lorraine (88)

Raw

## CHÈVRE FERMIER ALPILLES

This young *fermier* cheese is produced by a farm at the foot of the Alpilles, a range of small mountains in Provence. It has a delicate yet robust flavour, which improves with age. Affinage usually takes a minimum of ten days.

Ⴈ Bellet, Côtes de Provence

**ESSENTIAL FACTS**

⊖ 6 cm diameter, 2 cm high
⚖ 60 g
🝙 45%
⅄ All summer

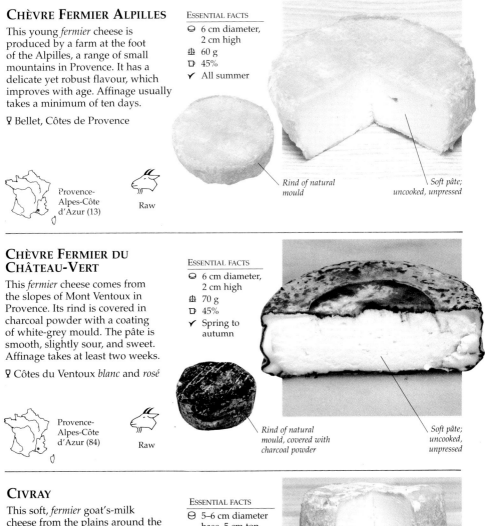

Rind of natural mould

Soft pâte; uncooked, unpressed

Provence-Alpes-Côte d'Azur (13)

Raw

---

## CHÈVRE FERMIER DU CHÂTEAU-VERT

This *fermier* cheese comes from the slopes of Mont Ventoux in Provence. Its rind is covered in charcoal powder with a coating of white-grey mould. The pâte is smooth, slightly sour, and sweet. Affinage takes at least two weeks.

Ⴈ Côtes du Ventoux *blanc* and *rosé*

**ESSENTIAL FACTS**

⊖ 6 cm diameter, 2 cm high
⚖ 70 g
🝙 45%
⅄ Spring to autumn

Rind of natural mould, covered with charcoal powder

Soft pâte; uncooked, unpressed

Provence-Alpes-Côte d'Azur (84)

Raw

---

## CIVRAY

This soft, *fermier* goat's-milk cheese from the plains around the town of Civray in the department of Vienne, comes from the same family as Chabichou (p. 79). The natural mould gives it a pleasant flavour and it has a fine pâte, with pronounced acidity and little sugar. Affinage takes a minimum of two weeks.

Ⴈ Haut Poitou

**ESSENTIAL FACTS**

⊖ 5–6 cm diameter base, 5 cm top, 5 cm high
⚖ 110–150 g
🝙 45%
⅄ Spring to autumn

Rind of natural mould

Soft pâte; uncooked, unpressed

Poitou-Charentes (86)

Raw

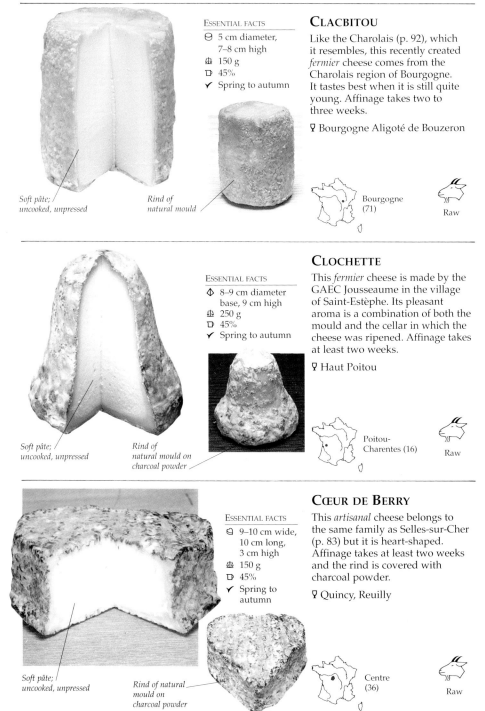

**ESSENTIAL FACTS**

⊖ 5 cm diameter,
7–8 cm high
⚖ 150 g
◻ 45%
✔ Spring to autumn

## CLACBITOU

Like the Charolais (p. 92), which it resembles, this recently created *fermier* cheese comes from the Charolais region of Bourgogne. It tastes best when it is still quite young. Affinage takes two to three weeks.

♉ Bourgogne Aligoté de Bouzeron

*Soft pâte;*
*uncooked, unpressed*

*Rind of*
*natural mould*

Bourgogne
(71)

Raw

**ESSENTIAL FACTS**

◈ 8–9 cm diameter
base, 9 cm high
⚖ 250 g
◻ 45%
✔ Spring to autumn

## CLOCHETTE

This *fermier* cheese is made by the GAEC Jousseaume in the village of Saint-Estèphe. Its pleasant aroma is a combination of both the mould and the cellar in which the cheese was ripened. Affinage takes at least two weeks.

♉ Haut Poitou

*Soft pâte;*
*uncooked, unpressed*

*Rind of*
*natural mould on*
*charcoal powder*

Poitou-
Charentes (16)

Raw

**ESSENTIAL FACTS**

⊖ 9–10 cm wide,
10 cm long,
3 cm high
⚖ 150 g
◻ 45%
✔ Spring to
autumn

## CŒUR DE BERRY

This *artisanal* cheese belongs to the same family as Selles-sur-Cher (p. 83) but it is heart-shaped. Affinage takes at least two weeks and the rind is covered with charcoal powder.

♉ Quincy, Reuilly

*Soft pâte;*
*uncooked, unpressed*

*Rind of natural*
*mould on*
*charcoal powder*

Centre
(36)

Raw

## LE CORNILLY

These three *artisanal* cheeses from the province of Berry show different stages in the affinage, which usually takes from three to four weeks – although sometimes there is none at all. They have very little smell and a nutty flavour.

♀ Quincy, Reuilly

ESSENTIAL FACTS

⊖ 5–8 cm diameter base, 5 cm diameter top, 7–9 cm high
⚖ 150–250 g
◻ 45%
✓ All year

Centre (36)

Raw

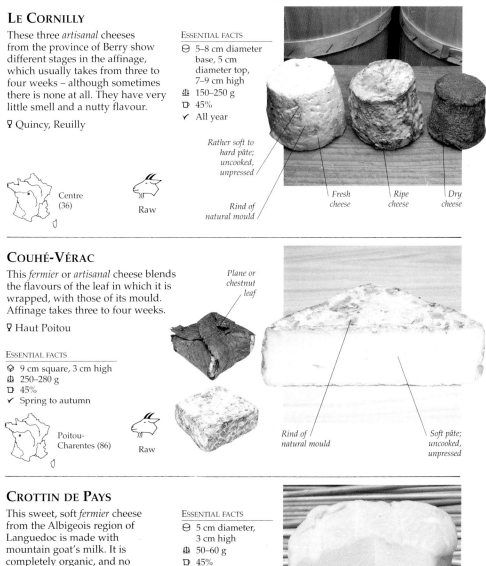

Rather soft to hard pâte; uncooked, unpressed

Rind of natural mould

Fresh cheese

Ripe cheese

Dry cheese

## COUHÉ-VÉRAC

This *fermier* or *artisanal* cheese blends the flavours of the leaf in which it is wrapped, with those of its mould. Affinage takes three to four weeks.

♀ Haut Poitou

ESSENTIAL FACTS

◈ 9 cm square, 3 cm high
⚖ 250–280 g
◻ 45%
✓ Spring to autumn

Poitou-Charentes (86)

Raw

Plane or chestnut leaf

Rind of natural mould

Soft pâte; uncooked, unpressed

## CROTTIN DE PAYS

This sweet, soft *fermier* cheese from the Albigeois region of Languedoc is made with mountain goat's milk. It is completely organic, and no chemical fertilizers are used on the pastures. Affinage takes around two weeks.

♀ Gaillac

ESSENTIAL FACTS

⊖ 5 cm diameter, 3 cm high
⚖ 50–60 g
◻ 45%
✓ All year except in January; best from spring to autumn

Midi-Pyrénées (81)

Raw

Rind of natural mould

Soft pâte; uncooked, unpressed

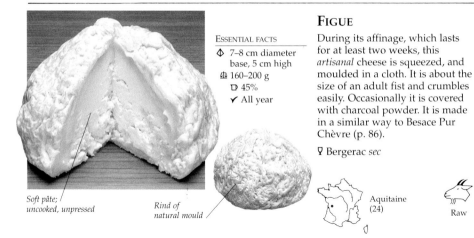

ESSENTIAL FACTS

◈ 7–8 cm diameter base, 5 cm high
⚖ 160–200 g
D 45%
✓ All year

*Soft pâte; uncooked, unpressed*

*Rind of natural mould*

## FIGUE

During its affinage, which lasts for at least two weeks, this *artisanal* cheese is squeezed, and moulded in a cloth. It is about the size of an adult fist and crumbles easily. Occasionally it is covered with charcoal powder. It is made in a similar way to Besace Pur Chèvre (p. 86).

♈ Bergerac *sec*

Aquitaine (24)

Raw

---

## FOURME DE CHÈVRE ARDÈCHE

This slightly sour *fermier* cheese needs an affinage of six weeks.

♈ St. Péray

ESSENTIAL FACTS

⊖ 9–10 cm diameter, 15 cm high
⚖ 1 kg
D 45%
✓ Spring to autumn

*Soft pâte; uncooked, unpressed*

*Rind of natural, blue and brown mould*

**Affinage of one month**

Rhône-Alpes (71)

Raw

---

ESSENTIAL FACTS

◔ 10 cm diameter, 3 cm high
⚖ 250 g
D 40%
✓ Spring to autumn

## FROMAGE DE CHÈVRE ARIÈGE

Acidity and sweetness are pronounced in this *fermier* cheese, which is made at a farm on a mountainside close to the town of Foix in the Central Pyrénées. Affinage takes at least ten days.

♈ Limoux, Vouvray *sec*

*Soft pâte; uncooked, unpressed*

*Rind of white mould*

Midi-Pyrénées (09)

Raw

## FROMAGE DE CHÈVRE DE COIN

The people of the village of Glénat used to make *fermier* goat's-milk cheeses mainly for their own consumption. Gradually, the cheeses started to be sold at the market, named after their village, and commercialized, athough they retain their homemade appearance. Affinage takes at least ten days.

♈ St. Pourçain

ESSENTIAL FACTS
- ◯ 6 cm diameter, 2 cm high
- ⬭ 50 g
- ◻ 45%
- ❤ Spring to autumn

Auvergne (15)

Raw

Rind of natural mould · Soft pâte; uncooked, unpressed

---

## FROMAGE DE CHÈVRE FERMIER (1)

The *fermier* cheese shown here was made on a farm at Cierp-Gaud in the Pyrénées, at the end of a narrow mountain trail called Cap del Mail, meaning top of the rock. It is small but well made, and smells slightly of goat. It can be eaten after the fourth day of affinage.

♈ Limoux, Vouvray *sec*

ESSENTIAL FACTS
- ◯ 5–6 cm diameter, 3 cm high
- ⬭ 100 g; 200 g (fresh)
- ◻ 45%
- ❤ February to November

Midi-Pyrénées (31)

Raw

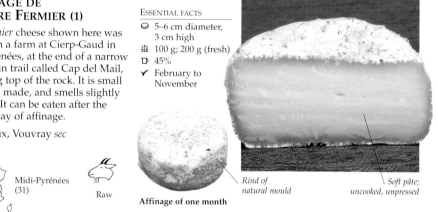
Rind of natural mould · Soft pâte; uncooked, unpressed

**Affinage of one month**

---

## FROMAGE DE CHÈVRE FERMIER (2)

This is a barely ripened, pleasantly sour *fermier* cheese that reflects the high quality of the milk from which it is made. In the town of Marciac in Gascogne, where it is produced, it is often eaten for breakfast, seasoned with ground pepper. Although it can be eaten fresh, affinage may take up to two weeks.

♈ Gaillac

ESSENTIAL FACTS
- ◯ 6 cm diameter, 3–4 cm high
- ⬭ 120 g
- ◻ 45%
- ❤ Spring to autumn

Midi-Pyrénées (32)

Raw

**Affinage of ten days**

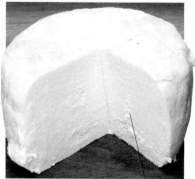
Rind of natural mould · Soft pâte; uncooked, unpressed

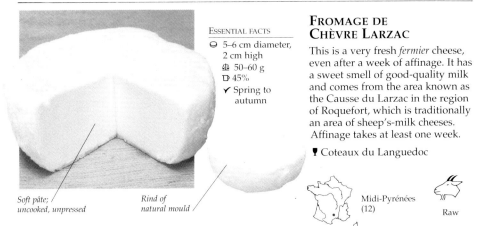

ESSENTIAL FACTS
- ⊖ 5–6 cm diameter, 2 cm high
- ⚖ 50–60 g
- ⊅ 45%
- ✓ Spring to autumn

*Soft pâte;*
*uncooked, unpressed*

*Rind of*
*natural mould*

## FROMAGE DE CHÈVRE LARZAC

This is a very fresh *fermier* cheese, even after a week of affinage. It has a sweet smell of good-quality milk and comes from the area known as the Causse du Larzac in the region of Roquefort, which is traditionally an area of sheep's-milk cheeses. Affinage takes at least one week.

♟ Coteaux du Languedoc

Midi-Pyrénées (12)

Raw

---

ESSENTIAL FACTS
- ⊖ 5–6 cm diameter, 2.5–3 cm high
- ⚖ 70 g
- ⊅ Not defined
- ✓ Spring to end of autumn

*Soft pâte;*
*uncooked, unpressed*

## FROMAGE FERMIER

This slightly spicy *fermier* cheese is produced in the village of Granges-sur-Vologne in the mountainous region of the Vosges in Lorraine. The cheese shown here has been ripened for four weeks and is dry, hard, and covered with a white, brown, and pale blue mould. Affinage takes at least ten days.

♟ Vin gris des Côtes de Toul (*rosé*)

Lorraine (88)

Raw

---

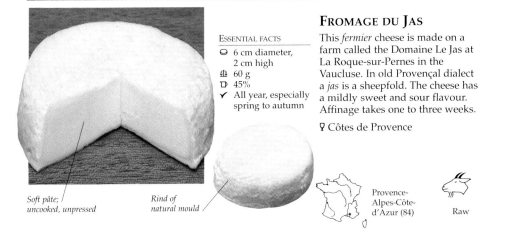

ESSENTIAL FACTS
- ⊖ 6 cm diameter, 2 cm high
- ⚖ 60 g
- ⊅ 45%
- ✓ All year, especially spring to autumn

*Soft pâte;*
*uncooked, unpressed*

*Rind of*
*natural mould*

## FROMAGE DU JAS

This *fermier* cheese is made on a farm called the Domaine Le Jas at La Roque-sur-Pernes in the Vaucluse. In old Provençal dialect a *jas* is a sheepfold. The cheese has a mildly sweet and sour flavour. Affinage takes one to three weeks.

♟ Côtes de Provence

Provence-Alpes-Côte-d'Azur (84)

Raw

## FROMAGE AU LAIT DE CHÈVRE / CHÈVRE DE PAYS

The village of Saint-Jean-de-Chapteuil, where the main industries are lace and shoemaking, has a population of just 1,700. A local farmer, J-A. Garnier, made the drum-shaped cheese shown here at the Domaine de Villeneuve. Affinage takes at least 15 days.

❢ St. Pourçain

**ESSENTIAL FACTS**

- ⊖ 5 cm diameter, 4 cm high
- ⚖ 100–120 g
- ▯ Not defined
- ✓ April to October

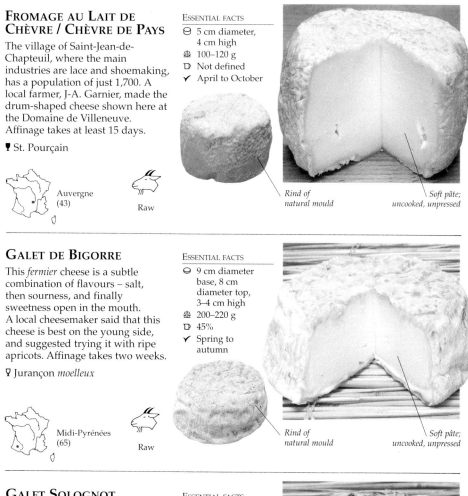

Auvergne (43)

Raw

*Rind of natural mould*

*Soft pâte; uncooked, unpressed*

---

## GALET DE BIGORRE

This *fermier* cheese is a subtle combination of flavours – salt, then sourness, and finally sweetness open in the mouth. A local cheesemaker said that this cheese is best on the young side, and suggested trying it with ripe apricots. Affinage takes two weeks.

♀ Jurançon *moelleux*

**ESSENTIAL FACTS**

- ⊖ 9 cm diameter base, 8 cm diameter top, 3–4 cm high
- ⚖ 200–220 g
- ▯ 45%
- ✓ Spring to autumn

Midi-Pyrénées (65)

Raw

*Rind of natural mould*

*Soft pâte; uncooked, unpressed*

---

## GALET SOLOGNOT

This *fermier* cheese has a strong-smelling mould and a balanced sweet-and-sour flavour. The mould is attractive and influences botht the smell and taste of the pâte. An unattractive mould does little to whet the appetite and gives the cheese an unpleasant aftertaste, even if the rind is removed. Affinage takes two weeks.

♀ Reuilly

**ESSENTIAL FACTS**

- ⊖ 7 cm diameter base, 6 cm diameter top, 3 cm high
- ⚖ 120 g
- ▯ 45%
- ✓ Spring to autumn

Centre (45)

Raw

*Rind of natural mould covered with charcoal powder*

*Soft pâte; uncooked, unpressed*

## GRAND COLOMBIER DES AILLONS

**ESSENTIAL FACTS**

- ⊖ 20 cm diameter, 3 cm high
- ⚖ 800–900 g
- 🗋 45%
- ✓ Spring to autumn

This *fermier* cheese is produced in the mountains of the Massif des Bauges in Savoie. It is usually made with goat's milk or a mixture of goat and cow's milk. The flavour increases as it matures. Affinage usually takes at least four weeks.

♀ Vin de Savoie

*Soft pâte; uncooked, unpressed*

*Dry, washed rind*

Rhône-Alpes (73)

Raw

## MONT D'OR DU LYONNAIS

**ESSENTIAL FACTS**

- ⊖ 10 cm diameter, 1–1.5 cm high
- ⚖ 120–140 g
- 🗋 45%
- ✓ Spring to autumn

The characteristics of this small *fermier* or *artisanal* goat's-milk cheese from Lyon, are the blue mould and reddish rind that appear after a long and very humid affinage of two to four weeks. The cheese has a strong taste of salt, and no acidity.

♀ Beaujolais, Mâcon

*Soft pâte; uncooked, unpressed*

*Rind of natural mould*

Rhône-Alpes (69)

Raw

## GALETTE DES MONTS DU LYONNAIS

**ESSENTIAL FACTS**

- ⊖ 10 cm diameter, 1.5 cm high
- ⚖ 100–140 g
- 🗋 45%
- ✓ All year

This *artisanal* cheese has a soft, gentle flavour, more like milk than cheese. The consistency is so runny that it is eaten with a spoon and is difficult to transport without its thin wooden container. It is made by only one cheesemaker in the Monts du Lyonnais. Affinage takes two to three weeks.

♀ Coteaux du Lyonnais

*Runny pâte; uncooked, unpressed*

*Rind of natural mould*

Rhône-Alpes (69)

Raw

## MÂCONNAIS

This *fermier* or *artisanal* cheese, also called Chevreton de Mâcon, is made solely from goat or cow's milk, or a mixture of the two depending on the season and manufacturer. The cheese shown is hard enough to make *fromage fort* (p. 140). A faint smell of spring herbs comes from the dense pâte. Affinage takes at least two weeks.

♀ Bourgogne Aligoté

ESSENTIAL FACTS

⊖ 4–5 cm diameter,
   3–4 cm high
⚖ 50–60 g
⊐ 45%
✔ All year

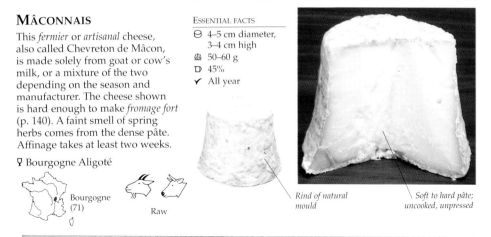

Bourgogne (71)

Raw

Rind of natural mould

Soft to hard pâte; uncooked, unpressed

## PAVÉ BLÉSOIS

Both square and rectangular versions of this *artisanal* cheese are produced in the Blésois region near the town of Blois on the River Loire. The rind has a dry surface covered with a silvery blue mould. When cut, the pâte is clean, fine-textured, and tingles on the tongue. Affinage takes two to four weeks.

♀ Sancerre, Pouilly Fumé

ESSENTIAL FACTS

◈ 8 cm square, 3–4 cm
   high (square)
◈ 11–12 cm long,
   6–7 cm wide,
   3.5 cm high (rectangle)
⚖ 250 g (square);
   300 g (rectangle)
⊐ 45%
✔ Spring to autumn

Rind of natural mould on charcoal powder

Centre (41)

Raw

Soft pâte; uncooked, unpressed

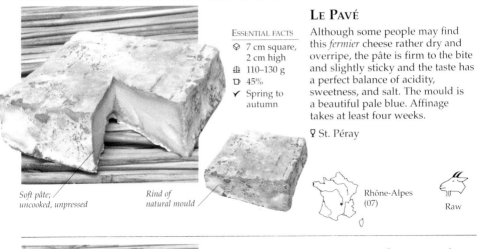

## LE PAVÉ

Although some people may find this *fermier* cheese rather dry and overripe, the pâte is firm to the bite and slightly sticky and the taste has a perfect balance of acidity, sweetness, and salt. The mould is a beautiful pale blue. Affinage takes at least four weeks.

♀ St. Péray

ESSENTIAL FACTS
◈ 7 cm square, 2 cm high
⚖ 110–130 g
🝑 45%
✔ Spring to autumn

Soft pâte; uncooked, unpressed

Rind of natural mould

Rhône-Alpes (07)

Raw

---

## PAVÉ DE LA GINESTARIÉ

This is an organic mountain goat's-milk cheese from the Albigeois region of Languedoc. It has an affinage of at least two weeks, but the *fermier* method of production is a secret. There are traces of straw on the rind as well as in the flavour. The straw absorbs water and its bacteria play a role in the ripening.

🍷 Coteaux du Languedoc, Collioure

ESSENTIAL FACTS
◈ 8 cm square, 2–2.5 cm high
⚖ 150–200 g
🝑 45%
✔ All year except January; best from spring to autumn

Soft pâte; uncooked, unpressed

Rind of spots of natural mould

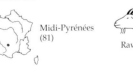

Midi-Pyrénées (81)

Raw

---

## POURLY

This *artisanal* cheese is produced in the limestone plateaux of the Auxerrois regions of Bourgogne. It is ideal for those who like a light goat's-milk cheese. Affinage usually takes two to four weeks, although the cheese may be eaten almost fresh, after the fifth day.

🍷 Sauvignon de St. Bris

ESSENTIAL FACTS
⊖ 7 cm diameter base, 6 cm diameter top, 6–7 cm high
⚖ 250–300 g
🝑 45%
✔ Spring to autumn

Soft pâte; uncooked, unpressed

Rind of natural mould

Bourgogne (89)

Raw

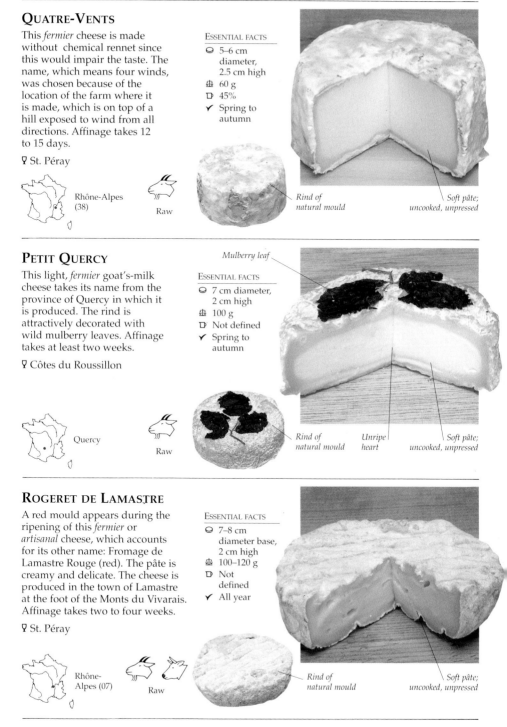

## QUATRE-VENTS

This *fermier* cheese is made without chemical rennet since this would impair the taste. The name, which means four winds, was chosen because of the location of the farm where it is made, which is on top of a hill exposed to wind from all directions. Affinage takes 12 to 15 days.

♈ St. Péray

Rhône-Alpes (38)

Raw

ESSENTIAL FACTS

⊖ 5–6 cm diameter, 2.5 cm high
⚖ 60 g
🌡 45%
✔ Spring to autumn

Rind of natural mould

Soft pâte; uncooked, unpressed

## PETIT QUERCY

This light, *fermier* goat's-milk cheese takes its name from the province of Quercy in which it is produced. The rind is attractively decorated with wild mulberry leaves. Affinage takes at least two weeks.

♈ Côtes du Roussillon

Quercy

Raw

*Mulberry leaf*

ESSENTIAL FACTS

⊖ 7 cm diameter, 2 cm high
⚖ 100 g
🌡 Not defined
✔ Spring to autumn

Rind of natural mould

Unripe heart

Soft pâte; uncooked, unpressed

## ROGERET DE LAMASTRE

A red mould appears during the ripening of this *fermier* or *artisanal* cheese, which accounts for its other name: Fromage de Lamastre Rouge (red). The pâte is creamy and delicate. The cheese is produced in the town of Lamastre at the foot of the Monts du Vivarais. Affinage takes two to four weeks.

♈ St. Péray

Rhône-Alpes (07)

Raw

ESSENTIAL FACTS

⊖ 7–8 cm diameter base, 2 cm high
⚖ 100–120 g
🌡 Not defined
✔ All year

Rind of natural mould

Soft pâte; uncooked, unpressed

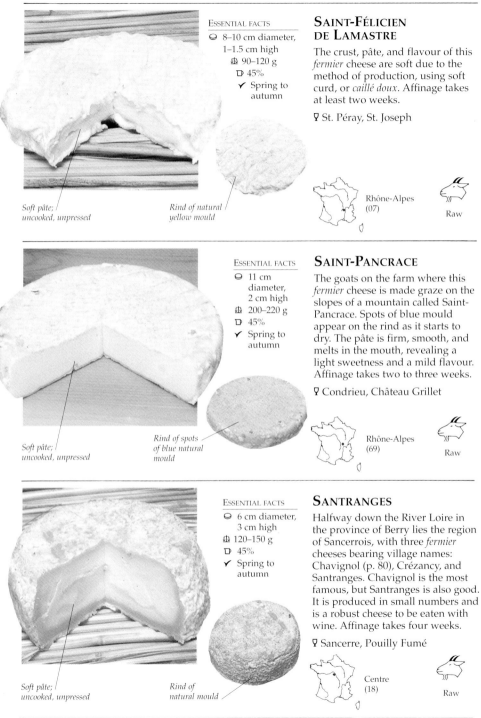

ESSENTIAL FACTS
- 8–10 cm diameter, 1–1.5 cm high
- 90–120 g
- 45%
- Spring to autumn

## SAINT-FÉLICIEN DE LAMASTRE

The crust, pâte, and flavour of this *fermier* cheese are soft due to the method of production, using soft curd, or *caillé doux*. Affinage takes at least two weeks.

♥ St. Péray, St. Joseph

*Soft pâte; uncooked, unpressed*

*Rind of natural yellow mould*

Rhône-Alpes (07)

Raw

ESSENTIAL FACTS
- 11 cm diameter, 2 cm high
- 200–220 g
- 45%
- Spring to autumn

## SAINT-PANCRACE

The goats on the farm where this *fermier* cheese is made graze on the slopes of a mountain called Saint-Pancrace. Spots of blue mould appear on the rind as it starts to dry. The pâte is firm, smooth, and melts in the mouth, revealing a light sweetness and a mild flavour. Affinage takes two to three weeks.

♥ Condrieu, Château Grillet

*Soft pâte; uncooked, unpressed*

*Rind of spots of blue natural mould*

Rhône-Alpes (69)

Raw

ESSENTIAL FACTS
- 6 cm diameter, 3 cm high
- 120–150 g
- 45%
- Spring to autumn

## SANTRANGES

Halfway down the River Loire in the province of Berry lies the region of Sancerrois, with three *fermier* cheeses bearing village names: Chavignol (p. 80), Crézancy, and Santranges. Chavignol is the most famous, but Santranges is also good. It is produced in small numbers and is a robust cheese to be eaten with wine. Affinage takes four weeks.

♥ Sancerre, Pouilly Fumé

*Soft pâte; uncooked, unpressed*

*Rind of natural mould*

Centre (18)

Raw

## SÉCHON DE CHÈVRE DRÔMOIS

This *fermier* cheese is called a *séchon*, which means a small, dry cheese. It is named after the River Drôme in the immense Dauphiné region of southeast France where it is produced. The flavour is rather salty as well as sweet. Affinage takes at least three weeks.

♈ St. Péray

**ESSENTIAL FACTS**

⊖ 5 cm diameter, 2 cm high
⚖ 50 g
Ⅾ 45%
✓ All year

Rhône-Alpes (26)

Raw

*Rind of natural mould*

*Soft to hard pâte; uncooked, unpressed*

---

## TARENTAIS

This *fermier* cheese comes from the Tarentaise region of Savoie. After four weeks of ripening, a slight blue mould covers the rind. After another week, a red and blue mould develops. Affinage takes from 15 days to three months; the cheese may also be eaten fresh.

♈ Crépy

**ESSENTIAL FACTS**

⊖ 6–7 cm diameter, 7 cm high
⚖ 250 g
Ⅾ 45%
✓ Spring to autumn

Rhône-Alpes (73)

Raw

*Rind of natural mould*

*Soft pâte; uncooked, unpressed*

---

## LA TAUPINIÈRE

This new *fermier* cheese is similar in shape to Gaperon (p. 150) and is made with highly concentrated milk. It is produced with great care and attention by M. Jousseaume at his farm at St. Estèphe in the province of Angoumois. During the two-week period of affinage, the cheese absorbs natural mould in the cellar, which gives it a good flavour.

♈ Haut Poitou

**ESSENTIAL FACTS**

⊖ 9 cm diameter base, 5 cm high
⚖ 220–250 g
Ⅾ 45%
✓ All year

Poitou-Charentes (16)

Raw

*Rind of natural mould on charcoal powder*

*Soft pâte; uncooked, unpressed*

Soft pâte;
uncooked, unpressed

Rind of
natural mould

ESSENTIAL FACTS

⊖ 6 cm diameter
base,
5 cm diameter top,
4–5 cm high
⚖ 170–200 g
◻ 45%
✔ Spring to autumn

# TOUCY

This goat's-milk cheese is made in
the Auxerrois region in northern
Bourgogne. It is light and easy to
eat. Both *fermier* and *artisanal*
versions are produced, with an
affinage of at least ten days.

♈ Sauvignon de St. Bris

Bourgogne
(89)

Raw

---

Soft pâte;
uncooked,
unpressed

Rind of natural
mould, covered with
charcoal powder

ESSENTIAL FACTS

⊖ 6–7 cm
diameter,
3 cm high
⚖ 90–100 g
◻ 45%
✔ Spring to
autumn

# VENDÔMOIS

This *fermier* goat's-milk cheese is
produced on farms in the
Vendômois region north of the
town of Vendôme. Although the
rind of the cheese shown here
would suggest that it is fully ripe,
the cut pâte is clearly rather young.
It is fine and slightly sour. Affinage
takes a minimum of ten days.

♈ Coteaux du Vendômois

Centre
(41)

Raw

---

Cheese soaked
in oil and
Provençal herbs
absorbs their
flavours

# CROTTIN DE BERRY À L'HUILE D'OLIVE

To make this Provençal speciality,
small goat's-milk cheeses with a
mild soft pâte are soaked in olive
oil flavoured with pepper, thyme,
rosemary, laurel, juniper berries,
and garlic. They are usually served
with bread or salad and tomatoes.

♈ Tavel *rosé*, Sancerre *rosé*

Provence-
Alpes-Côte-
d'Azur

Not
defined

## CHÈVRE À L'HUILE D'OLIVE ET À LA SARRIETTE

Small, young Provençal goat's-milk cheeses are soaked in olive oil with berries and savory leaves to make this local speciality. Choose a cheese with no mould, which would discolour the mixture. The savory must be quite dry.

♀ Bandol *rosé*

*Olive oil flavoured with dried savory and berries*

Provence-Alpes-Côte-d'Azur (04)      Not defined

---

# Seasonal goat's-milk cheeses

Jean-Pierre Moreau is the owner of the Elevage Caprin de Bellevue, where he, his wife, and two employees raise 200 goats and eight billy-goats. All the goats belong to the pedigree white Saanen (top right) and brown Alpine breeds, whose quality is reflected in his cheeses. M. Moreau himself takes the cheeses to Paris twice a week.

The flavour of a goat's-milk cheese varies according to a number of factors: the breed of goat, what the animals are fed on, the way they are raised, the protein and fat content of the milk, the shape of the cheese, and the methods of coagulation and drainage, to name but a few. The goats first give birth at a year old, and subsequently once a year, between January and mid-March. Two or three kids are born to each goat; surplus kids are sold off immediately since their value diminishes as they grow. At the age of two, goats begin to give more milk, and continue to produce it for about five years. Around 200 goats give some 700 litres of milk, which is used to make 12 different cheeses.

Seasonal cheeses are made by traditional methods using milk produced after the birth of the kid in spring. Fresh spring milk, from goats grazing on lush grass outdoors, is used to make spring cheeses from April to May. Modern goat's-milk cheeses are made using milk from animals kept in sheds and fed on hay. Thanks to artificial insemination and frozen curd, goat's-milk cheeses can be made and sold even in winter, but they lack the flavour of the seasonal cheeses.

107

## CHEVRETTE DES BAUGES

In the mountain region of Savoie, a cheese made from a blend of goat and cow's milk is called a *chevrette*, while a pure goat's-milk cheese is a *chevrotin*. Today, this *fermier* cheese is made only by older producers, on two or three farms, and is in danger of dying out. The top picture shows a cheese made from three-quarters goat's milk and one-quarter cow's milk and was photographed at a cheese shop in Thonon, near Lake Geneva.

The cheese in the lower picture was made with equal proportions of the same milks; it was found in a shop in Chambéry. The owners of both cheese shops are well known for their Savoie cheeses and they also ripen them according to their own methods. Both claim that the mould that forms on a *chevrette* depends on the type of food the animals eat, their exact location on the mountainsides, and even on whether they are milked in the morning or evening.This explains why each of these cheeses has such an individual taste. Affinage takes one to three months.

♀ Seyssel

*Rind of natural mould*

*Semi-hard pâte; uncooked, pressed*

**Cheese made with three-quarters goat's milk, and one-quarter cow's milk**

ESSENTIAL FACTS

- ◯ 10–15 cm diameter, 5 cm high
- ⚖ 500 g–1 kg
- ⌷ Not defined
- ✓ Early spring to early winter

**Cheese made with equal proportions of goat and cow's milk**

Rhône-Alpes (73, 74)

Raw

## CHEVROTIN D'ALPAGE, VALLÉE DE MORZINE

The *fermier* goat's-milk cheese shown here was made in a *chalet* in the Vallée de Morzine in Savoie. Its moist surface still shows traces of the cloth used to wrap it during affinage, which can take up to four months. The milk used to make this cheese comes from goats grazing on flower meadows in the Alps, which gives the pale yellow pâte a sugary smell and a taste of honey. Throughout the pâte there are small holes, which are characteristic of a pressed cheese. Chevrotin *d'alpage* was inspired by another great cheese, Reblochon (p. 175).

♥ Vin de Savoie

*Semi-hard pâte sinks under finger pressure; uncooked, pressed*

**Affinage of 14 weeks**

*Moist rind of natural white and reddish-brown mould*

Rhône-Alpes (74)

Raw

**ESSENTIAL FACTS**

- ⊖ 17–20 cm diameter, 4 cm high
- ⚖ 1–1.3 kg
- ⊡ Not defined
- ✔ Autumn to winter

---

## CHEVROTIN DES ARAVIS

This *fermier* goat's-milk cheese is made in a *chalet* in the Chaîne des Aravis in Savoie. Its appearance and flavour are quite different from those of the goat's-milk cheeses of the Loire. It has a moist, yellowish-orange rind stained with white mould. The pâte is rounded, mild, fine-textured, and melting at the edges – rather like Reblochon (p. 175), which is made using very similar methods of production. Affinage requires 95% humidity and takes three to six weeks, during which time the cheese is washed in brine, turned, and lightly pressed by hand.

♥ Vin de Savoie

*Soft pâte; uncooked, slightly pressed by hand*

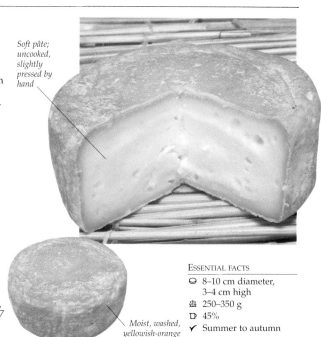

Rhône-Alpes (73, 74)

Raw

*Moist, washed, yellowish-orange rind, with a floury natural mould*

**ESSENTIAL FACTS**

- ⊖ 8–10 cm diameter, 3–4 cm high
- ⚖ 250–350 g
- ⊡ 45%
- ✔ Summer to autumn

Rind of natural mould

## CHEVROTIN DE MACÔT

One of the prime requirements of a good *fromagerie* is the *cave d'affinage*, since this is where the cheese is "finished". This cheese is made in an adapted bomb shelter from World War II. This space of around 300 square metres cut into the mountainside offers the ideal cool, dark, damp conditions

When it leaves the farm where it is made in the Tarentaise region of Savoie, this *fermier* cheese is white. It is taken to be ripened by a *fromager*. Affinage takes between one and three months. The cheese is left to rest for a month, during which time the yellow and pink mould opens up on the surface. The pâte ripens slowly.

♀ Vin de Savoie

### ESSENTIAL FACTS
- ⊖ 10–11 cm diameter, 6 cm high
- ⚖ 500–600 g
- ⛉ 45%
- ✔ June to December

Semi-hard pâte; uncooked, pressed

**Affinage of one month**

Rhône-Alpes (73)

Raw

---

Semi-hard pâte; uncooked, pressed

## CHEVROTIN DU MONT CENIS

This *fermier* goat's-milk cheese comes from the area around Mont Cenis in Savoie. Because of its relatively large size, it requires a long affinage of up to six months. The rind, which is washed in brine, is regularly rubbed with a cloth soaked in liquid *morge* (p. 21). As the rind develops, it protects the cheese against bad mould but allows contact between the inside of the cheese and the natural environment in the cellar. The cheese shown has been ripened for a full six months. The rind is still smooth and the elastic pâte begins to turn sticky.

♀ Crépy

### ESSENTIAL FACTS
- ⊖ 45 cm diameter, 8 cm high
- ⚖ 8 kg
- ⛉ 45%
- ✔ Best from autumn onwards

Washed rind

Rhône-Alpes (73)

Raw

## CHEVROTIN DE MONTVALEZAN

This *fermier* cheese was discovered by a *fromager* who then helped the cheesemaker to produce it in the Tarentaise region of Savoie. Its appearance reflects the enthusiasm and quality of their work together. It has a compact, fine, ivory pâte, which is sticky and smells of mould. Affinage takes from four to five weeks.

*Semi-hard pâte; uncooked, pressed*

♉ Roussette de Savoie

Rhône-Alpes (73)

Raw

*Rind of natural mould*

ESSENTIAL FACTS

⊖ 10–12 cm diameter, 6 cm high
⚖ 500–600 g
🜄 45%
✓ Spring to autumn

---

## CHEVROTIN DE PEISEY-NANCROIX

At an altitude of 1,300 m, the tiny villages of Peisey and Nancroix in Savoie have a total of only 481 inhabitants between the two of them. Their local goat's-milk cheese is *fermier* produced with an affinage of up to six months, which is a long time considering its small size. After affinage, the change in the crust is impressive; the pâte is rather sticky. This is a goat's-milk cheese of quality, with a mature taste.

*Semi-hard pâte; uncooked, pressed*

♉ Roussette de Savoie

Rhône-Alpes (73)

Raw

*Rind of natural mould*

ESSENTIAL FACTS

⊖ 10–12 cm diameter, 6–7 cm high
⚖ 550–600 g
🜄 Not defined
✓ Spring to autumn

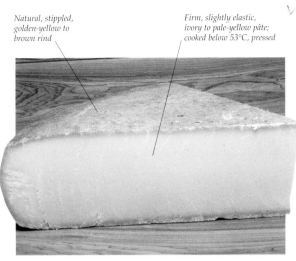

Natural, stippled, golden-yellow to brown rind

Firm, slightly elastic, ivory to pale-yellow pâte; cooked below 53°C, pressed

**Affinage of approximately one year**

ESSENTIAL FACTS

- ◒ 40–70 cm diameter, 9–13 cm high
- ⚖ 35–55 kg
- ⦂ 62 g per 100 g cheese
- ☡ 45%; 27.9 g min. per 100 g cheese
- ✓ All year

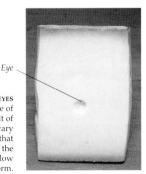

Eye

**THE EYES**
The "eyes" in the pâte of a Comté are the result of careful affinage. They vary from the size of a pea to that of a small cherry. If the affinage is prolonged at low temperatures, no eyes form.

## COMTÉ (AOC)

With Beaufort, this cheese, also called Gruyère du Comté, is the richest and most popular cheese in France. It is traditionally produced in the mountains of the Jura, where local farmers bring their milk down to the *fruitières*, which are local cooperatives managed by a group of villages. It takes as many as 530 litres of milk, equivalent to the daily production of 30 cows, to make one Comté cheese.

### Appearance and flavour
The surface of the cheese shown here is broad and flat with a moist, cool, grey, yellow, and ochre rind. When it is cut, it reveals a firm and supple pâte that melts in the mouth, leaving a sweet taste. The salt is strong but balanced and the flavour has a nutty tang. Comté is a nourishing and versatile cheese: it is a good accompaniment to an apéritif, or may be eaten in a salad, with fruit, in a sandwich, or cooked in a croque-monsieur or a fondue.

### Production and affinage
Consumed by 40% of the French population, Comté has the highest production figures of all French cheeses – some 38,000 tonnes per year. The AOC restricts production to the Franche-Comté, eastern Bourgogne, and parts of Lorraine, Champagne, and the Rhône-Alpes (see map below for specific departments). Quality is strictly controlled, and each year 5% of cheeses fail to pass the AOC tests. Affinage must take place within the AOC specified areas and needs 90 days from the date of production at below 19°C with a minimum humidity level of 92%. The cheeses are regularly wiped and rubbed with brine. The rind must be treated with *morge* and stippled.

♀ Côtes du Jura (*jaune*), Vin de Paille *doux*

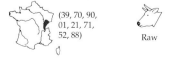

(39, 70, 90, 01, 21, 71, 52, 88)

Raw

# How to cut a Comté

To cut a whole Comté in two or four, first use a cutting wire. Thereafter, it may be cut with a kitchen knife.

**1.** The cheese is first cut in half.

**2.** Each half is then halved.

**3.** A right-angle is cut off each quarter.

**4.** A wedge is then cut off the side of each quarter.

**5.** A slice is cut off the end of the quarter.

**6.** A second slice is cut parallel to the last.

**7.** The remaining quarter is cut into wedges.

**8.** Each quarter is cut to the same pattern.

## AOC Regulations: Comté

**1.** The milk must be transported immediately after milking to the place of production. If the milk is refrigerated and kept at 14–18°C, renneting must be carried out within 14 hours. If the milk is kept at 4°C, renneting must occur within 24 hours, 36 hours in winter.

**2.** The milk may be heated once to a maximum of 40°C, but only at the renneting. Systems or machinery that would allow the rapid heating to above 40°C before renneting may not be kept on the premises.

**3.** The salt must be applied to the surface of the cheese directly or with brine.

**4.** The green *casein* label must be applied to the side of the cheese, bearing the date of production.

**5.** Grated cheese may not be sold as Comté.

AOC GRANTED 1976

## Scale of Marks for AOC Assessment of Comté

Comté is graded on a scale of 1 to 20. The minimum score for a pass is an average above 12. Cheeses with marks of 15 to 20 have green *casein* labels; those with 12 to 15 show brick-red *casein* labels.

The minimum score for taste is 3 out of 9. A score of 0 in the following areas leads to elimination from the test: shape, rind, holes, and pâte. Cheeses thus eliminated are sold as Gruyère.

| Aspect | Marks | Ideal conditions for reference |
|---|---|---|
| Overall appearance | 1/20 | Rounded sides; clear-cut form: no joint between sides, top, and bottom; well-proportioned; no bulging, no stretching. |
| Quality of rind on top, bottom, and sides | 1.5/20 | Treated with *morge*; stippled (with cloth marks); solid (not crumbly); clean (dry, smooth, not stained or coated); even (light orange to ochre); no defects, no cracks. |
| Appearance of the cut and eyes | 3.5/20 | Holes should be present: 10 to 20 eyes on a half cheese; round, clear, cherry sized, well spread, no grooves or other defects. |
| Quality of pâte | 5/20 | Even colour (creamy to light orange-yellow); supple (slightly elastic); smooth (not too moist or oily); medium resistance to deformation; fine pâte (no little particles when the cheese is reduced in the mouth); should not stick to the palate. |
| Quality of taste | 9/20 | Simple (no defects); nutty (walnut); fruity (apricot, dried fruits); "lactic" (milk, butter); lightly roasted (caramel); grassy (hay); balanced (sour, salty, sweet, bitter); no tingling, lingering taste. |

# Corse

The island of Corsica, called Corse in French, lies in the Mediterranean 170 km south of France's Côte d'Azur and 83 km west of Piombino on the Italian coast. The highest point is Monte Cinto, which is covered in snow for much of the year.

Corsicans see themselves as independent and some even refer to France as "the Continent". The language is closer to Italian than French and the independence movement is active.

Due to its strategic position and commercial potential, the island has been coveted, invaded, and dominated by different powers throughout history – Greece, Rome, the Saracens, Pisa, Genoa, and for the last 200 years France. The Greeks introduced sheep, wine, and olives to the island, and the Saracens their goats.

Most of Corsica has a Mediterranean climate, but above 1,500 m, it gets colder and more alpine. The range of climates

has permitted around 2,000 species of plant to become established, all of which are resistant to fierce heat, arid conditions, strong winds, and intense cold. Of these, species, 78 are unknown elsewhere. The *maquis*, which is the rocky landscape where many of these bushy and herby plants grow wild, shows an explosion of colours in spring, and provides excellent grazing for goats and sheep.

The mixed climate, varied terrain, robust vegetation, and near-wild sheep and goats are ideal ingredients for a rich variety of cheeses that are quite different from those of the mainland. Corsican cheeses are generally small or medium-sized and marked by the *faisselle* (colander) when moulded. They tend to be salty and highly flavoured, with a pronounced smell. Due to a long affinage, many of them are strong-tasting and are best eaten with local red wines.

**AERIAL VIEW OF THE PLATEAU DU NIOLO**
The mountainous Niolo region in the centre of Haute Corse is home to many herds of semi-wild goats and sheep whose milk is used for making a vast range of Corsican cheeses.

MAP OF
CORSICA

## FROMAGE CORSE

M. Manenti's home and cheese-making *atelier*, where this *fermier* cheese is made, lie some 360 m up Col San Bastiano in Calcatoggio, which is itself 411 m high. The herds of ewes and goats are taken into the mountains at the end of June or beginning of July, and come down again in October. The ewes stay outdoors all year round. The rennet (p. 15) that makes the milk coagulate is homemade from an enzyme called chymosin that is found in the stomach of a young goat. The stomach is dried indoors for at least 40 days, thinly cut, and soaked in a litre of warm water for two days. In the past, the reed colander used to strain the cheese was also made at home. After 100 days, the cheese is covered with mould. It is salty, with a fine texture. Affinage takes at least two months.

❦ Patrimonio

ESSENTIAL FACTS

- ⊜ 11–13 cm diameter, 3–4 cm high
- ⚖ 500 g
- ♉ 48%
- ✓ Spring to autumn

Corse-du-Sud (2A)

Raw

Dried kid's stomach containing cheese

**Affinage of four months**

*Soft pâte, slightly elastic to finger pressure; uncooked, unpressed*

**Affinage of ten hours**

**Affinage of eight days**

**Affinage of five months**

*Washed rind*

*Fresh, white pâte*

**Very fresh Brocciu, still hot and steaming**

ESSENTIAL FACTS
- 🧀 Colander-shaped, in different formats
- ⚖ Generally 500 g (as shown) to 1 kg
- 🌡 40–51%
- ✔ Spring to autumn (fresh goat's cheeses); winter to early summer (fresh ewe's cheeses); all year, if matured

# BROCCIU / FROMAGE DE LACTOSÉRUM (AOC)

The Corsican name for this cheese is Brocciu, while in French it is called Broccio. The origin of the name may be *brousse*, which is another word for *fromage frais* made from goat or ewe's milk. Brocciu is an unusual cheese since it is the first AOC cheese to be made from *lactosérum,* or whey, which is usually discarded during cheese production. Because some proteins and other nutritional elements remain in it, whey makes a useful by-product. Brocciu, which is similar to Italian ricotta, is popular with Corsicans and is sold at local markets in returnable baskets.

### Production
First the whey is heated to 35°C and salted, then whole milk (10 to 15% of its volume) is added. This blend is mixed while being further heated to 90°C. Solid white particles floating on the surface are skimmed, transferred to a colander, and drained. Production may be *fermier*, *artisanal*, or *coopérative*.

### How to eat Brocciu
Brocciu is usually eaten fresh, hot or cold, within 48 hours of production, although if drained and salted it can be ripened like other cheeses. The pâte is soft, sweet, and smells of milk, and feels liquid in the throat. Brocciu is excellent eaten for breakfast with jam or salt and pepper. It can also be served with local *marc* poured on it, or used as a filling for omelettes or cannelloni. *Fiadone* is a tasty, lemon-flavoured sponge cake made with brocciu, eggs, sugar, and grated lemon rind.
The AOC was granted in 1983.

❑ *Marc* de Corse

Corsica

Raw, whole

## DIFFERENT TYPES OF BROCCIU

**1.** Brocciu in its traditional Corsican basket, from the Domaine de la Porette, near Corte.

**2.** Brocciu from a Parisian *fromager*.

**3.** Brocciu from Ajaccio market.

**4.** Brocciu from Lyon market.

**5.** Brocciu *poivré* – pepper Brocciu from a market at Sainte-Maure.

*Soft pâte; uncooked, unpressed*

## CALENZANA (LE NIOLO)

This is a well-known *fermier* cheese from the Niolo plateau in the northern part of Corsica. It has an affinage of at least three months. The cheese shown here is rather white. The rind is wet, and the pâte is heavy and crumbles like clay, and has a strong taste.

❡ Patrimonio

*Natural rind*

ESSENTIAL FACTS

⬨ 10 cm square, 4–5 cm high
⚖ 600 g
🗍 Not defined
✔ Spring to autumn

Haute-Corse (2B)

Raw

---

## LE FIUM'ORBO

This *artisanal* cheese, named after a small river in the north of Corsica, has a sticky rind, marked by the colander in which it was moulded. It has a concentrated flavour, and the pâte sinks under light finger pressure, with no elasticity. Affinage takes at least two months, during which time the cheese is turned every two days.

❡ Vin de Corse

*Soft pâte with no elasticity; uncooked, unpressed*

ESSENTIAL FACTS

⬭ 10–12 cm diameter, 4 cm high
⚖ 400–450 g
🗍 50%
✔ November to end June (ewe's); January to end June (goat's)

*Natural mould rind*

Haute-Corse (2B)

Raw

# FLEUR DU MAQUIS

This *artisanal* cheese is called the "flower of the *maquis*" which is French name for the scrubby Corsican landscape.

*Chillis, juniper berries, savory and rosemary*

Fleur du Maquis

ESSENTIAL FACTS

- ◈ 10–12 cm square, 5–6 cm high
- ⚖ 600–700 g
- 🗇 Fleur du Maquis: 45%; Brin d'Amour: not defined
- ✓ Winter to summer

*Soft pâte, with no elasticity; uncooked, unpressed*

*Natural rind, covered with savory and rosemary*

Brin d'Amour

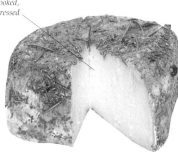

# BRIN D'AMOUR

Both this cheese and the Fleur du Maquis above have a strong scent of dried herbs that bites on the tongue. Their pâte is fine-textured and ivory in colour, and tastes slightly sour. Both types are occasionally made in France, where they are more popular than in their native Corsica. They are both *artisanal* cheeses with an affinage of at least one month.

♀ Vin de Corse, Côtes de Provence

Haute-Corse (2B)

Raw

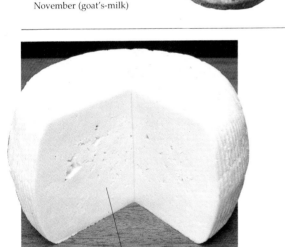

# A FILETTA (LA FOUGÈRE)

*A filetta* means "the fern" in Corsican. This *artisanal* cheese, decorated with a sprig of fern, comes from Isolaccio, which lies 45 km south of the town of Bastia. It has a faint smell of the cellar and fern leaves. Young cheeses may be exported to the mainland. Affinage takes three to four weeks, during which time the cheese is turned.

♀ Patrimonio

*Soft pâte with no elasticity; uncooked, unpressed*

*Rind of natural mould with colander marks and decorated with fern*

ESSENTIAL FACTS
◒ 10 cm diameter, 3–4 cm high
⚖ 300–350 g
🥛 45%
✓ December to June (ewe's-milk); March to November (goat's-milk)

 Haute-Corse (2B)

 Raw

# FROMAGE DE BREBIS

The *fermier* cheese shown here was made in November in Santa-Maria-Siché with milk from the farm of M. Cianfarani. This photograph was taken only a week later. The white rind looks fresh, but the pâte is elastic. The first milk from the morning's milking makes it slightly bitter. Affinage usually takes at least three months.

♀ Patrimonio

*Washed rind*

ESSENTIAL FACTS
◒ 11–13 cm diameter, 7 cm high
⚖ 1 kg
🥛 50%
✓ Spring to autumn

*Soft, elastic, rubbery pâte; uncooked, unpressed*

Corse-du-Sud (2A)

 Raw

## FROMAGE FERMIER BREBIS

This *fermier* sheep's-milk cheese has a wet rind and sticky pâte and belongs to the same family as Venaco (p.130). It is best eaten from spring to autumn. Production starts at the beginning of winter and continues until summer. Cheesemaking commences as soon as the ewes on the farm begin to produce milk on 7 December. Every day of the 45 days of affinage, the cheeses are all washed with a little water and turned. At the beginning of affinage, the cheese has almost no smell.

♀ Patrimonio

*Soft pâte, with no elasticity; uncooked, unpressed*

ESSENTIAL FACTS

- ◒ 9–11 cm diameter, 4 cm high
- ⚖ 350–400 g
- ⛁ 45%
- ✓ Best from spring to autumn

*Washed rind*

Haute-Corse (2B)

Raw

HANDMADE CHEESES
Although this might look like a washed-rind cheese, it is only rubbed with a moistened hand and turned several times.

*Fresh cheese*

*Pâte sinks under finger pressure and is so moist that it crumbles*

*Rind and pâte reveal the quality of the milk*

**①**

Young cheese, around two months old

*Colander marks on rind*

**②**

Mature cheese

*Pâte is riddled with holes and slightly elastic*

*Patches of white, green, and straw-coloured mould cover the light brown rind*

## FROMAGE PUR LAIT DE BREBIS

The four *fermier* cheeses shown here are all of the same type, but the length of affinage – from two months to a year – gives them each a very different character.

♀ Vin de Corse

ESSENTIAL FACTS

- ◯ 12–15 cm diameter, 5–6 cm high
- ⚖ 500–700 g
- ⏲ Not defined
- ✓ Winter to summer

*Holes made by the cheesemite, le ciron*

**③**

**④**

Old, hard cheese

*Brittle pâte with a spicy taste*

Affinage of one year

Corse-du-Sud (2A)

Raw

## FROMAGE CORSE

There are hardly any cheese shops in Corsica, so people buy cheese at the morning market. Cheesemakers also sell their own cheeses, which become known by the maker's name – for example, Mme Nicole's cheese. The *fermier* cheese shown is so young that it is still exuding whey; pâte and salt are not yet integrated. It was bought at the supermarket in Calacuccia.

❦ Ajaccio

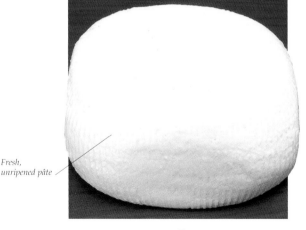

*Fresh,
unripened pâte*

Haute-Corse
(2B)

Raw

ESSENTIAL FACTS

◈ 11 cm square,
5 cm high
⚖ 570 g
▯ Not defined
✔ Winter to early
summer

---

## FROMAGE CORSE NIOLO

The *fermier* cheese shown was bought at a market in Lyon. It was sold under the name of "Niolo" but according to Corsican cheese experts it is of the *bastelicaccia* type made in the Ajaccio area. The mould is blue and reddish-brown and the rind is moist. The pâte sinks a little under finger pressure. It is a little young for a Corsican cheese, but it has flavour. Affinage takes at least three months.

❦ Patrimonio *rosé*

*Soft pâte;
uncooked,
unpressed*

*Washed rind,
marked by colander*

Haute-Corse
(2 B)

Raw

ESSENTIAL FACTS

◔ 11–12 cm diameter,
4.5 cm high
⚖ 450 g
▯ 45%
✔ Winter to early
summer

123

## FROMAGE FERMIER DE CHÈVRE DE LA TAVAGNA

The Giancoli family's house lies on the coast in a mountainous area about an hour's drive south of Bastia. For eight months of the year they make some 70 *fermier* cheeses per day. When the airtight package in which the cheese is packed is opened, a pungent smell fills the air and you can see the paper wrapper, bearing the marks of the colander. The cheese itself looks moist and is hard, like soap. It has been ripened for seven months. Affinage usually takes two months, during which time the cheese is regularly wiped with a moist cloth.

♀ Château Chalon (*jaune*), Arbois *jaune*, ❏ Marc de Corse,

ESSENTIAL FACTS

*Soft pâte; uncooked, unpressed*

◈ 9–10 cm wide, 11 cm long 4 cm high

⚖ 300–400 g

◻ 45%

✔ All year

*Natural rind*

Haute-Corse (2B)

Raw

---

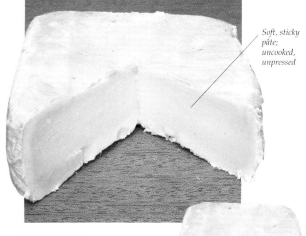

## LE NIOLO

The Corsican village of Casamaccioli has only 140 inhabitants. It is here, deep in the mountains, that the Santini brothers produce Le Niolo cheese. It is a *fermier* cheese with a strong smell, a sticky consistency, and a taste that tingles on the tongue. The smell grows and never disappears. In Paris, when people think of Corsican cheeses, this is what comes to their minds. Affinage takes at least three months.

♀ Château Chalon (*jaune*), Arbois *jaune*, ❏ Marc de Corse

*Soft, sticky pâte; uncooked, unpressed*

ESSENTIAL FACTS

◈ 10–13 cm square, 4 cm high

⚖ 400–500 g

◻ 50%

✔ Spring to autumn

*Washed rind, marked by colander*

Haute-Corse (2B)

Raw

## Le Mouflon

This *fermier* cheese is made from raw goat's milk in Calgèse in southern Corsica. Affinage, which usually lasts for three months, takes place in the mountain town of Calacuccia in northern Corsica.

♀ Patrimonio

ESSENTIAL FACTS

◈ 12 cm square,
   3 cm high
⚖ 400–500 g
◻ 50%
✔ Best in summer

*Washed rind*

Corse-du-Sud
(2A)

Raw

*Pâte breaks like hard clay, with no elasticity; uncooked, unpressed*

**THE MOUFLON**
Although cheesemakers think of it as a goat, the *mouflon* is a wild mountain sheep, the ancestor of domestic European sheep, with curved horns, but no beard. *Mouflons* are still found today, mainly in Sardinia and Corsica, where they are known as *muflone* and *mufoli*. Although they are now an endangered species, they used to be eaten roasted or stewed in much the same way as mutton or venison.

# PÂTE DE FROMAGE

*Pâte de fromage*, meaning cheese paste (p. 140), is a Corsican speciality. Ripened cheese is milled, put into a container, and ripened again. Some locals say that it is best when it is infested with the *ciron,* or cheese mite. This is an *artisanal* cheese with an affinage of five to six months in vats.

♈ Château Chalon (*jaune*), Arbois *jaune,* ▢ *Marc* de Corse

ESSENTIAL FACTS
- In a pot
- 200 g net
- 50%
- All year

Haute-Corse (2B)

Raw, whole

---

# A FILETTA

It is said that this cheese – a *pâte de fromage* (cheese paste) – was formerly made in all Corsican homes. The smell of A Filetta is so strong that it stings the eyes. It is an *artisanal* cheese with an affinage of five to six months.

♈ Château Chalon (*jaune*), Arbois *jaune,* ▢ *Marc* de Corse

ESSENTIAL FACTS
- In a pot
- 230 g net
- 45%
- All year

Haute-Corse (2B)

Raw

## SAN PETRONE

This is another *pâte de fromage* made from mature milled cheese, shaped without including further additives, and ripened for seven to eight months. There is no rind. The pâte looks like dough that has been lightly kneaded. It is sticky, with a strong salty, sharp, and tingling taste, which resembles that of *fromage fort*. Production is *artisanal*.

♈ Château Chalon (*jaune*), Arbois *jaune*, ❑ *Marc* de Corse

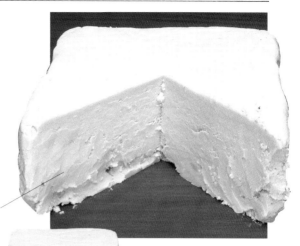

*Dough-like pâte*

Haute-Corse
(2B)

Raw

ESSENTIAL FACTS

◈ 10–11 cm square, 5 cm high
⚖ 500 g
▷ 45%
✔ Produced from December to end of June; available all year

## LE VIEUX CORSE

This *pâte de fromage* is wrapped in three layers of wax paper. The pâte is stained with blue mould. It is salty, spicy, and tasty. The Corsicans eat it thickly spread on bread like butter. This is an *artisanal* cheese with an affinage of at least three months.

♈ Château Chalon (*jaune*), Arbois *jaune*, ❑ *Marc* de Corse

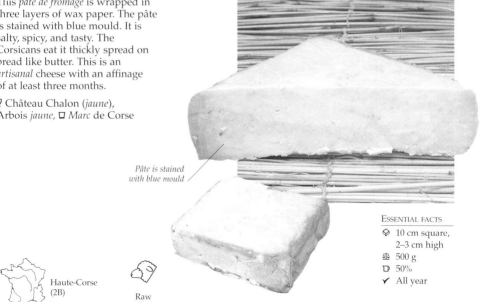

*Pâte is stained with blue mould*

Haute-Corse
(2B)

Raw

ESSENTIAL FACTS

◈ 10 cm square, 2–3 cm high
⚖ 500 g
▷ 50%
✔ All year

*Rind of natural mould*

*Semi-hard pâte; uncooked, pressed*

ESSENTIAL FACTS
- ⊖ 17–18 cm diameter, 8–9 cm high
- ⚖ 2 kg
- ⏦ Undefined
- ✔ Summer to winter

## TOME CHÈVRE

This is an excellent *fermier* cheese made by M. Andreani from the village of Piaggiola near Sartène. According to the cashier at the local supermarket he sometimes comes to sell his cheeses himself. This cheese is very different from the goat's-milk cheeses of the mainland. The mould looks like a dry stone covered with reddish lichen, and the pâte is so shiny that it resembles candle wax and has to be broken with a hammer. It smells slightly of the cellar in which it is matured. Affinage takes at least three months. This cheese is probably related to a Sardinian cheese called Fleur de Sardaigne (flower of Sardinia), which is said to date from Roman times.

♀ Patrimonio

Corse-du-Sud (2A)

Raw

---

*Semi-hard pâte; uncooked, pressed*

*Rind of natural mould*

ESSENTIAL FACTS
- ⊖ 16 cm diameter, 6 cm high
- ⚖ 1.5 kg
- ⏦ Undefined
- ✔ All year

## TOME DE CHÈVRE

This very dry *fermier* cheese smells of hay. Perhaps it is the smell of the flowers that grow in the *maquis* (mountain scrub) on which the goats feed. It has an affinage of at least three months. The precise origin of the cheese shown here is unknown.

♀ Patrimonio

Throughout Corse

Raw

## Tomme Corse

Bite into the hard pâte of this *artisanal* cheese and an almost coppery flavour of salt, sweetness, red pepper, and sourness explodes in the mouth. It goes particularly well with a vintage Corsican wine. Compare Ossau *fermier* (p. 54) or Salers (p. 71) with this Corsican cheese.

🍷 Vin de Corse (vintage)

*Semi-hard pâte; uncooked, pressed*

*Rind of natural mould*

Haute-Corse (2B)

Raw

**Essential facts**

- ⊖ 20 cm diameter, 8 cm high
- ⚖ 2 kg
- ⊐ 47%
- ✓ All year

## Tomme Corse

The *coopérative* A. Pecurella, where this cheese is made, was founded in 1975. A *pecurella* is the Corsican name for the ewe that produces the rich, strongly aromatic milk used to make this cheese. The piece shown here is a year old and very crumbly. Tomme Corse has an affinage of three months to one year at 12°C and 85% humidity. The locals are very partial to it.

🍷 Vin de Corse (vintage)

*Semi-hard pâte becomes granular with age; uncooked, pressed*

*Rind of natural mould*

Corse-du-Sud (2A)

Raw

**Essential facts**

- ⊖ 20 cm diameter, 8–10 cm high
- ⚖ 2.5 kg
- ⊐ 48%
- ✓ All year

**Affinage of one year**

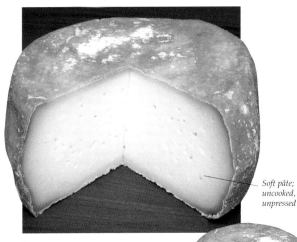

## U Rustinu

Corsican cheeses do not usually have specific names and are simply called cheese or *brocciu*. Sometimes the wholesaler will name them himself. This one was made by Joseph Guidicelli. His cheeses are known by two names: U Rustinu, which is a geographical name, and U Muntanacciu, which is Corsican for a mountain. U Rustinu is an *artisanal* cheese with an affinage of at least three months, during which time it is turned regularly.

Ⴘ Patrimonio

*Soft pâte; uncooked, unpressed*

*Moist red rind of white and red mould*

### Essential Facts

- ⊖ 10 cm diameter, 5 cm high
- ⚖ 450 g
- ⅅ 45%
- ✔ Produced from December to late June; best in spring

 Haute-Corse (2B)

 Raw

---

## Le Venaco

With Niolo (p. 124), Calenzana (p. 118), and Brocciu (p. 116), Venaco is one of the most typical Corsican cheeses. The name originally derived from the place of production, Venaco, a town in the centre of Corsica, but it is no longer made there. It is a *fermier* cheese made from ewe or goat's milk, with an affinage of at least two months.

❢ Ajaccio

*Soft, sticky pâte; uncooked, unpressed*

### Essential Facts

- ⊖ 9 cm diameter, 3–4 cm high
- ⚖ 350 g
- ⅅ 45%
- ✔ Produced from winter to early summer; best from spring to autumn

*Washed rind*

Haute-Corse (2B)

 Raw, whole

## Dreux à la Feuille / Feuille de Dreux

The ancient town of Dreux lies in a cereal-producing region to the north of Chartres, some 80 km from Paris. The flat, thin cheeses produced there ripen gently under the cover of chestnut leaves, which stop them from sticking to each other. A faint smell of the chestnut leaf mingles with a pleasant scent of mould. The patchy white mould turns to a reddish-brown late in the cheese's affinage, which lasts two to three weeks. This *artisanal* cheese used to be eaten as a snack by workers in the fields.

❦ Touraine

*Soft pâte; uncooked, unpressed*

*Rind of white mould decorated with chestnut leaf*

Centre (28)

Raw or pasteurized

ESSENTIAL FACTS

⊖ 14–16 cm diameter, 2–3 cm high
⚖ 300–350 g
🌡 30–40%
✔ All year

---

## Emmental Grand Cru

This cheese has a red *casein* label, which is a kind of guarantee of its quality. This label gives details of the place of production, fat content, and licence number of the maker. Emmental Grand Cru is a large *coopérative* or *industriel* cheese with a cooked and pressed pâte like that of Beaufort (p. 26) and Comté (p. 112). It is produced using raw milk in the Franche-Comté, and parts of Rhône-Alpes, Champagne-Ardenne, Bourgogne, and Lorraine (see map below for specific departments). The pâte is smooth; its aroma and taste are sweet. Affinage takes at least ten weeks.

❦ Vin de Savoie, Givry, Rully, Mercurey

*Dry, natural, washed and brushed, ochre rind*

*Firm ivory to pale yellow pâte; cooked, pressed*

*Holes should be 1.5–3 cm in diameter*

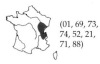

(01, 69, 73, 74, 52, 21, 71, 88)

Raw

ESSENTIAL FACTS

⊖ 70 cm–1 m diameter, 13–25 cm high
⚖ 60–130 kg
⁘ 62 g min. per 100 g cheese
🌡 45% min., 27.9 g per 100 g cheese
✔ All year

*Hard, ivory to pale yellow pâte, with cherry-to walnut-sized holes; cooked, pressed*

*Hard, dry ochre to light-brown rind*

# EMMENTAL

This *industriel* cheese is almost identical to Emmental Grand Cru but is made with pasteurized milk.

❢ Vin de Savoie, Givry, Rully, Mercurey

### ESSENTIAL FACTS

- ⊖ 70 cm–1 m diameter, 13–25 cm high
- ⚖ 60–130 kg
- ⸭ 60 g per 100 g cheese
- ♉ 45% min., 27 g per 100 g cheese
- ✓ All year

## HOW EMMENTAL GRAND CRU IS MADE

The whole process of making this Emmental takes at least 10 weeks.

### Coagulation

It takes 800 to 900 litres of milk to make a 70-kg Emmental. The milk is heated to 33°C at the renneting stage and coagulates within 30 minutes. The curd is milled to help the whey separate, and then heated and cooked for 90 minutes at a maximum of 53°C.

### Moulding

The curd is put into moulds and pressed for 24 hours. The *fromage blanc* is then floated in brine for 48 hours. The brine salts the cheese and forms the rind.

### Affinage

The cheese rests in a cellar at 10–13°C for four to five days, then the temperature is raised to 16–18°C. After a week, the cheese is transferred to a cellar, at 21–25°C and 60% humidity, where it stays for a month. Natural bacteria in the cheese transform oxygen into $CO_2$ to form holes, while the pâte becomes more elastic, fine-textured, and tasty. When the surface of the cheese bulges, it is moved back to a cellar at 16–18°C, then to another cellar at 10–13°C.

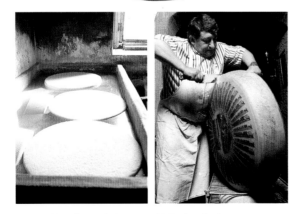

All regions of France

Pasteurized

*Fromage blanc* floats in brine to salt cheese and form rind

M. Boujon, the *fromager*, guillotines his giant cheese

## EPOISSES DE BOURGOGNE (AOC)

Napoleon is said to have been partial to this cheese and ate it with Chambertin wine. Although it was very popular at the beginning of the 20th century, production did not survive World War II. M. Berthaut of the village of Epoisses revived it in 1956. A single farm in Bourgogne currently makes all the cheeses of the *fermier* category. There are also *artisanal* versions and both a large and a small version are produced.

This is a strong-smelling, washed-rind cheese, with an aroma of *marc*. The fine-textured pâte melts in the mouth, with a mixture of salt, sweet, metallic, and milky flavours. Affinage takes place in specified areas and lasts for at least four weeks; the cheese is first washed in water or brine, then *marc* is added to the liquid. The cheese is washed one to three times a week, with gradually increasing quantities of *marc*.

♈ Pouilly-Fuissé, Sauternes (*moelleux*), ☐ Marc de Bourgogne

*Cheese ripens from outside in*

*Supple, soft, light beige pâte; uncooked, unpressed*

*Smooth, washed rind sometimes wrinkled; ivory, orange to brick-red colour, depending on age*

ESSENTIAL FACTS

⬤ 16.5–19 cm diameter, 3–4.5 cm high (large); 9.5–11.5 cm diameter, 3–4.5 cm high (small)
⚖ 700–1100 g; 250–350 g
‰ 40 g min. per 100 g cheese
ⷁ 50% min. per 100 g cheese
✓ All year

### AOC REGULATIONS: EPOISSES DE BOURGOGNE

**1.** The coagulation of the milk for a period of 16 hours must be caused mainly by lactic acid.

**2.** The curd should be roughly cut. It must not be broken.

**3.** After drainage, the cheese must be salted with dry salt.

AOC GRANTED 1991

Bourgogne (21, 89); Champagne-Ardenne (52)

Whole

---

## L'AMI DU CHAMBERTIN

This *artisanal* cheese is made in the village of Gevrey-Chambertin in Bourgogne. Affinage takes at least four weeks.

☐ *Marc* de Chambertin

ESSENTIAL FACTS

⬤ 9 cm diameter, 4 cm high
⚖ 250 g
ⷁ 50%
✓ All year

Bourgogne (21)

Pasteurized

*Moist, red rind, washed with water and Marc de Bourgogne*

**Fourme d'Ambert**

*Natural rind of red or white mould*

**Fourme de Montbrison**

*Pâte of blue mould; uncooked, unpressed*

## FOURME D'AMBERT / FOURME DE MONTBRISON (AOC)

These two cheeses are made in two regions around the towns of Ambert and Montbrison, now joined by the AOC, which has streamlined methods of production. The word *fourme* comes from the Latin *forma,* meaning form or shape; it is thought that the word *fromage* may have the same roots.

As with Roquefort (p. 178), the blue mould is introduced first, then air is injected into the pâte through a syringe to help it develop (p. 181). This is one of the mildest of all the blue cheeses. Its rind is rather dry, the pâte creamy and firm, with a smell of the cellar. Production is *coopérative* or *artisanal;* there is no *fermier* version. Affinage within AOC specified areas takes a minimum of 28 days from the date of production, but is more usually about two months.

The AOC was granted in 1976.

♀ Sauternes *moelleux,* Rivesaltes (VDN)

ESSENTIAL FACTS
- ⊖ 13 cm diameter, 19 cm high
- ⚖ 1.5–2 kg
- ⁂ 50 g min. per 100 g cheese
- ◻ 50% min., 25 g min. per 100 g cheese
- ✓ All year

Rhône-Alpes (42); Auvergne (63, 15)

Pasteurized

## FRINAULT

In any good ashed cheese, the pâte dries slowly under its extra coating and compacts without growing hard. The ancient method of applying ashes to the moist surface of cheese to protect it comes from the Orléanais region of Central France. Originally, only the ash of vine shoots was used. The cut cheese shown here is less ripe than the uncut cheese. Frinault reveals its quality in the mouth and has a mild aftertaste. It is an *industriel* cheese, with an affinage of three to four weeks.

❦ Touraine

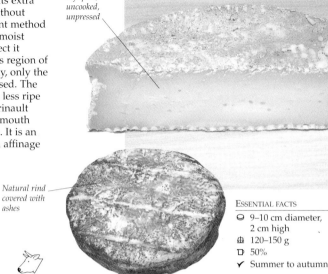

*Soft pâte; uncooked, unpressed*

*Natural rind covered with ashes*

Centre
(18, 45)

Pasteurized

ESSENTIAL FACTS

☉ 9–10 cm diameter, 2 cm high
⚖ 120–150 g
🗓 50%
✓ Summer to autumn

---

# Types of milk used in cheese production

French cheeses are made from cow, goat, and sheep's milk. The type of milk used to make a cheese determines its taste. The most highly concentrated milk of all is ewe's milk, which gives strong, robust, full-flavoured cheeses, with a lingering aftertaste.

The annual quantity of milk produced by one cow over 305 days of milking is 6,065 kg; a goat produces 644 kg over 240 days; and a ewe produces 200 kg over 180 days.

Cheese may be made from either pasteurized or raw milk. Raw milk is not heat treated prior to cheesemaking and is usually used shortly after milking or within 12 hours; if chilled immediately to 4°C, it may be

stored for up to 24 hours. Raw milk contains natural bacteria and is considered to produce cheese with complex taste and flavour. All *fermier* cheeses belong to this category. Raw milk is compulsory for some AOCs.

Pasteurized milk is treated at low or high temperatures. Pasteurization at low temperatures usually involves heating the milk to 72°C for 15 seconds and immediately chilling it to 4°C. This process reduces the level of bacteria in the milk, allowing it to be stored for a long time, and is widely used in factory-produced cheeses. Mass-produced cheeses made from pasteurized milk are simple in appearance and taste.

WEIGHT AND COMPOSITION OF DIFFERENT TYPES OF MILK

|  | COW'S MILK | GOAT'S MILK | SHEEP'S MILK |  |
|---|---|---|---|---|
| Fats | 35–45 g | 30–42 g | 65–75 g |  |
| Proteins | 30–35 g | 28–37 g | 55–65 g | **(From** *Les* |
| Sugars | 45–55 g | 40–50 g | 43–50 g | *Productions* |
| Minerals | 7–9 g | 7–9 g | 9–10 g | *Laitières,* **Vol. 1,** |
| Water | 888–915 g | 892–925 g | 838–866 g | **Tableaux des** |
| Approx. net weight: | 1,032 g | 1,030 g | 1,038 g | **Calories, 1993)** |

# Fromage allégé

*Allégé*, meaning light, is a fashionable term used to refer to foods that are low in fat, such as certain kinds of yoghurt, butter, margarine, and *fromage blanc*. A cheese may be described as *allégé* when the fat content shown on the label is between 20–30%. The classification for the fat content of cheeses is as follows:

- *Maigre* – less than 20%
- *Allégé* – 20 to 30%
- *Normal* – 40 to 50%
- *Double crème* – 60 to 75%
- *Triple crème* – more than 75%
- Some *fermier* cheeses have no clearly defined fat content. This is due to the slight daily variations in their milk.
- Processed cheese (*fromage fondu,* p. 230) has a minimum 40% fat content; light processed cheese (*fromage fondu allégé*) has 20 to 30% fat.

According to the regulations of the *Journal Officiel* governing cheese production, a product must contain more than 23 g dry matter per 100 g to qualify as cheese; 43 g for processed cheese; and 31 g for light processed cheese.

There is a close link between fat content and taste. Cheeses with a fat content of 40–50% are generally firm, with a rounded flavour. High-fat cheeses tend to be soft and spread easily on bread, rather like butter.

Low-fat cheeses have neither the flavour of a cheese with a *normal* fat content, nor do they have the melting, smooth texture of the latter. They do, however, offer an alternative for people who may be following a low-fat diet or watching their cholesterol intake, but who do not wish totally to forgo the pleasure of eating cheese.

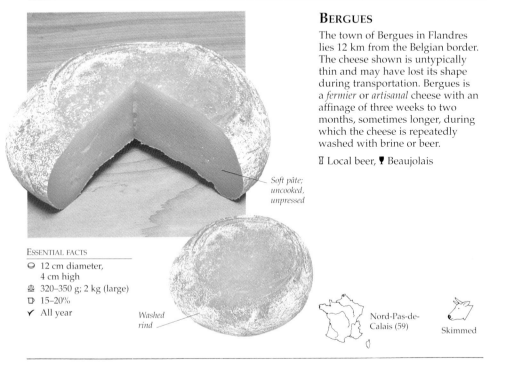

*Soft pâte; uncooked, unpressed*

*Washed rind*

## BERGUES

The town of Bergues in Flandres lies 12 km from the Belgian border. The cheese shown is untypically thin and may have lost its shape during transportation. Bergues is a *fermier* or *artisanal* cheese with an affinage of three weeks to two months, sometimes longer, during which the cheese is repeatedly washed with brine or beer.

🍺 Local beer, 🍷 Beaujolais

ESSENTIAL FACTS
- ◯ 12 cm diameter, 4 cm high
- ⚖ 320–350 g; 2 kg (large)
- ▯ 15–20%
- ✓ All year

Nord-Pas-de-Calais (59)

Skimmed

## LE BOURRICOT

This cheese from Cantal in the Auvergne is produced in an *industriel* dairy and has a slight smell of the straw in which it was ripened. Affinage takes eight weeks on straw.

❦ St. Pourçain

*Natural rind*

*Semi-hard pâte; uncooked, pressed*

Auvergne
(15)

Skimmed

**ESSENTIAL FACTS**
- ⊜ 12 cm diameter, 4 cm high
- ⚖ 500 g
- ʊ 30%
- ✔ All year

## FROMAGE CENDRÉ

Locally, this *artisanal* cheese is also known as Cendré de Champagne and is a speciality of the time of the grape harvest. The white wood ash on the rind keeps the flies away out in the vineyards, but is removed with a wet brush before the cheese is eaten. The smell is musty, of the cellar. During affinage the cheeses are left to cure in ashes for more than two months.

❦ Bouzy, Coteaux Champenois

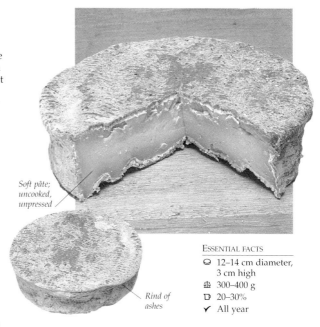

*Soft pâte; uncooked, unpressed*

*Rind of ashes*

Champagne-
Ardenne (51)

Skimmed

**ESSENTIAL FACTS**
- ⊜ 12–14 cm diameter, 3 cm high
- ⚖ 300–400 g
- ʊ 20–30%
- ✔ All year

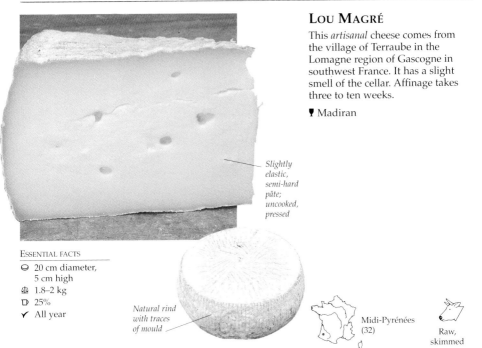

## LOU MAGRÉ

This *artisanal* cheese comes from the village of Terraube in the Lomagne region of Gascogne in southwest France. It has a slight smell of the cellar. Affinage takes three to ten weeks.

**?** Madiran

*Slightly elastic, semi-hard pâte; uncooked, pressed*

ESSENTIAL FACTS

◯ 20 cm diameter, 5 cm high
⚖ 1.8–2 kg
🗁 25%
✓ All year

*Natural rind with traces of mould*

Midi-Pyrénées (32)

Raw, skimmed

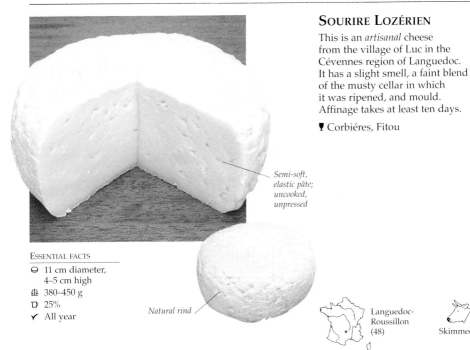

## SOURIRE LOZÉRIEN

This is an *artisanal* cheese from the village of Luc in the Cévennes region of Languedoc. It has a slight smell, a faint blend of the musty cellar in which it was ripened, and mould. Affinage takes at least ten days.

**?** Corbiéres, Fitou

*Semi-soft, elastic pâte; uncooked, unpressed*

ESSENTIAL FACTS

◯ 11 cm diameter, 4–5 cm high
⚖ 380–450 g
🗁 25%
✓ All year

*Natural rind*

Languedoc-Roussillon (48)

Skimmed

## TOMME DE LOMAGNE

This *artisanal* cheese, with a slight smell of the cellar, is produced in the Lomagne region of Gascogne. Affinage takes two months.

❧ Madiran

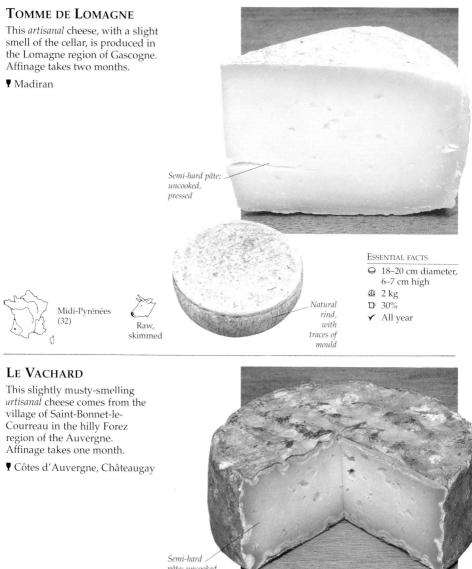

Semi-hard pâte; *uncooked, pressed*

Natural *rind, with traces of mould*

Midi-Pyrénées (32)

Raw, skimmed

ESSENTIAL FACTS

◯ 18–20 cm diameter, 6–7 cm high
⊕ 2 kg
▯ 30%
✓ All year

## LE VACHARD

This slightly musty-smelling *artisanal* cheese comes from the village of Saint-Bonnet-le-Courreau in the hilly Forez region of the Auvergne. Affinage takes one month.

❧ Côtes d'Auvergne, Châteaugay

Semi-hard *pâte; uncooked, pressed*

Rind of *natural mould*

Rhône-Alpes (42)

Raw, skimmed

ESSENTIAL FACTS

◯ 12–13 cm diameter, 3 cm high
⊕ 600 g
▯ 30%
✓ All year

# Fromage fort

Originally, *fromage fort* was made at home by grating and breaking leftover bits of cheese, and mixing them with, and letting them ferment in, one or more liquids such as whey, milk, or vegetable broth. Oil, *eau-de-vie*, or wine was added to stabilize the mixture, and herbs, spices, salt, and wine or cider, to season it. It was then left for months, to be served when finished with wine. *Fromage fort* is a local product, especially in wine-producing regions where each area has its own tradition. The names too are individual – for example, Cachat or Cacheilla, from areas of goat's-milk or half-goat's-milk cheeses. The Lyonnais, Mâconnais, Beaujolais, Dauphiné, and the Massif du Ventoux are the main areas where *fromage fort* continues to be made.

M. Voy, chief *fromager* and proprietor of the Ferme Saint-Hubert cheesemongers in Paris says: "Our *fromage fort* is strong.

We put it in a covered stoneware pot. If the pot did not have its lid on and you took it down the Metro, people would avoid you like the plague". Cheeses with a strong smell and taste, such as Epoisses (p. 133), Langres (p. 151), and Maroilles (p. 154) are used to make the *fromage fort du Lyonnais* sold in the Ferme Saint-Hubert. The mixture is soaked in *Marc* de Bourgogne until the pâte is completely smooth. Depending on the season, if the smell of cheese in the shop is not strong enough, the pot is stirred every now and then and left open to "scent" the air.

*Fromage fort* is sold by the ladleful. It tingles on the tongue and is good on toasted garlic bread or as an accompaniment to an apéritif. On tasting, a variety of flavours opens in the mouth, leaving a complex aftertaste. The cheese goes well with *Marc* de Bourgogne.

Stoneware pot keeps *fromage fort* at a constant temperature

### FROMAGE FORT DU LYONNAIS

This is a Lyonnais speciality made with hardened cow or goat's-milk cheeses left to ferment in a covered stoneware pot at home or in a cheese shop. The strong, piquant smell and flavour go better with *marc* than with wine.

◻ *Marc*, ♀ Château Chalon (*jaune*) or Arbois Jaune

Rhône-Alpes (69)

Not defined

## CACHAT

Both Cachat and the Confit d'Epoisses shown below are made by Georges Carbonel and his wife at their Restaurant in Aix-en-Provence. Cachat is made with young goat's-milk cheeses (Banon, p. 24) soaked in *marc*. The cheese turns creamy from the fifteenth day onwards.

Provence-
Alpes-Côte
d'Azur (13)    Not defined

**Cachat in an earthenware dish**

## CONFIT D'EPOISSES

Originally from the village of Epoisses, the Confit is made with a young Epoisses cheese, which is soaked in white Burgundy and a little *marc* for a week; then the liquid is discarded and replaced with more white wine. Epoisses de Bourgogne (p. 133) is one of the strongest washed-crust cheeses. Its smell is pungent and the taste of salt is pronounced. After a week in *marc,* it tingles on the tongue, and tastes sharp and copperish. Two weeks later, it turns creamy. The salt appears to be well integrated and there is a sweetness that might be called metallic. It should be eaten with bread.

M. Carbonel says that in the past, there used to be many flavoured cheeses made with salt, pepper, saffron, garlic, rosemary, thyme, and mustard. Meat was expensive, so people would eat a lot of bread with a little cheese. The cheeses had such a strong flavour that they made the bread taste better.

❑ *Marc* de Bourgogne

Provence-
Alpes-Côte
d'Azur (13)    Not defined

**Confit d'Epoisses**

## CACHAILLE

ESSENTIAL FACTS

- 🏺 Sold in a pot
- ⚖ 200 g net
- ⧖ Not defined
- ✓ All year

This *fromage fort* comes from the village of Puimichel. It is made by grating dry cheese into an earthenware pot, and adding *eau-de-vie*, pepper, olive oil, and fresh cheese up to three days old. It must be stirred well. Cachaille will keep for up to 20 years, if periodically topped up with new cheese. Affinage takes two to three months.

🍷 Coteaux Varois *rosé*

Provence-Alpes-Côte d'Azur (04)

Raw

## FROMAGÉE DU LARZAC

ESSENTIAL FACTS

- 🏺 Sold in an earthenware pot
- ⚖ 160 g net
- ⧖ 50%
- ✓ All year

Like Roquefort (p. 178) this sweet-tasting *fromage fort* comes from the Causse du Larzac in Rouergue. It is an *artisanal* cheese, made in an earthenware pot.

🍷 Sainte Croix du Mont *moelleux*, Rivesaltes (VDN)

Midi-Pyrénées (12)

Not defined

## PATEFINE FORT

ESSENTIAL FACTS

- 🏺 Sold in a plastic pot
- ⚖ 200 g net
- ⧖ Not defined
- ✓ All year

This *artisanal* cheese from Saint-Georges-d'Espéranche in the department of Isère is sold in a plastic pot. The ingredients are 90% cow's-milk cheese, white wine, spices, salt, and pepper. The cheese is served spread on country bread and toast. Its flavour is sour.

🍷 St. Joseph

Rhône-Alpes (38)

Not defined

# Fromage frais

*Fromage frais* (fresh cheese) has to be made in the following way:
• It must be unripened and made from milk coagulated by lactic fermentation.
• Bacteria, such as lactic ferment, must be active in the cheese when sold.
• It must contain 10 to 15 g dry matter per 100 g of cheese.
• It should be eaten soon after production. The consume-by date must be clearly indicated.
• Pasteurized milk is usually used. There are some *fermier*, raw-milk *fromages frais*.

• Depending on the fat content, *maigre, allégé, double*, and *triple-crème* versions (p. 213) are produced.

COMPARISONS BETWEEN THE COMPOSITION OF FROMAGE FRAIS AND OTHER CHEESES PER 100 G

|  | WATER | DRY MATTER | FAT CONTENT |
|---|---|---|---|
| Fromage frais | 85 g | 15 g | 45% (c. 7 g) |
| Camembert | 55 g | 45 g | 45% (c. 20 g) |
| Cantal | 43 g | 57 g | 45% (c. 25 g) |
| Comté | 38 g | 62 g | 45% (c. 28 g) |
| Roquefort | 44 g | 56 g | 52% (c. 29 g) |

## BROUSSE DU ROVE

The word *brousser* means to beat or stir in Provençal. This *artisanal* cheese is called Brousse because its curd is beaten before being drained. It was also known as *fromage frais de corne*, meaning fresh cheese in a horn, because it used to be poured into sheep's horns. It is liquid, light, sweet, and mild, with a slight smell of milk.

♥ Côtes de Provence *blanc* or *rosé*

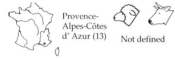

Provence-Alpes-Côtes d' Azur (13)  Not defined

ESSENTIAL FACTS
🧀 Sold in 9-cm-high plastic cones
🥛 45%
✓ All year; December to June (ewe's-milk cheese)

## CERVELLE DE CANUT / CLAQUERET LYONNAIS

This is the traditional way of eating *fromage frais* in the Lyonnais region. Shallots, garlic, parsley, chervil, chives, and other herbs are mixed with well-drained, fresh, white *fromage blanc* (p. 145). The cool, sour flavour goes well with toasted bread. The cheese is occasionally served chilled at the end of a meal.

♥ St. Véran, Mâcon

Rhône-Alpes (69)   Not defined

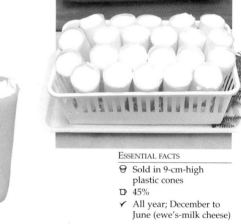

## CHÈVRE FRAIS

ESSENTIAL FACTS

⊖ 5–6 cm
diameter
4 cm high
⚖ 125 g
🗋 45%
✓ All year

This *artisanal* cheese is made in the same region as Selles-sur-Cher AOC (p. 83) in the province of Berry. It has a gentle, sweet smell of goat's milk.

⛉ Quincy

Centre
(41)

Not defined

## FAISSELLE DE CHÈVRE

ESSENTIAL FACTS

⛉ Sold in a pot
🗋 Not defined
✓ Spring to
autumn

The name of this *fermier* cheese from Rouergue comes from the word *faisselle*, meaning the basket in which the curd is drained. The *industriel* version of Faisselle, made with cow's milk, can be found anywhere in France. It is sold in plastic pots and is usually eaten with a spoon.

❢ Côtes d'Auvergne

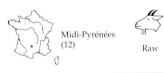

Midi-Pyrénées
(12)

Raw

## FONTAINEBLEAU

ESSENTIAL FACTS

🗋 60%
✓ All year

This creamy *fromage frais* is thought to originate from a village near the Forêt de Fontainebleau. It is an *artisanal* blend of whipped cream and *fromage frais* that may be made by the *fromager*. The flavour is mild, sweet, and light, more like a cream cake than a cheese. Try it with crystallized fruit.

⛉ Maury, Banyuls (VDN);
❢ Bordeaux (with crystallized fruit)

*Shaped in a
gauze-lined container*

Ile-de-France
(77)

Pasteurized

## FROMAGE BLANC

There are two kinds of *fromage blanc*. The first is young cheese that has been drained and shaped in a mould. The second (shown here) is cheese that has undergone lactic fermentation only. It is slightly drained and sold by weight. *Fromage blanc* makes a refreshing, milky dish with a slightly sweet-and-sour taste.

🍷 Beaujolais, 🍷 Coteaux du Layon *moelleux*, Vouvray *moelleux* (dessert)

ESSENTIAL FACTS
- 🥣 Sold in a pot
- ⊅ 40%
- ✔ All year

 Throughout France

 Pasteurized

*Creamy consistency goes well with salt, pepper, and chives, or as a dessert with jam, honey or fruit*

## FROMAGE BLANC FERMIER

This *fromage blanc* is a *fermier* cheese made in the small town of Marciac in the department of Gers in Gascogne. Like the Fromage Blanc shown above, it makes a refreshing, milky dish and has a slightly sweet-and-sour taste.

🍷 Tursan

ESSENTIAL FACTS
- 🥣 9 cm wide, 10 cm long, 3.5 cm high
- ⚖ 200 g
- ⊅ Not defined
- ✔ Spring to autumn

 Midi-Pyrénées (32)

 Raw

## FROMAGE FRAIS DE NÎMES

This *artisanal*-produced *fromage frais* comes from Languedoc. It is decorated with a bay leaf, the aroma of which blends with the milk of the cheese. It has a smooth texture and a mildly acidic flavour with a hint of sweetness.

🍷 Faugères

ESSENTIAL FACTS
- 🥣 8 cm diameter, Less than 2 cm high
- ⚖ 150 g
- ⊅ Not defined
- ✔ All year

 Languedoc-Roussillon (30)

 Raw

*Bay leaf decorates and flavours cheese*

145

Bay leaf / Juniper berry

## GARDIAN

ESSENTIAL FACTS

- 🧀 6–7 cm diameter, 3 cm high
- ⚖ 250 g
- 🥛 45%
- ✓ December to summer (ewe's-milk cheese); all year (cow's-milk cheese)

These little *fromages frais* are produced in the Provençal department of Boûches-du-Rhône. They are made with cow or ewe's milk, sprinkled with pepper and *herbes de Provence*, and decorated with bay leaves. Production is solely *fermier*.

🍷 Côtes de Provence *rosé*

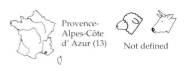

Provence-Alpes-Côte d' Azur (13)

Not defined

## GASTANBERRA

ESSENTIAL FACTS

- 🧀 Sold in an earthenware pot
- 🥛 45–50%
- ✓ December to June

*Gastanberra* means coagulated ewe's milk in the Pays Basque, which is where this *fermier* cheese is produced. One woman makes the cheese, while her daughter-in-law takes it to market. The buyer must return the earthenware pot in which the cheese is sold. It tastes like solidified milk.

🍷 Irouléguy

Aquitaine (64)

Raw

## GOURNAY FRAIS

ESSENTIAL FACTS

- 🧀 10 cm wide, 10 cm long, 3.5 cm high
- ⚖ 250 g
- 🥛 45%
- ✓ All year

This is an *artisanal* cheese from Pays de Bray in the department of Seine-Maritime in Normandie. It has a sweet smell of milk and a light flavour.

🍷 Bordeaux, Bourgogne, Côtes du Rhône

Haute-Normandie (76)

Not defined

## PETIT-SUISSE

These popular *artisanal* and *industriel* cheeses were invented in around 1850 by a Swiss worker in a cheese dairy in Normandie. Sold by the half-dozen, they have a sweet-and-sour flavour, with a very soft pâte. These little cheeses are often served with jam or coffee.

❢ Bordeaux, Bourgogne, Côtes du Rhône

**ESSENTIAL FACTS**

- ⊖ 3 cm diameter, 4 cm high
- ⬚ 30 g
- ⦂ 23% min;
- ⫘ 40% min.
- ✓ All year

*Very soft, fresh, even-textured pâte*

Throughout France

Pasteurized, with cream

## SÉGALOU

The name of this *fermier* cheese derives from the area of production, called Ségala, in the south of the Quercy. Ségala is a poor region in the Tarn, where only rye (*seigle*) can be grown. Although fresh, the cheese shown here has already begun to ripen. It is supple and made from good milk, and has a lingering aftertaste.

❢ Gaillac, Cahors

**ESSENTIAL FACTS**

- ⬙ 4 cm diameter in the middle, 15 cm long
- ⬚ 250 g
- ⫘ 45%
- ✓ All year

Midi-Pyrénées (81)

Raw

## VACHE FRAIS

This unsalted *fermier* cheese is produced in the Béarn by M. A. Penen. Rennet is added to the milk from the evening milking, and one hour later the curd is moulded and left to drain overnight. The fresh cheese is taken to market on the next day.

❢ Tursan

**ESSENTIAL FACTS**

- ⊖ 8 cm diameter, 4 cm high
- ⬚ 280 g
- ✓ All year

Aquitaine (64)

Raw

# Fromage de lactosérum

*Fromages de lactosérum* are obtained by the coagulation or precipitation of *lactosérum*, or whey. These low-fat cheeses may be concentrated, and other dairy products may be added. One of the most famous whey cheeses is Brocciu (p. 116) from Corsica, which is the only whey cheese to have been granted AOC status.

Whey is the liquid extracted when the milk coagulates during cheesemaking. Most of the protein and fat remains in the curd and becomes the main constituent of the cheese, but some of it is lost in the thin, milky whey, which is commonly called *petit-lait*. This liquid still contains a number of nutritious elements, such as protein, fat, and minerals.

*Fromage de lactosérum* is made from a secondary coagulation (usually by heat) to recoup the residual protein and fat before the whey is finally discarded. It is a useful and profitable by-product of cheese.

Whey cheeses should have a sweet, mild milky flavour and may be spread on bread as a savoury snack, or eaten as a dessert on their own or with jam.

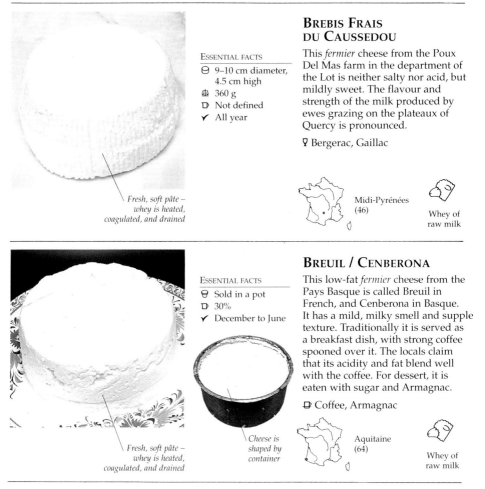

## BREBIS FRAIS DU CAUSSEDOU

ESSENTIAL FACTS

- ⊖ 9–10 cm diameter, 4.5 cm high
- ⚖ 360 g
- ⊐ Not defined
- ✓ All year

This *fermier* cheese from the Poux Del Mas farm in the department of the Lot is neither salty nor acid, but mildly sweet. The flavour and strength of the milk produced by ewes grazing on the plateaux of Quercy is pronounced.

♀ Bergerac, Gaillac

Midi-Pyrénées (46)

Whey of raw milk

*Fresh, soft pâte – whey is heated, coagulated, and drained*

## BREUIL / CENBERONA

ESSENTIAL FACTS

- ⊖ Sold in a pot
- ⊐ 30%
- ✓ December to June

This low-fat *fermier* cheese from the Pays Basque is called Breuil in French, and Cenberona in Basque. It has a mild, milky smell and supple texture. Traditionally it is served as a breakfast dish, with strong coffee spooned over it. The locals claim that its acidity and fat blend well with the coffee. For dessert, it is eaten with sugar and Armagnac.

⊡ Coffee, Armagnac

Aquitaine (64)

Whey of raw milk

*Fresh, soft pâte – whey is heated, coagulated, and drained*

*Cheese is shaped by container*

## GREUILH

This is a *fermier* cheese from the Vallée d'Ossau in Béarn. Greuilh may be eaten by itself or as a dessert with jam. It is light and refreshing and goes especially well with quince jam. Sold in vacuum-packs, this cheese should be consumed within 21 days.

❢ Tursan

**ESSENTIAL FACTS**

⊞ Sold in vacuum-packs of 2 to 3kg; also sold by weight

ᴅ Not defined

✔ December to end of June

Fresh, soft pâte – whey is heated, coagulated, and drained

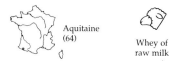

Aquitaine (64)

Whey of raw milk

---

## SÉRAC

This *fermier* cheese from Savoie is delicious by itself or on toast with herbs and olive oil. A version of this cheese is made with whey from Beaufort cheese (p. 26).

♀ Roussette de Savoie

**ESSENTIAL FACTS**

Size varies according to size of container

ᴅ Not defined

✔ Spring to autumn (goat's-milk cheese); all year (cow's-milk cheese)

Fresh, soft pâte – whey is heated, coagulated, and drained

Rhône-Alpes (73)

Whey of raw ewe or goat's milk

---

# Nutritional values of cheese

Cheese is recommended for children and old people because of its high nutritional value. Compared with milk, it contains the same nutrients although in greater concentration, with fats, proteins, minerals (calcium, phosphorus), and vitamins (A, B,), but less water. The proteins change into amino acids which the digestive system can absorb. Calcium, joins with the amino acids and can similarly be absorbed. Cheese also contains a lot of beta carotene (vitamin A); the only elements lacking are vitamin C and fibre. Eaten with fruit and vegetables, cheese offers an almost complete diet.

NUTRITIONAL VALUES OF CHEESE PER 100 G

|  | PROTEINS | FAT CONTENT | CALCIUM | ENERGY |
|---|---|---|---|---|
| *Fromage frais* (fresh cheese) | 6.5–9.6 g | 0.9–4 g | 75–170 mg | 44–160 kcal |
| Soft cheese (e.g. Camembert) | 20–21 g | 20–23 g | 150–380 mg | 260–350 kcal |
| Uncooked, pressed cheese (e.g. Tomme) | 24–27 g | 24–29 g | 657–865 mg | 326–384 kcal |
| Cooked, pressed cheese (e.g. Comté) | 27–29 g | 28–30 g | 900–1100 mg | 390–400 kcal |
| Blue mould cheese (e.g. Roquefort) | 20 g | 27–32 g | 722–870 mg | 414 kcal |

## GAPERON

The name Gaperon may derive from the word *gap* or *gape*, which means buttermilk in the local dialect of the Auvergne. In the past, when butter was made in a butter churn, the liquid left in the churn called *lait de beurre* (buttermilk) or *lait battu* (beaten milk), was mixed with fresh milk to make Gaperon.

This *artisanal* cheese has a hard, dry rind, while the pâte, which contains garlic and ground pepper, is elastic. The flavour is tingling and rough. This is a low-fat cheese, cured on a hook by the fire, which explains the tang of smoke. Affinage takes one to two months.

**♟** Côtes d'Auvergne

*Semi-hard pâte; uncooked, pressed*

*Rind of natural mould*

- ⊖ 8–9 cm diameter base, 8–9 cm high, suspended from yellow string
- ⚖ 250–350 g
- ⏹ 30–45%
- ✔ All year

Auvergne (63)

Raw, pasteurized, whole, partly skimmed

## GRATARON D'ARÈCHES

The *fermier* cheese shown here was ripened for four weeks and is salty and sticky. It was made from strong milk in a *chalet* in the Beaufort region of Savoie. During the affinage of four weeks, this cheese is rubbed with brine and turned.

**♟** Crépy, Seyssel

*Soft pâte; uncooked, slightly pressed*

- ⊖ 9–11 cm diameter, 3–4 cm high
- ⚖ 300–400 g
- ⏹ 45%
- ✔ Spring to autumn

*Washed rind*

Rhône-Alpes (73)

Raw

## LANGRES (AOC)

As the name indicates, this *artisanal* cheese originates from the high plains of Langres, in Champagne. It is shaped like a cylinder and has a 5-mm deep well on top called a *fontaine*, a kind of basin into which Champagne or *marc* may be poured. This is a pleasant way to eat this cheese and is characteristic of wine-producing regions.

The surface of the cheese is sticky, wet, and shiny, and has a pronounced smell. The pâte is firm and supple, and melts in the mouth, releasing a complex mixture of aromas. The salt too is strong, yet Langres is a milder cheese than Epoisses de Bourgogne (p. 133). The cheeses shown are completely ripe.

Langres is produced in a large and a small version. Affinage usually takes five to six weeks within the areas specified by the AOC. The cheeses are placed in a cellar at a humidity of 95%, where they are regularly rubbed with brine, either using a damp cloth or by hand. The minimum permitted affinage is 21 days for large cheeses and 15 days for small ones. A red dye extracted from the seeds of the American annatto tree is applied to colour the rind. This is called *rocou* in French and is also added to other cheeses and butter.

❑ *Marc* de Champagne

White to light-beige pâte,
becomes softer towards centre;
uncooked, unpressed

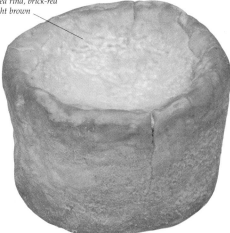

Smooth, fine-textured,
washed rind, brick-red
to light brown

### AOC REGULATIONS: LANGRES

**1.** The sliced curd must be neither washed nor kneaded. (Concentrated or reconstituted milk is not allowed.)

**2.** It is permitted to add annatto to the brine, applied when rubbing the cheese, in order to impart a red colouring to the rind.

AOC GRANTED 1975

Champagne-Ardenne (52);
Lorraine (88);
Bourgogne (21)     Pasteurized

ESSENTIAL FACTS

◯ 16–20 cm diameter, 5–7 cm high (large);
7.5–9 cm diameter, 4–6 cm high (small)

⚖ 800 g min. (large); 150 g min. (small)

•• 42 g min. per 100 g cheese

❐ 50% min., 21 g min. per 100 g cheese

✙ All year

# LIVAROT (AOC)

This *artisanal* or *industriel* cheese was named after a village in Normandie. Its nickname is the Colonel because it is bound with straps of rush or paper reminiscent of a Colonel's stripes.

Both the smell and taste of Livarot have lessened over the years. It should be very ripe when chosen, and a finger should sink into the pâte. There should, however, be no smell of ammonia since this could indicate that the cheese was past its best.

Livarot is very strong tasting. The rind is washed and coloured with annatto (p. 148), and sticks to the fingers. The ripe pâte has no elasticity and feels heavy and moist on the tongue. The cheese dissolves in the mouth, with a spicy flavour, close to that of hung meat.

Affinage takes at least three weeks, usually one to two months, during which time the cheese is washed in water or light brine and turned regularly.

♀ Tokay, Pinot Gris d'Alsace *vendage tardive*, ♥ Pomerol *jeune*

ESSENTIAL FACTS

◯ 12 cm diameter of mould, 4–5 cm high
⚖ 450 g
⁑ 230 g min. per cheese
ᗡ 40% min., 92 g min. per cheese
✓ All year

*Soft pâte, uncooked, unpressed*

*Moist, washed rind*

Basse-Normandie (14, 61)

Raw or pasteurized

## MAMIROLLE

The flavour of this brick-shaped cheese from the village of Mamirolle in the department of Doubs is sweet; the consistency of the pâte is elastic and fine. Mamirolle is a washed-rind cheese made by students of the École Nationale d'Industrie Laitière, a college with a high standard of learning that is difficult to get into. The cheese is also made by the Union Agricole Comtoise at Besançon. Affinage takes at least 15 days, during which time the cheese is washed in brine with annatto.

♥ Arbois

*Semi-hard, elastic pâte; uncooked, pressed*

Franche-Comté (25)

Pasteurized

*Moist, brick-red, washed rind*

**ESSENTIAL FACTS**

- 15 cm long, 6–7 cm wide, 4 cm high
- 500–650 g
- 45%
- All year

---

# Buying, storing, and tasting cheese

**Buying cheese**
- Choose a reputable, well-managed shop, with helpful assistants. It should be clean and the cheeses cut in front of you. More important than variety is the quality and condition of the cheeses on sale.
- Learn to choose cheese first by eye and then by taste. With time your eyes and tongue will begin to work together.
- Do not buy more than you can eat. Larger pieces of pressed or cooked pressed cheeses (e.g. Emmental) usually keep well, as do well-ripened goat's-milk cheeses. Avoid pre-packed cheeses since they are often inferior to those cut in a shop.

**Keeping and storing cheese**
- Cheeses contain living organisms that must not be cut off from air, yet it is important not to let a cheese dry out. As a rule, big pieces of cheese keep well.
- The ideal place for storing cheese is a cool, dark, well-ventilated room. Although dark, refrigerators are often too airless.

- Cover the cut sides of a cheese only and let it breathe through its rind or crust. Wrap soft cheeses loosely. Use waxed or greaseproof paper rather than cling film.
- Do not store cheese with strong-smelling foods. As a cheese breathes it will absorb other aromas and may spoil.
- Small quantities of cheese may be stored in a refrigerator for short periods as long as they are wrapped in waxed or greaseproof paper as described above.

**Tasting cheese**
- Let cold cheese warm up for about half an hour before eating to allow the flavour and aroma to develop. Cover it with a damp cheesecloth if the air is very dry.
- Cut the cheese into pieces, with an equal portion of rind as well as the heart and outer bits of the pâte (p. 221).
- Remove hard crusts depending on taste.
- Offer bread and wine with the cheese. There is nothing to beat well-matured cheese, crusty fresh bread, and a good wine.

# Maroilles

*Moist, brick red, washed rind*

A Mignon (below and right), the small version of Maroilles

## MAROILLES (AOC)

This cheese is said to have been created in AD 962 by a monk. Maroilles, also called Marolles, is a powerful *fermier* or *industriel* cheese. The pâte is golden, soft, and oily. The sweet taste lingers in the mouth. Affinage takes at least five weeks within the specified areas, although two to four months are more usual. During this time, the cheese is regularly turned and brushed and its rind changes from yellow, to orange, and finally red. Repeated turnings and washings eliminate the natural white mould and promote the development of bacteria (red ferments) that form the distinctive red rind.

♀ Châteauneuf-du-Pape

ESSENTIAL FACTS

◈ 12.5–13 cm square, 6 cm high
⚖ 700 g
⁂ 360 g min. per cheese
⬭ 45% min.,162 g min. per cheese
✓ All year

### AOC REGULATIONS: MAROILLES

1. The divided curd must not be washed.

2. Use of fungicides is forbidden.

3. Three sizes are permitted:
**Sorbais:** 12–12.5 cm square, 4 cm high, weight 550 g with a minimum of 270 g dry matter. Affinage of at least four weeks.
**Mignon:** 11–11.5 cm square, 3 cm high, weight 350 g with a minimum of 180 g dry matter. Affinage of at least three weeks.
**Quart:** 8–8.5 cm square, 3 cm high, weight 180 g with a minimum of 90 g dry matter. Affinage of at least two weeks.

AOC GRANTED 1976

*Soft pâte; uncooked, unpressed*

Picardie (02); Nord-Pas-de-Calais (59)

Raw or pasteurized

## BAGUETTE LAONNAISE

This is an *industriel* cheese from the ancient city of Laon. It is usually brick-shaped, but baguette-shaped cheeses also exist in the Avesnois and Thiérache areas. They are all strong and of the same family as Maroilles. No one seems to know whether the production of this cheese started after World War I or II. Affinage takes two months.

❢ Coteaux Champenois, Bouzy

ESSENTIAL FACTS
⬦ 6 cm wide, 15 cm long, 6 cm high
⚖ 500 g
🌡 45%
✔ All year

*Moist, red, washed rind*

*Soft pâte; uncooked, unpressed*

**Small format baguette of 250 g**

Picardie (02)

Pasteurized

---

## BOULETTE D'AVESNES

This *fermier* or *industriel* cheese is named after Avesnes, an ancient city near the Belgian border. It is made from buttermilk or Maroilles *fromage blanc* flavoured with parsley, pepper, tarragon, and cloves, then shaped by hand and dyed with annatto or covered with paprika. Affinage takes two to three months; the *fermier* version is washed with beer.

❢ Bourgogne Passetoutgrains

ESSENTIAL FACTS
◈ 6–8 cm diameter at base, 10 cm high
⚖ 180–250 g
🌡 45%
✔ All year

*Moist, dark red-coloured rind with annatto or covered with paprika*

*Soft-flavoured pâte; uncooked, unpressed*

Nord-Pas-de-Calais (59)

Raw or pasteurized

---

## BOULETTE DE CAMBRAI

The region of Cambrai produces cereals and sugar beet, and is known for its *andouillettes* (tripe sausages). Boulette de Cambrai is made by hand from *fromage frais*, to which salt, pepper, tarragon, parsley, and chives are added. It is only eaten fresh. Production may be *fermier* or *artisanal*, with no affinage.

❢ Bourgogne Passetoutgrains, Beaujolais

ESSENTIAL FACTS
◈ 7–8 cm base, 8 cm high
⚖ 200 g
🌡 45%
✔ All year

*No rind*

*Fresh pâte*

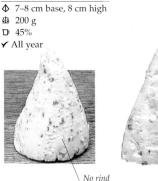

Nord-Pas-de-Calais (59)

Raw or pasteurized

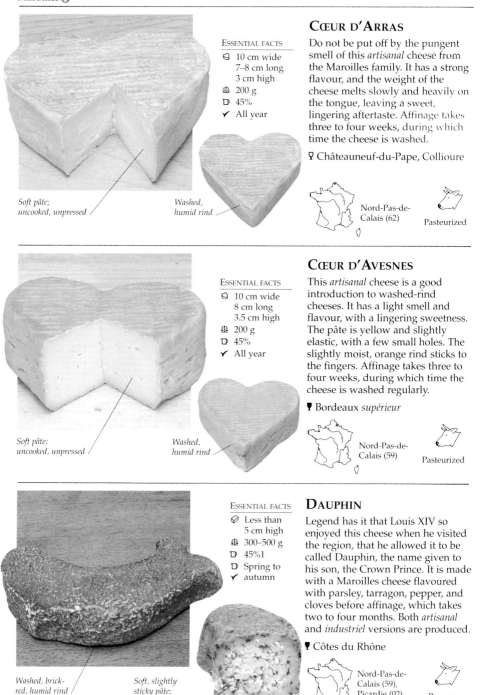

## CŒUR D'ARRAS

ESSENTIAL FACTS
- ⊖ 10 cm wide
  7–8 cm long
  3 cm high
- ⚖ 200 g
- ▯ 45%
- ✓ All year

Do not be put off by the pungent smell of this *artisanal* cheese from the Maroilles family. It has a strong flavour, and the weight of the cheese melts slowly and heavily on the tongue, leaving a sweet, lingering aftertaste. Affinage takes three to four weeks, during which time the cheese is washed.

♥ Châteauneuf-du-Pape, Collioure

*Soft pâte; uncooked, unpressed*

*Washed, humid rind*

Nord-Pas-de-Calais (62)

Pasteurized

## CŒUR D'AVESNES

ESSENTIAL FACTS
- ⊖ 10 cm wide
  8 cm long
  3.5 cm high
- ⚖ 200 g
- ▯ 45%
- ✓ All year

This *artisanal* cheese is a good introduction to washed-rind cheeses. It has a light smell and flavour, with a lingering sweetness. The pâte is yellow and slightly elastic, with a few small holes. The slightly moist, orange rind sticks to the fingers. Affinage takes three to four weeks, during which time the cheese is washed regularly.

♥ Bordeaux *supérieur*

*Soft pâte; uncooked, unpressed*

*Washed, humid rind*

Nord-Pas-de-Calais (59)

Pasteurized

## DAUPHIN

ESSENTIAL FACTS
- ◈ Less than 5 cm high
- ⚖ 300–500 g
- ▯ 45%1
- ▯ Spring to
- ✓ autumn

Legend has it that Louis XIV so enjoyed this cheese when he visited the region, that he allowed it to be called Dauphin, the name given to his son, the Crown Prince. It is made with a Maroilles cheese flavoured with parsley, tarragon, pepper, and cloves before affinage, which takes two to four months. Both *artisanal* and *industriel* versions are produced.

♥ Côtes du Rhône

*Washed, brick-red, humid rind*

*Soft, slightly sticky pâte; uncooked, unpressed*

Nord-Pas-de-Calais (59), Picardie (02)

Raw or pasteurized

## GRIS DE LILLE

Also known as Puant de Lille, Puant Macéré, and Vieux Lille, this cheese is a ripened Maroilles soaked for three months in brine to give a salty taste. *Puant* means strong smelling and this cheese does have a putrefied smell – but the stronger it grows, the more the locals like it. It is said that northern miners ate this *artisanal* or *industriel* cheese down the pit.

🍺 Local beer, 🍷 Champagne

**ESSENTIAL FACTS**
◈ 13 cm square 5-6 cm high
⚖ 700 g–1 kg
🗓 45%
✔ All year

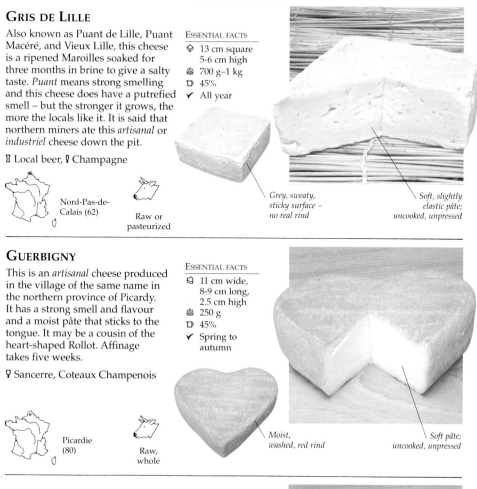

Nord-Pas-de-Calais (62)

Raw or pasteurized

Grey, sweaty, sticky surface – no real rind

Soft, slightly elastic pâte; uncooked, unpressed

## GUERBIGNY

This is an *artisanal* cheese produced in the village of the same name in the northern province of Picardy. It has a strong smell and flavour and a moist pâte that sticks to the tongue. It may be a cousin of the heart-shaped Rollot. Affinage takes five weeks.

🍷 Sancerre, Coteaux Champenois

**ESSENTIAL FACTS**
◖ 11 cm wide, 8-9 cm long, 2.5 cm high
⚖ 250 g
🗓 45%
✔ Spring to autumn

Picardie (80)

Raw, whole

Moist, washed, red rind

Soft pâte; uncooked, unpressed

## ROLLOT

The first Rollot was a *fermier* cheese produced in the village of the same name. It has a distinct, salty flavour with a lingering bitterness. The cheese shown here is still young and mild but will be very strong when it ripens. There is also a heart-shaped *industriel* version. Affinage takes four weeks.

🍷 Sancerre, Coteaux Champenois

**ESSENTIAL FACTS**
◖ 7–8 cm diameter, 3.5 cm high
⚖ 280–300 g
🗓 45%
✔ Spring to autumn

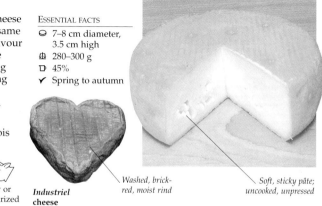

Picardie (80)

Raw or pasteurized

**Industriel cheese**

Washed, brick-red, moist rind

Soft, sticky pâte; uncooked, unpressed

Affinage of
three weeks

Fresh, non-AOC cheese

## MUNSTER / MUNSTER-GÉROMÉ (AOC)

This cheese is made under different names on either side of the Vosges mountains, in Alsace to the east, and Lorraine to the west. In Alsace it is called Munster, while in Lorraine it is known as Géromé. In 1978, the AOC Munster-Géromé united these two cheeses.

**Appearance and flavour**
The chief characteristics of this cheese are firstly the pungent smell, and secondly the soft, smooth pâte, with the consistency of melting chocolate. The rind is brick-red, and the pâte is fine-textured and golden, slightly sticky, and sweet, with the flavour of rich milk, as long as the cheese has been properly matured.

When this cheese is young, the rind is orange-yellow, while the pâte is pale cream with the consistency of brittle soap. A ripe Munster smells very strong. Locally, the cheese is eaten with cumin or potatoes boiled with their skins on. Cumin-flavoured Munster may be bought ready-made.

Alsace (67, 68);
Lorraine (88, 54, 57);
Franche-Comté (70, 90)

Raw or pasteurized

### The Munster cows

The milk used to make Munster comes from Vosgiennes cows, a breed that was imported from Scandinavia in the 18th century. The animals are strong and yield good-quality milk that is high in protein.

### Production and affinage

*Fermier, industriel,* and *coopérative* versions of this cheese are produced. Concentrated or reconstituted milk is not permitted. Affinage must take place within the areas specified by the AOC and needs a minimum of three weeks (two weeks for Petit-Munster), although two to three months are more usual. During affinage, the cheeses are stored in a cellar at 11–15°C and 95–96% humidity, where they are rubbed with a light brine by cloth or by hand every two to three days. This causes the characteristic yellow to reddish-orange rind to develop.

♀ Gewürztraminer, Tokay, Pinot Gris d'Alsace

ESSENTIAL FACTS

- ⊖ 13–19 cm diameter, 2.4–8 cm high; 7–12 cm diameter, 2–6 cm high (Petit-Munster)
- ⚖ 450 g min; 120 g min. (Petit-Munster)
- ⦂ 44g per 100 g cheese
- ♉ 45% min., 19.8 g per 100 g cheese
- ✓ All year; summer to winter (*fermier*)

---

#### AOC REGULATIONS: MUNSTER

**1.** The divided curd must be neither washed nor kneaded before moulding.

**2.** If the cheese is ripened in a region other than the place of production, the label must indicate the place of production and the place of affinage.

AOC GRANTED 1978

---

Munster flavoured with cumin

*Rind is a yellow to reddish-orange in colour due to red ferments (Bacterium linens)*

**Affinage of one week**

*Soft pâte; uncooked, unpressed*

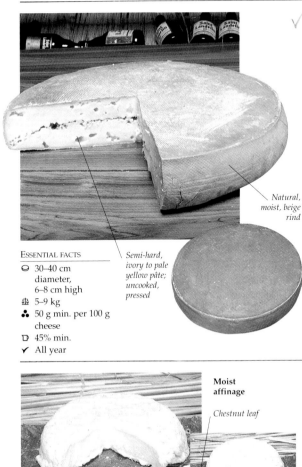

## MORBIER

The rind of Morbier is natural and rubbed, and the pâte is supple and sweet. It is a mild cheese, originally made for personal consumption by the cheesemakers of Comté. In the past, soot was sprinkled on the fresh curd to prevent a rind from forming and keep insects away, as it rested for the night at the bottom of a barrel. In the morning, leftover pieces of cheese were put on top to make the Morbier. Today, the black layer is a harmless vegetable product and purely decorative. The shape is round, with bulging sides and a horizontal black furrow through the middle. Production may be *artisanal, fermier, coopérative,* or *industriel.* Affinage takes at least 30 days, usually two months.

🍷 Crépy, Seyssel

*Natural, moist, beige rind*

*Semi-hard, ivory to pale yellow pâte; uncooked, pressed*

ESSENTIAL FACTS
- ⬭ 30–40 cm diameter, 6–8 cm high
- 🧀 5–9 kg
- ⁑ 50 g min. per 100 g cheese
- 🗇 45% min.
- ✓ All year

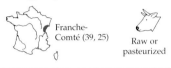

Franche-Comté (39, 25)

Raw or pasteurized

---

**Moist affinage**

*Chestnut leaf*

**Normal affinage**

*Soft pâte; uncooked, unpressed*

*Rind of natural mould*

## MOTHAIS À LA FEUILLE

This *fermier* goat's cheese has a sticky rind and a melting pâte with a soft flavour. Goat's cheeses are usually ripened in drier and better ventilated cellars than other cheeses. This one, however, has an affinage of three to four weeks in a cellar at almost 100% humidity, with no ventilation. The cheese rests on a chestnut or plane leaf to retain as much moisture as possible, and is turned every four to five days.

🍷 Fleurie, 🍷 Champagne *rosé,* ☕ Coffee

ESSENTIAL FACTS
- ⬭ 10 cm diameter, 3 cm high
- 🧀 250 g
- 🗇 45%
- ✓ Spring to autumn

Poitou-Charentes (79)

Raw

## MUROL

Traces of cloth are visible on the rind of this *industriel* cheese. The pâte is yellow when ripe, fine-textured, and very elastic. Its smell and flavour are mild. Murol is a Saint-Nectaire cheese (p. 184) with a hole in the middle. (The piece cut out makes the Murolait shown below.) Affinage takes one month.

ESSENTIAL FACTS

- ☉ 12 cm diameter, 5–4 cm high
- ⚖ 450–500 g
- ᗡ 45%
- ✓ All year

*Washed, orange-red, humid rind*

*Semi-hard, elastic pâte; uncooked, pressed*

## MUROLAIT

This cheese was made from the piece cut out of the Murol above.

❢ Fleurie, ♢ Champagne *rosé*

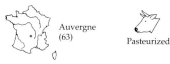

Auvergne (63)

Pasteurized

ESSENTIAL FACTS

- ☉ 3.5 cm diameter, 4.5 cm high
- ⚖ 50 g

*Red paraffin wax*

## NANTAIS / CURÉ

This is a cheese with many names, including Curé Nantais and Fromage du Pays Nantais dit du Curé, as well as the above. Originally round, and made by the *curé*, or curate of Vendée, it was brought into this region, which previously lacked cheeses, by a monk who was fleeing from the French Revolution. The rind is smooth and wet, the pâte golden and supple, with a few small holes. This is a strong, small-scale *industriel* cheese. Affinage takes one month.

♢ Muscadet, Gros Plant

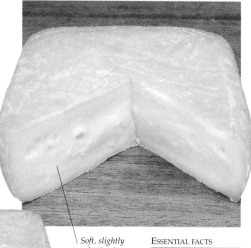

Pays de la Loire (44)

Pasteurized

*Soft, slightly elastic pâte; uncooked, unpressed*

*Washed, wet, orange-pink rind*

ESSENTIAL FACTS

- ◈ 8–9 cm square, 2.5–3 cm high
- ⚖ 170–200 g
- ᗡ 40%
- ✓ All year

*Rind "fleurie", meaning covered in a "bloom" of white mould*

**Carré, or square-shaped version**

**Bonde, or cylinder-shaped version**

## NEUFCHÂTEL (AOC)

This *fermier*, *industriel*, or *artisanal* cheese comes from the town of Neufchâtel in the Pays de Bray in northern Normandie. It may date from as far back as AD 1035, when Hugues I of Gournay, a town close to Neufchâtel, offered it as a donation to the Abbey of Sigy. Parisians discovered it through the famous food guide of the time, *Almanach des Gourmands*, (1803–1812). Neufchâtel lies only 132 km from Paris and the proximity boosted the popularity of the cheese in the capital.

The rind of the cheese is dry and velvety and crumbles when pinched, while the firm but supple pâte sinks under finger pressure.

Six different versions of Neufchâtel are produced: *bonde* and *double bonde*, which are a small and large cylinder; *carré*, which is square; *briquette*, which is a small brick shape; and a *cœur* and *grand cœur*, a large and small heart.

Following a good affinage of at least ten days, usually three weeks, after renneting the cheese develops

*Soft, firm, smooth pâte with no holes; uncooked, slightly pressed*

a covering of fine white mould. The mould flavours the cheese and gives it a pronounced mouldy smell. The flavour goes well with a good, crusty bread.

🍷 Pomerol, St. Emilion

Haute-Normandie (76); Picardie (60)

Raw or pasteurized

◇ *Bonde*: 4.5 cm diameter, 6.5 cm high
⚖ 100 g
◇ *Double bonde*: 5.8 cm diameter,
   8 cm high
⚖ 200 g
◇ *Carré*: 6.5 cm square, 2.4 cm high
⚖ 100 g
◇ *Briquette*: 5 cm wide, 7 cm long,
   3 cm high
⚖ 100 g
◙ *Cœur*: 10 cm wide, 8.5 cm long,
   3.2 cm high
⚖ 200 g
◙ *Grand cœur*: 14 cm wide, 10.5 cm
   long, 5 cm high
♣ 40 g min. per 100 g cheese
D 45% min., 18 g min. per 100 g cheese
✓ Summer to winter (raw cheeses);
   all year (pasteurized cheeses)

AOC REGULATIONS:
NEUFCHÂTEL

1. The drained curd must be kneaded
until it becomes uniform.

2. Pieces of mature, blooming
Neufchâtel are added to the curd.

AOC GRANTED 1977

*Cœur*, or small, heart-
shaped version

*Rind of
white mould*

*Firm,
young, heart*

## BONDARD /
## BONDE / BONDON

The point of affinage reached by
the cheese shown here is just right.
It has a white, velvety mould that
forms a thick rind. The fat content
is high and the pâte melting. When
eaten with the rind, it tingles on the
tongue and is rather salty.
Production may be *fermier* or
*artisanal*, with an affinage of two
weeks to two months.

♀ Jasnières

ESSENTIAL FACTS

◇ 5 cm diameter,
   8 cm high
⚖ 200 g
D 50–60%
✓ Summer to winter

*Rind of
white,
velvety
mould*

Haute-
Normandie
(76)

Enriched
with cream

*Soft pâte;
uncooked,
unpressed*

## OLIVET CENDRÉ

This *artisanal* cheese is made in Olivet, a town on the River Loire. In May and June, the milk produced by cows grazing on the lush pastures is very rich and the cheeses made during this period are kept for the harvesting season, when there will be a lot of people to feed as they work in the fields and vineyards. Olivet ripens slowly and used to be preserved in vine ashes. The pâte is slightly resistant to the bite and has a slight scent of mould. Affinage in ashes takes at least one month.

❢ Sancerre

*Soft pâte; uncooked, unpressed*

*Ash-grey rind*

- ⊖ 10–12 cm diameter, 3 cm high
- ⚖ 250–300 g
- ⊡ 40–45%
- ⋎ All year

Centre (45)

Pasteurized

---

## OLIVET AU FOIN

This recently introduced cheese is a variation on the Olivet Cendré shown above. The white mould contains a few strands of hay. There is also a version covered in crushed pepper.

❢ Sancerre

*Soft pâte; uncooked, unpressed*

*Rind of white mould with a few strands of hay*

- ⊖ 10 cm diameter, 2 cm high
- ⚖ 250 g
- ⊡ 45%
- ⋎ All year

Centre (45)

Pasteurized

## PALOUSE DES ARAVIS (PUR CHÈVRE D'ALPAGE)

This is a *fermier* cheese from the town of Grand-Bornand in the chain of mountains called the Aravis on the edge of the Alps. In the local dialect, *palouse* means a dry disc, which aptly describes this cheese. The cheeses are made in a *chalet* during the summer, and cured over a long period. The pâte is drained under pressure and the rind is washed at the beginning of the affinage, then left for the mould to expand naturally, and dry out. Affinage takes between five and ten months. The rind is as hard as a rock, and the pâte is dry and rough with a concentrated flavour.

♀ Vin Jaune du Jura, Alsace

Semi-hard pâte; uncooked, pressed

Rind of natural mould

ESSENTIAL FACTS

⊖ 16–19 cm diameter, 3 cm high
⚖ 800 g
D Not defined
✓ Summer to winter

Rhône-Alpes (74)

Raw

---

## PAVÉ D'AUGE

In the centre of almost every old French town, there is usually a church in a square of rough paving stones, called *pavés*. This *fermier* or *artisanal* cheese is shaped like one of those stones. It has a mild and supple pâte, with a relatively high fat content. The dry or washed rind bears a slight resemblance to Pont l'Evêque (p. 172). If you can find a Pavé d'Auge *fermier* that has rested long enough in its cellar, you will be able to taste the quality of the Normandie milk used in its production. Affinage takes two to three months.

Ⅱ Cidre du pays d'Auge,
♀ Champagne

Soft pâte; uncooked, unpressed

Dry or washed rind

ESSENTIAL FACTS

◈ 11 cm square, 5–6 cm high
⚖ 600–800 g
D 50%
✓ Summer to winter

Basse-Normandie (14)

Raw or pasteurized

## Le Pavé du Plessis

The pâte of this cheese bounces slightly under finger pressure because it is full of small holes. Its taste is soft, with a flavour of sweet salt. Le Pavé is an *artisanal* cheese from the Fromagerie du Plessis in Normandie, with an affinage of two to three months.

❢ Haut Médoc, Margaux

*Soft, yellow pâte; uncooked, unpressed*

ESSENTIAL FACTS

◈ 11–12 cm square, 5 cm high
⬙ 500 g
🗗 50%
✓ All year

*Rind of natural, dry, white or orange-red mould*

Haute-Normandie (27)

Raw

## Pavé de Roubaix

Roubaix is a town in the north of France, which grew with the expansion of the textile industry. It is said that this cheese was a permanent fixture on the tables of the weavers and a symbol of wealth. Pavé de Roubaix has a dry, rock-hard rind, and the pâte is of the same carrot-orange colour as that of Mimolette (p. 36). It is an *artisanal* cheese, with an affinage at 15°C of one or even two years, during which time it is turned and brushed once a month. Sadly, there are only two or three people making this cheese and it is in danger of disappearing altogether.

♀ Banyuls (VDN)

*Semi-hard pâte; half-cooked, pressed*

ESSENTIAL FACTS

◈ 13 cm wide, 27 cm long, 8 cm high
⬙ 3.3 kg
🗗 45%
✓ All year

*Natural, hard, dry rind*

Nord-Pas-de-Calais (59)

Pasteurized

## PÉLARDON DES CÉVENNES

This young goat's-milk cheese comes from the Cévennes region near Alès in Languedoc, where all small goat's-milk cheeses are called *pélardon*. It has almost no rind and a compact, nutty pâte. The balance of acidity and salt is just right and there is a full, rich, milky flavour with a lingering aftertaste. Both *fermier* and *artisanal* versions are produced, with an affinage of two to three weeks. The cheese is a candidate for AOC status.

♀ Clairette du Languedoc

*Soft pâte; uncooked, unpressed*

*Rind of natural mould*

**Affinage of two to three weeks**

Languedoc-Roussillon (30, 48)

Raw

### ESSENTIAL FACTS

- ◷ 6–7 cm diameter, 2–3 cm high
- ⚖ 60–100 g
- ◷ 45%
- ✓ Spring to autumn

---

## PÉLARDON DES CORBIÈRES

This *fermier* goat's-milkcheese, another *pélardon,* comes from Lagrasse in the Corbières region on the Mediterranean coast. After one week of ripening, the rind shows a bloom of natural mould, and the pâte is supple. The flavour is slightly acidic, with no sweetness. This is a *fermier* cheese, with an affinage that lasts from one week onwards.

♀ Côtes du Roussillon

*Soft pâte; uncooked, unpressed*

*Rind of natural mould*

Languedoc-Roussillon (11)

Raw

**Affinage of more than three weeks**

### ESSENTIAL FACTS

- ◷ 6–7 cm diameter, 2 cm high
- ⚖ 70–80 g
- ◷ 45%
- ✓ All year

# Persillé

The blue goat's-milk cheeses that are produced throughout the mountainous Savoie region are called *persillés*. The blue colour within the pâte comes from a very subtle natural mould that only becomes visible after a minimum affinage of three months. These cheeses may be made with pure goat's milk, or from a mixture of different milks. Cow's-milk cheeses with internal blue moulds are most commonly known as *bleus*, although they may sometimes be called *persillés*, depending on the way the mould is distributed through the pâte. Cheeses in which the pâte is delicately marbled with the blue mould are described as *marbré*. If there are definite veins of blue mould, the cheese is described as *veiné* or *veineux*.

**ESSENTIAL FACTS**

⊖ 6–8 cm diameter, 6–8 cm high
⚖ 250–550 g
🜄 45%
✓ Best in early summer

*Soft pâte; uncooked, unpressed*

*Rind of natural mould*

## PERSILLÉ DE LA TARENTAISE

This *fermier* cheese from the Tarentaise area of Savoie has the typically acid tang of a young goat's-milk cheese. It has a white, fine-textured pâte with a blue mould that is not yet apparent in the cheese shown here. Affinage usually takes one-and-a-half months, but may be shorter than that.

♈ Crépy

Rhône-Alpes (73)

Raw

**ESSENTIAL FACTS**

⊖ 9–10 cm diameter, 8 cm high
⚖ 500–600 g
🜄 Not defined
✓ April to December

*Soft pâte; uncooked, unpressed*

*Rind of natural mould*

## PERSILLÉ DE LA HAUTE-TARENTAISE

The Haute-Tarentaise, where this *fermier* cheese is made, lies at the source of the River Isère, which rises just one kilometre away from the Swiss border. It has an affinage of two to three months.

♈ Crépy

Rhône-Alpes (73)

Raw

## PERSILLÉ DE TIGNES

The original village of Tignes in Savoie, where this cheese was first made, was submerged in 1952 by an artificial lake. This cheese comes from the new village that was built to replace it. The younger cheese (shown top right), has a raw, salty taste. As the cheese ripens, the crust hardens, and the pâte dries, becomes spicy, and breaks easily. It is said that the mustard-coloured crust is a sign that the goats were fed on grass growing on sulphurous soil. This *fermier* cheese has an affinage of at least one-and-a-half months.

♈ Crépy

**Affinage of one-and-a-half months**

*White, blue, natural mould is not visible*

*Soft pâte; uncooked, unpressed*

ESSENTIAL FACTS

⊖ 9.5–11 cm diameter, 9–10 cm high
⚖ 680–975 g
🕽 Not defined
✔ Best in summer

**Affinage of six months**

*Slightly bluish pâte*

Rhône-Alpes (73)

Raw

---

## PERSILLÉ DU SEMNOZ

The rock-hard crust on this *fermier* cheese is formed by a light brown mould. The pâte is greyish-yellow, with a blue mould that is not yet visible in the cheese shown here. The sticky consistency is evidence of the quality of the milks used in its production – usually equal parts of goat and cow's milk. Affinage takes one to two months.

♈ Crépy

Rhône-Alpes (74)

Raw

ESSENTIAL FACTS

⊖ 9–11 cm diameter, 6 cm high
⚖ 400–450 g
🕽 45%
✔ April to December

*Rind of natural mould*

*Semi-hard pâte; uncooked, pressed*

# Picodon

*Dry, thin rind of
natural moulds;
sometimes no mould*

**Ripe
Picodon de
l'Ardèche**

*Soft, white pâte
cuts cleanly*

❶

**Well-matured
Picodon de
l'Ardèche,**

*Smooth, fine-
textured pâte*

❷

**Young
Picodon de
l'Ardèche**

❸

**Picodon de
la Drôme**

❹

## ✓ Picodon (AOC)

The region of Picodon straddles
the River Rhône. The department
of the Drôme lies to the east of the
river, and the Ardèche to the west.
The name of this cheese derives
from the ancient language, Langue
d'Oc, and means spicy.

The climate of the lower Rhône
is dry. Mountain grass and shrubs,
with strong aromas and flavours,
grow short and thick there. The
goats that feed on the mountain
devour everything, including the
shoots and leaves of trees. Their
milk is the basis of this spicy
cheese. Its pâte is so dry that the
best way of getting all the taste
out of it is to suck it.

Pélardon (p. 167) is often
mistaken for Picodon. This is not
surprising, given the similarity of
their names and the fact that both
are southern mountain cheeses that
look like stones and weigh less
than 100 g. Production may be
*fermier*, *artisanal*, or *industriel*, with
an affinage of at least twelve days
from the day of renneting, although
three to four weeks is more usual.
AOC regulations forbid the
addition of concentrated or
powdered milk, lactic protein,
and frozen curd.

♀ Rivesaltes (VDN)

ESSENTIAL FACTS

- ◒ 5–8 cm diameter,
  1–3 cm high
- ⚖ 50–100 g
- ⁂ 40 g min. per 100 g cheese
- ⏷ 45% min., 18 g min.
  per 100 g cheese
- ✓ All year; spring to autumn (*fermier*)

Rhône-Alpes
(07, 26);
Provence-
Alpes-Côte
d'Azur (84);
Languedoc-
Rousillon (30)

Whole

The Picodons shown on these two pages demonstrate the variations in appearance and taste that may be found in these cheeses.

**1. Picodon de l'Ardèche**
This cheese weighs 55 g.

**2. Picodon de l'Ardèche**
After an affinage of four weeks, this cheese weighs just 40 g. It has a sticky pâte that smells of dry mould and has good acidity.

**3. Picodon de l'Ardèche**
This 60-g cheese has an acid, salty flavour. It still needs another week.

**4. Picodon de la Drôme**
This cheese weighs 45 g. The saltiness and sweetness have blended and there is little acidity.

**5. Picodon de Crest**
This cheese is made with rich, high-quality milk, and its flavour has a good blend of salt, sweetness, and acidity. It weighs 60 g.

**6. Picodon de Dieulefit**
This young cheese weighs 90 g and has a white mould and a soft pâte.

**7. Picodon de Dieulefit**
This cheese has shrunk to half its original size and weighs 40 g. The rind is hard and coloured by the mould. On tasting, the sun of Provence and the aroma of herbs and grass open up in the mouth as the cheese slowly melts.

**8. Picodon du Dauphiné**
This cheese is well ripened.

**9. Picodon à l'huile d'olive**
This cheese has been covered and marinated in olive oil flavoured with bay leaves.

---

**AOC Regulations: Picodon**

**1.** The milk must be coagulated with a low quantity of rennet. (Concentrated or powdered milk, lactic protein, and frozen curd are not allowed.)

**2.** The cheese must be salted with dry (fine or semi-coarse) salt.

**3.** The label may say *affinage méthode Dieulefit*. This method of affinage consists of rubbing the surface of the cheese by hand and with water, after which the cheese is left to mature and soften for more than a month in covered earthenware jars.

AOC GRANTED 1983

Picodon de
Crest

Young
Picodon de
Dieulefit

*Soft, young
cheese*

Well-ripened
Picodon de
Dieulefit

*Pâte becomes
hard and
brittle as it
ripens*

Picodon du
Dauphiné

Picodon à
l'huile d'olive

## Pont-l'Evêque (AOC)

Essential facts

- 10.5–11 cm square, 3 cm high
- 350–400 g
- 140 g min. per cheese
- 45%, 63 g min. per cheese
- All year

This washed-rind cheese is probably the oldest Norman cheese still in production. Some people say that Pont-l'Evêque originated in an abbey, but this story has never been substantiated. A document from the 12th century says that "a good table always finishes with a *dessert d'angelot*", which may be the old name for Pont l'Evêque. During the 17th century, cheeses made in the village of Pont l'Evêque were sent all over France and were popular.

It takes three litres of milk to make one Pont l'Evêque of 350–400 g. After washing, the rind is moist and ochre in colour. The pâte is creamy yellow, fine-textured, and smooth. It sinks under finger pressure but has no elasticity. As the cheese ripens, the rind grows sticky and reddens, and small holes spread through the pâte. Further ripening will result in a pâte that glistens with fat when cut. There are lingering traces of sweetness in the taste. Cheeses that are washed and turned during their affinage are strong, but this mature flavour is not present in younger cheeses.

Production of Pont l'Evêque may be *fermier*, *artisanal*, *coopérative*, or *industriel*. However, of the 3,727 tonnes produced in 1991, just over 2% (8 tonnes) were *fermier* cheeses. Affinage takes place within the specified areas at least two weeks from the date of production, although six weeks is more usual. During affinage, the cheeses are washed, brushed, and turned.

🍷 Condrieu, 🍺 Cider

*Soft pâte; uncooked, unpressed*

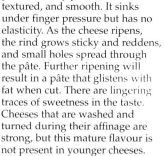

*Washed, moist or dry rind*

### AOC Regulations: Pont-l'Evêque

**1.** The curd must be divided, kneaded, and drained.

**2.** Three different sizes are produced:
**Petit-Pont-l'Evêque** (Small size): 8.5–9.5 cm square, 85 g minimum dry matter per cheese.
**Demi-Pont-l'Evêque** (half-size): 10.5–11.5 cm x 5.2–5.7 cm, 70 g minimum dry matter per cheese.
**Grand-Pont-l'Evêque** (large size): 19–21 cm square, 650–850 g minimum dry matter per cheese.

AOC granted 1976

Basse-Normandie (14, 50, 61); Haute-Normandie (27, 76); Pays-de-la-Loire (53)

Raw or pasteurized

## PORT-SALUT

This cheese is related to Port-du-Salut (below), with which it is often confused. It is produced in Entrammes in the department of Mayenne in northwest France.

The rind of the cheese is slightly moist and uniformly coloured, with regular traces of the plastific-covered cloth used in production. It has a very faint smell. The pâte is elastic under finger pressure and sticks to the knife when cut. It is cream-coloured, soft, and supple, with little acidity and a slight aftertaste, the result of successful *industriel* cheesemaking. The development of production from monastery to large industry is proof of the great demand for this cheese. Affinage takes one month.

*Semi-hard pâte; uncooked, pressed*

❦ Chinon, Bourgueil

Pays de la Loire (53)

Pasteurized

*Washed rind artificially coloured with beta carotene*

ESSENTIAL FACTS

- ◷ 20 cm diameter, 4 cm high
- ⚖ 1.3–1.5 kg;
- ◷ 50%
- ✓ All year

## PORT-DU-SALUT / ENTRAMMES

This cheese was first made in an abbey in around 1830. The method of production was then passed on to other abbeys. In 1959, the production rights and name were granted to the Société Anonyme des Fermiers Réunis. At this point, Port-Salut (above) began to be produced.

A few monks continued to make real Port-du-Salut, naming their cheese Entrammes, after the village where the Abbaye du Port-du-Salut once stood. They were forced to stop, unable to keep up with modernization. Although their method of production is still followed in abbeys and monasteries across France, Port-du-Salut is rare. Affinage takes at least one month.

*Washed rind*

*Semi-hard pâte*

❦ Chinon, Bourgueil

Pays de la Loire (53)

Pasteurized

ESSENTIAL FACTS

- ◷ 10 cm diameter, 4 cm high
- ⚖ 300 g
- ◷ 40–42%
- ✓ All year

## PITHIVIERS AU FOIN

This cheese is produced in the small town of Bondaroy, near Pithiviers. It is also call Bondaroy au Foin. Farmers used to make it in summer, when milk was plentiful, and keep it in hay until the autumn or winter. During the grape harvests, when many people were hired, it would be served after meals or as a snack. Today, it is available all year round, but it has lost the pleasant smell of hay of the old *fermier* cheeses. The rind is white, with a slight smell of the mould. This is an *artisanal* cheese with an affinage of three weeks.

*Soft pâte; uncooked, unpressed*

❦ Chinon, Bourgueil

ESSENTIAL FACTS

*Rind of white mould sprinkled with hay*

- ◒ 10–12 cm diameter, 2.5 cm high
- ⚖ 300 g
- ◗ 45%
- ✓ All year

Centre (45)

Pasteurized

---

## RACLETTE

*White to light yellow pâte, with small holes; supple and firm; uncooked, pressed*

This Savoie cheese, which is also called Fromage à Raclette, may be either round or square. The name derives from *racler*, meaning to scrape, and describes the way in which it is traditionally prepared and eaten in the mountains. The cheese is cut and heated on a spit so that it melts and can be scraped off with a knife. It is usually accompanied by potatoes boiled in their skins and pickles. Its pâte is slightly hard, but melts well, with a light smell of mould when warm, and a full, milky flavour. This is an *artisanal* or *industriel* cheese, with an affinage of at least eight weeks.

❦ Vin de Savoie, Hautes Côtes de Beaune

ESSENTIAL FACTS

- ◒ 28–36 cm diameter, 5.5–7.5 cm high;
- ◇ 28–36 cm square, 5.5–7.5 cm high
- ⚖ 4.5–7 kg (both formats)
- ❖ 53 g min. per 100 g cheese
- ◗ 45% min., 23.85 g min. per 100 g cheese
- ✓ All year

*Thin, golden-yellow to light brown rind with uncoated sides*

Throughout France

Raw or pasteurized

# REBLOCHON DE SAVOIE / REBLOCHON (AOC)

Freshness, youth, and tenderness are the most noticeable features of this mountain cheese from Savoie. The name derives from the verb *reblocher*, which means "to pinch a cow's udder again". This is because Reblochon is made with the thicker, richer milk from the second milking of Abondance, Montbéliard, and Tarine cows.

Reblochon is a well-proportioned cheese with a thin, orange-yellow to pink, tight, velvety rind. Its fresh, clear aroma comes from the mould, and it has a moist, smooth and supple, fatty pâte. The flavour opens in the mouth, leaving a delicately nutty aftertaste.

Production may be *fermier* (sometimes in a *chalet*), *coopérative* (*fruitière*), or *industriel*, with an affinage of at least two (usually three to four) weeks from the date of production. The temperature of the cellar must be kept below 16°C. A regular and a small version (Petit Reblochon) are produced.

🍷 Vin de Savoie, Pommard

Reblochon bought
in Thonon-les-Bains

*Yellow to orange, washed rind with natural white mould*

*Smooth, soft, ivory pâte; uncooked, slightly pressed*

ESSENTIAL FACTS

◯ 9–14 cm diameter, 3–3.5 cm high
⚖ 240–550 g
⣿ 45 g min. per 100 g cheese
ᴅ 45% min; 20.25 g min. per 100 g cheese
✓ From summer (*fermier* and *chalet*-made cheeses)

---

AOC REGULATIONS:
REBLOCHON

1. The milk must be brought to the place of production as quickly as possible after each milking.

2. Renneting must be done within 24 hours of the last milking.

3. *Fermier* cheeses must bear a green *casein* label.

AOC GRANTED 1976

Rhône-Alpes (73, 74)

Raw, whole

**Reblochon bought in Paris**

# Rigotte

It is thought that cheeses very similar to *rigotte* may have been produced as early as Roman times.

The name *rigotte* is a local name for cheese in the regions of Isère, Rhône, and the Loire. The word probably derives from the French *recuit* or Italian *ricotta*, both of which mean recooked. Despite the possible origins of the name, however, *rigotte* is not produced by recooking the milky whey, which is the method used to produce most whey cheeses (see *fromage de lactosérum* on p. 148–149). *Rigotte* used to have a comparatively low fat content, but now it is almost always between 40 and 45%. Made mostly in factories or *artisanal* dairies and almost always of cow's milk, *rigotte* is normally allowed a week to drain before it goes on sale in shops and markets. *Rigottes* are usually eaten while firm to the touch but soft inside and slightly sharp in flavour.

## RIGOTTE D'ECHALAS

ESSENTIAL FACTS

⊖ 5 cm diameter, 4 cm high
⚖ 85g
⊡ 50%
✓ All year

This is an *artisanal* cheese from Echalas in the Lyonnais province. It is best eaten with toast. The rind on the cheese shown has just formed. The fat content is almost 50%, which accounts for its smoothness. Affinage takes at least two weeks.

❡ Bourgogne

Rhône-Alpes (69)

Pasteurized

*Soft pâte, uncooked, unpressed*

*Rind of natural mould*

## RIGOTTE DE SAINTE-COLOMBE

ESSENTIAL FACTS

⊖ 5 cm diameter, 3.5 cm high
⚖ 60–80 g
⊡ 50%
✓ All year

This *artisanal* cheese from Saint-Genix-sur-Guiers in Savoie should be eaten young. The rind on the cheese shown has not yet finished developing. The pâte is yellow, rich, fine-textured, and smooth, with a slightly sour flavour. Affinage takes at least 15 days.

❡ Vin de Savoie, Hautes Côtes de Beaune

Rhône-Alpes (73)

Pasteurized

*Soft pâte; uncooked, unpressed*

*Rind of natural mould*

## RIGOTTE DE CONDRIEU

This is a *fermier* cheese from the Lyonnais province. Most *rigottes* are made with cow's milk, but this is a pure goat's-milk cheese and therefore quite rare. The pâte is fine-textured and robust, with a delicate aroma of honey and acacia. Affinage takes up to three weeks, although the cheese can be eaten fresh.

♥ Condrieu

ESSENTIAL FACTS

- ⊖ 4 cm diameter, 1.5–3 cm high
- ⚖ 30 g
- ▯ 45%
- ✓ Spring to autumn

*Soft pâte; uncooked, unpressed*

*Rind of natural mould*

Rhône-Alpes (69)

Raw, whole

**Fresh white cheese**

---

## RIGOTTE DES ALPES

This *industriel* cheese from the Dauphiné has a slightly sour but pleasant taste. When soaked in white wine for several days, it gains a new flavour. It must be eaten with wine, and perhaps sprinkled with fresh ground pepper. Affinage takes at least ten days.

♥ Crépy, Seyssel

ESSENTIAL FACTS

- ⊖ 4 cm diameter, 3.5 cm high
- ⚖ 50 g
- ▯ 45%
- ✓ All year

Rhône-Alpes (38, 69)

Pasteurized

*Soft pâte; uncooked, unpressed*

*Almost no rind; reddish-yellow exterior, coloured with annatto*

*Moist, soft, ivory and blue pâte crumbles under finger pressure; uncooked, unpressed*

ESSENTIAL FACTS

- ⊖ 19–20 cm diameter, 8.5–10.5 cm high
- ⊜ 2.5–2.9 kg
- ♣ 56 g min. per 100 g cheese
- ▷ 52% min., 29.12 g min. per 100 g cheese
- ✓ All year

VARIED APPEARANCE
The three Roquefort cheeses shown here were made by different producers and illustrate the variations in colour and texture that can be caused by slight variations in methods of production.

# ROQUEFORT (AOC)

A cheese like Roquefort is said to date back to the time of Pliny in ancient Rome and is mentioned in his book of AD 79. In 1411, Charles VI granted the people of Roquefort the monopoly of ripening the cheese in their caves as they had done for hundreds of years. In 1925, they obtained an AOC, the first in France. Very soon, though, there were imitations.

## Legal protection

In 1961, the Tribunal de Grande Instance at Millau decreed that although the cheeses could be made in many regions of southern France (see map below for specific departments), they could only be classed as true Roqueforts if they were ripened in the natural caves of Mont Combalou in the commune of Roquefort-sur-Soulzon. This eliminated imitation and the modern monopoly was established.

## Appearance and flavour

With Stilton and Gorgonzola, Roquefort is one of the three greatest blue cheeses in the world. It has a clean, forceful flavour with strong salt, very different from the sweetness of milk. The pâte is damp and crumbly and should be cut with a pre-warmed knife. The cheese melts in the mouth, leaving an amazing flavour of mould and salt. When mature, it is exceedingly strong. Roquefort goes well with pasta or salad. It is rich and spicy and is best eaten at the end of a dinner, for example after venison, accompanied by a bottle of Sauternes. A young Roquefort might be accompanied by Bandol or Muscat de Rivesaltes, served with raisin bread. Match a ripe, grey-blue-veined Roquefort with Banyuls, a naturally sweet wine from Roussillon.

♥ Sauternes, Banyuls (VDN)

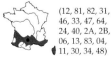 (12, 81, 82, 31, 46, 33, 47, 64, 24, 40, 2A, 2B, 06, 13, 83, 04, 11, 30, 34, 48)

 Raw, whole

## Production and affinage

Today, some 3.3 million cheeses per year are cured at Roquefort-sur-Soulzon. After Comté (p. 112) Roquefort is France's second most popular cheese. Around 60% of them are made by one company, the Société des Caves et des Producteurs Réunis. Roquefort is an *artisanal* or *industriel* cheese – there is no *fermier* version. All the cheeses carrying the name of Roquefort have been ripened for at least three months in natural caves as defined by the AOC. The usual affinage is four months, but may be extended by up to nine months. In a young cheese, the mould is pale and green; it becomes bluer and then grey as it ripens, while small, blue-grey holes begin to form. If the cheese is left for a long time, the mould becomes dominant.

Cheese produced by the Société des Caves et des Producteurs Réunis

Affinage of ten days

Affinage of one month

Affinage of three months

---

### AOC REGULATIONS: ROQUEFORT

**1.** The milk may not be delivered by the producers fewer than 20 days after lambing.

**2.** The renneting must take place within 48 hours at the latest after the last milking.

**3.** The cultures of *Penicillium roqueforti* used to produce the cheese must be prepared in France, from traditional sources in the micro-climate of the natural caves in the specified area of the commune.

**4.** Dry salt must be used for salting.

**5.** The producers must keep a register available to the agents of control in which the quantities of milk delivered by the producers as well as the weight and number of cheeses made are entered every day.

**6.** The whole process of conditioning and packing Roquefort cheeses from the moment they enter the caves until they are sold must take place exclusively in the commune of Roquefort. The refrigeration rooms used for storage before the cheeses are sold must also be situated in the commune of Roquefort.

FULL AOC GRANTED 1979,
FOLLOWING THE ORIGINAL LAW OF 1925

Affinage of six months

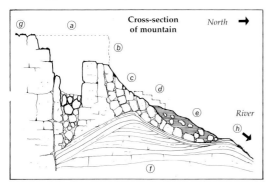

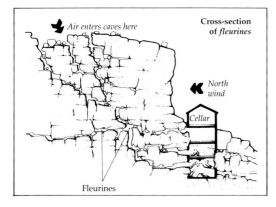

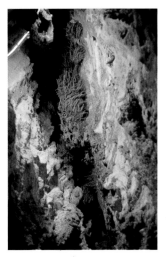

THE CAVES
This underground labyrinth of tunnels has changed little since the 17th century, and extends over a depth of 11 levels. Electricity was installed about 100 years ago. The insides of the caves are dark and cold. Except in the main alley, the rock along the walls is damp, if not wet. There is a constant through-draught of moist air.

THE FLEURINES
The *fleurines* are similar to chimneys, providing a sophisticated ventilation system through the caves.

## The home of Roquefort

The birthplace of Roquefort lies on a chalky mountain, called the Combalou or Cambalou. It has a flattish top, with slightly elevated sides, and resembles a saddle. The village of Roquefort hangs on a cliff to the north. Some two-thirds of the village are built into its side.

The mountain's partial collapse was caused by water erosion in prehistoric times. This geological accident occurred three times; the third opened a series of caves in the debris. Vertical faults and fissures in these caves provide natural ventilation and are known as *fleurines*. These chimneys or wind holes may be up to 100 m high and connect the caves to the outside world. They serve as an immense storage area that maintains a constant temperature of 9°C and humidity of 95%.

### Temperature and ventilation

In winter, when the outside temperature is low, warm air from the caves is expelled through the *fleurines*. The greater the number of fresh cheeses being ripened, the higher the temperature in the caves. In summer, the temperature outside is higher than that within. Hot air is cooled at the shaded northern surface of the cliff and falls to the muddy scree, where it is humidified and the draught from the caves can suck it in. In this way, the *fleurines* provide a highly sophisticated system of ventilation. A process of self-seeding of the mould occurs naturally thanks to the minuscule cheese particles attached to the walls of the caves. These serve as a kind of culture pool for *Penicillium roqueforti* and yeasts. When wind blows through the *fleurines*, the air becomes laden with their spores.

(From *Rocailleux Royaume de Roquefort*, by Robert Aussibal, 1985.)

### Penicillium roqueforti

The blue mould that is found only in the caves of Roquefort is called *Penicillium roqueforti*. It lives in the soil and ferments the cheeses. Bread is used to extract it from its environment. Round rye and wheat loaves are specially baked and left where the air-flow is strong. After six to eight weeks, they are covered with mould, inside and out. The crust is discarded, the crumb dried. Any bad mould is discarded.

Eight days after production, the white cheeses are taken to the caves, where they are pierced with needles. Carbon dioxide caused by fermentation in the pâte escapes, and spore-laden air is introduced. The mould multiplies until it spreads more or less evenly throughout. Then the cheese is wrapped in tinfoil in order to eliminate contact with the air and prevent bad mould. It is thus an artificial environment that encourages the development of the mould. The cheese is wrapped four weeks after its arrival in the cave.

### The ewes of Roquefort

A law of July 1925 decreed that Roquefort must be made from ewe's milk only. Before then, small proportions of cow or goat's milk were allowed. It takes four-and-a-half litres of milk to make one kilogramme of Roquefort. The ewes are Lacaune, Manechs, Basco-Béarnaise, and four Corsican breeds. A good ewe produces some 200 litres of milk over six or seven months, equivalent to 45 kg of Roquefort.

With the increase in demand for Roquefort at the beginning of the 20th century, the milk-producing regions were extended to the Pyrénées and Corsica. In 1930, producers of ewe's milk united with the makers of Roquefort to register the Label de la Brebis Rouge. This meant that minimum standards regarding such things as the fodder and quality of milk were laid down. The first milking machine appeared in 1932, and the maximum number of ewes milked by hand rose from 20 to 40 per day per farmer. Today, 300 ewes can be milked by one person in a single hour. Hygienic conditions have also been improved, with the milk being transferred automatically into vats.

The main cellar

Sheep eating while being milked by a milking machine

181

## SAINT-MARCELLIN

This small cheese from the Dauphiné region is mild, acidic, and salty. As it matures from a fresh to a dry, ripe cheese the flavours develop. Saint-Marcellin is often made with cow's milk, but originally it was a goat's-milk cheese. Production may be *fermier*, *artisanal*, or *industriel,* with an affinage of two to six weeks.

❢ Côtes de Ventoux, Gigondas, Châteauneuf-du-Pape

ESSENTIAL FACTS
- ⊖ 7 cm diameter, 2–2.5 cm high
- ⚖ 80 g min.
- ♣ 50 g min. per 100 g cheese
- ▽ 40% min., 20 g min. per 100 g cheese
- ✓ All year

Raw or pasteurized

Rhône-Alpes (38, 26)

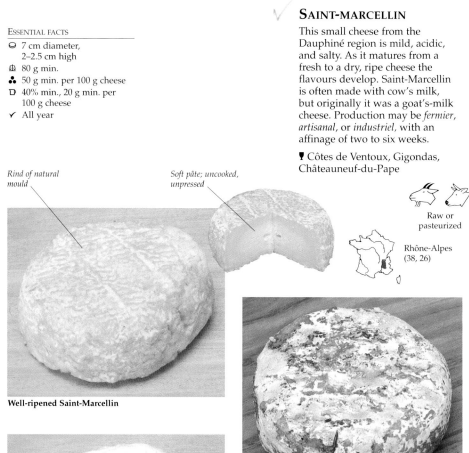

*Rind of natural mould*

*Soft pâte; uncooked, unpressed*

**Well-ripened Saint-Marcellin**

**Fresh Saint-Marcellin**

**Dry cheese, with a robust, ripe flavour**

**Ripe cheese with a fine flavour**

*Raffia band for carrying more than one cheese at a time*

**Ripe Saint-Marcellin**

# LE PITCHOU

This is an *artisanal* speciality made by marinating Saint-Marcellin cheeses in grapeseed oil with ample amounts of *herbes de Provence*. The cheese has a strong, salty flavour with some sourness. It is particularly good eaten with bread.

℣ Côtes du Rhône

 Rhône-Alpes (38)

Pasteurized

**Young Saint-Marcellin**

**Le Pitchou**

ESSENTIAL FACTS
- 🥛 Sold in a pot
- ⟱ 50%
- ✓ All year

*Golden-orange rind of natural mould*

*Fine, pure-white pâte*

**Goat's-milk Saint-Marcellin.**

*Rind of white, yellow, or red, natural moulds, according to level of ripening*

*Semi-hard pâte; uncooked, pressed*

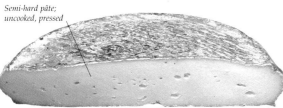

**Affinage of just over six weeks**

ESSENTIAL FACTS

- ◯ 21 cm diameter, 5 cm high
- ⚖ Approx. 1.7 kg
- ◯ Petit Saint-Nectaire: 13 cm diameter, 3.5 cm high
- ⚖ 600 g
- ♣ 52 g min. for 100 g of ripened cheese; 48 g min for 100 g of *fromage blanc*
- ◻ 45% min., 23.4 g min. per 100 g
- ✓ Best in summer (*fermier*); all year (*industriel*)

MARK OF QUALITY
*Casein* label of Saint-Nectaire *fermier*, indicating number of the department (63), and the codes of the maker (RG) and commune (Y).

## SAINT-NECTAIRE (AOC)

Like Cantal (p. 68) and Salers (p. 70), this cheese, which is typical of the Auvergne, was brought to the table of Louis XIV by the Maréchal de Sennecterre. It has a greyish-purple rind, with dots and stains of white, yellow, and red moulds. The pâte is supple with a silky texture, heavy on the tongue, and resistant to the bite. It melts in the mouth to reveal a slight acidity. It also tastes of well-marinated salt, walnut, copper, and spices.

The soil, wild grass, and rich raw milk produced by Salers cows all contribute to this complex taste. Saint-Nectaire made with pasteurized milk does not have the same interesting combination of flavours. This cheese must be fully ripe before eating. Affinage takes five to eight weeks. If it is any shorter than that, the smell and the taste do not develop sufficiently.

One of the characteristics of Saint-Nectaire is its distinctive smell, which could be described as old, the smell of a dark and humid cellar, of rye straw, on which it ripened, and of mould.

❦ St. Estèphe

AOC REGULATIONS:
SAINT-NECTAIRE

**1.** The *fromages blancs* may be frozen before they enter the *cave d'affinage*. They must be thawed at below 12°C.

**2.** The rind may be coloured using E153, E160, E172, or E180.

**3.** The green elliptic *casein* label must indicate Saint-Nectaire *fermier* and the registration number of the place of production for *fermier* cheeses. The label for *industriel* cheese is square.

**4.** All *affineurs* of Saint-Nectaire must be declared to the controlling commission.

AOC GRANTED 1979

Auvergne (15, 63)

Raw or pasteurized

## How Saint-Nectaire is Made

Saint-Nectaire is a *fermier*, *coopérative*, or *industriel* cheese from Auvergne and is cured and ripened within specified areas (departments of Cantal and Puy-de-Dôme) at a temperature of 6–12°C and almost 100% humidity. Production on the farms of Saint-Nectaire starts immediately after the morning and evening milkings. Around 15 litres of milk are needed for one cheese.

### Coagulation

The milk is heated to 31–33°C. After renneting, it is left to rest for about one hour. The temperature and resting period depend on the weather and the amount of milk used. The curd is milled to the size of wheat grains. The whey is discarded. Finally, the curd is gathered into a big mass, called the *tomme*.

### Moulding and pressing

The *tomme* is cut into small cubes of about 2 cm that are pressed into the mould by hand. Four to six moulds are stacked, then pressed. The whey is discarded. The cheeses are taken out of the moulds and the *casein* labels are applied. Next, the cheeses are salted, returned to the moulds, and pressed for 12 hours, and then turned and pressed again for another 12 hours. The cheeses are taken out of their moulds and transferred to the drying room, at 9–12°C, for two to three days.

### Affinage

The cheeses go into the *cave d'affinage* – at 9–11°C and 90–95% humidity – and are placed on rye straw. Ater two to three days they are washed in brine. Eight days later, they are washed for the second time. After one to two weeks of ripening, they are taken to the *affineur*. Only 5% of Saint-Nectaire are ripened at the farm.

Affinage takes a minimum of three to eight weeks, until the cheese is covered in a red or yellow mould.

**Affinage of one week**

**Affinage of just under a month**

**Affinage of ten weeks on straw**

*White, yellow, and, red mould*

Saint-Nectaire *fermier*

## SAINT-PAULIN

*Semi-hard pâte; uncooked, pressed*

This is one of many cheeses modelled on Port-du-Salut (p. 173). Once made exclusively in monasteries, both a large and a small version are now produced by private companies, both *artisanal* and *industriel*, in Bretagne and Maine. Saint-Paulin was the first cheese to be made with pasteurized milk, around 1930. Production of the raw-milk version, shown here, did not begin until 1990. The rind is thin and moist, the pâte tender with a sweet and discreetly salty taste. Affinage takes two to three weeks.

❢ Bordeaux *jeune fruité*

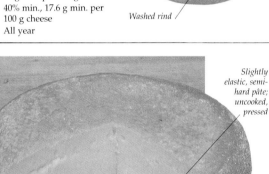

*Washed rind*

ESSENTIAL FACTS

- ◒ 20 cm diameter, 4–6 cm high; 8–13 cm diameter, 3–4.5 cm high, (small)
- ⚖ 1.8–2 kg; 500 g–1.5 kg (small)
- ⦂ 44 g min. per 100 g cheese
- ⛢ 40% min., 17.6 g min. per 100 g cheese
- ✓ All year

 Throughout France

 Pasteurized

## LE SAINT-WINOC

*Slightly elastic, semi-hard pâte; uncooked, pressed*

The name of this *fermier* cheese derives from the Abbey of Saint-Winoc in the extreme north of France, where it used to be made. Today, Mme Degraeve is probably the only person to continue its production there. Its beer-washed rind is slightly moist, and the pâte sinks under finger pressure, but springs back gently. The cheese shown here is extremely young. With further ripening, the taste and smell will become pungent, a characteristic of beer-washed-rind cheeses. Affinage takes at least three weeks.

🍺 Local beer, ♀ Crémant d'Alsace

ESSENTIAL FACTS

- ◒ 9–11 cm diameter, 4 cm high
- ⚖ 300–350 g
- ⛢ Not defined
- ✓ All year; Best to spring to

 Nord-Pas-de-Calais (59)

 Raw, skimmed

*Washed, pale orange rind*

## SOUMAINTRAIN

This *fermier*, *artisanal*, or *industriel* cheese from Bourgogne has a light, creamy pâte and is generally eaten young. The method of affinage that is used for similar to Epoisses (p. 133) and Langres (p. 151) and usually takes six to eight weeks, during which time the cheese is washed in brine.

❑ *Marc* de Bourgogne

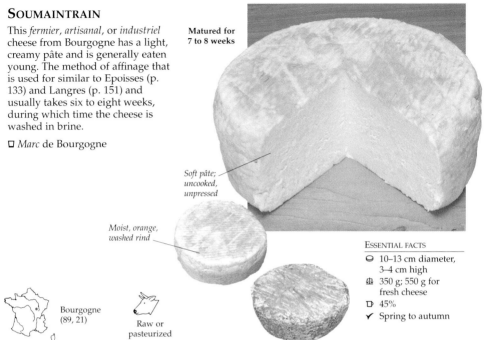

**Matured for 7 to 8 weeks**

*Soft pâte; uncooked, unpressed*

*Moist, orange, washed rind*

Bourgogne (89, 21)

Raw or pasteurized

ESSENTIAL FACTS
- ◯ 10–13 cm diameter, 3–4 cm high
- ⚖ 350 g; 550 g for fresh cheese
- ⅁ 45%
- ✔ Spring to autumn

## TAMIÉ

The Abbey of Tamié was founded in 1131 in the Bauges area of Savoie. It is an old monastery where cheese is still made by Trappist monks. Tamié is wrapped in blue paper, which is decorated with the white cross of Malta. It is a mild cheese from the same family as Reblochon (p. 175). Production is solely *artisanal*, with an affinage of at least one month, during which time the cheeses are washed in brine twice a week.

♀ Roussette de Savoie

*Semi-hard pâte; uncooked, pressed*

Rhône-Alpes (73)

Raw, whole

*Moist, pink, washed rind*

ESSENTIAL FACTS
- ◯ 18–20 cm diameter, 4–5 cm high
- ⚖ 1.3 kg; 500 g
- ⅁ 50%
- ✔ All year

# Tomme

Small cheeses made on small farms are generally called *tommes* or *tomes*, the spelling varying between the two forms. The names probably derive from Greek *tomos* and Latin *tomus*, meaning a slice or piece. These cheeses, which may be found in all regions of France, require little milk and do not keep for long but are easy to sell. *Tommes* may be made from cow, goat, or ewe's milk, or a mixture of milks. They are usually small to medium in size, and rounded in shape. The pâte may be unheated and pressed and therefore elastic; or soft and fresh as in Aligot (p. 74). The best-known *tomme* is probably Tomme de Savoie, made from cow's milk. There are goat's *tommes* in Savoie as well as in the Pyrénées. The following pages give details of the great variety of *tommes* to be found in France.

## Tomme de Savoie

The name Tomme de Savoie is a generic term, usually combined with the name of the village of production. It is said that there are nearly as many *tommes* in Savoie as there are mountains and valleys. Their rinds are hard and grey, with patches of yellow or red mould. The pâte has a sticky texture, with a smell of cellar and mould and a softer, more gentle taste than might be expected. *Tommes* made in the mountains are pressed to eliminate as much water as possible, so that they keep for longer. This also makes the pâte firm, hard, and elastic, with small holes. If there is not enough milk to make a large cheese such as Beaufort (p. 26), *tomme* is made instead. Butter is made with the cream and the remaining skimmed milk is used to make cheese. This is why *tommes* are traditionally low in fat (20–40%), although today whole-milk *tommes* are not uncommon. Some Tommes de Savoie have a regional quality guarantee – the "label Savoie" – indicated by a label showing four red hearts. Tomme de Savoie is currently a candidate for AOC status.

Tomme de Savoie

## TOMME DE SAVOIE

The cheeses shown here are all types of Tomme de Savoie. Production may be *fermier* (sometimes made in a *chalet*), *artisanal, coopérative,* or *industriel*, and affinage takes at least four weeks. Although most Tommes de Savoie are low in fat, a very low-fat version, Tomme de Savoie *maigre*, is also produced with a fat content of as little as 5%. The Vieille Tomme à la Pièce, shown below, is a Tomme de Savoie that has been given a very long affinage. The rind and pâte are riddled with holes, and the cheese has partially disintegrated.

Besides the Tommes de Savoie shown here, there is also the Tomme Label Savoie (see Tomme de Lullin on pages 194–195), which is produced according to regulations that are as strict and precise as those of the AOC. Affinage of this cheese takes at least six weeks.

🍷 Vin de Savoie, Hautes Côtes de Beaune

**Tomme de Savoie *maigre*: 5% fat content**

*Rind of dry, hard, grey natural mould with patches of red and yellow*

**Tomme de Savoie *maigre*: 30% fat content**

*Semi-hard pâte; uncooked, pressed*

ESSENTIAL FACTS

◯ 18–30 cm diameter, 5–8 cm high
⚖ 1.5–3 kg
🝙 40% min.
✓ All year (pasteurized); end of spring (raw milk); summer to winter (*chalet*)

**Vieille Tomme à la Pièce**

Rhône-Alpes (73, 74)

Raw or pasteurized

*Rind of natural mould*

ESSENTIAL FACTS

◯ 17–19 cm diameter,
   5–6 cm high
⚖ 1.5 kg
▭ 30–40%
✔ All year, depending
   on affinage

*Semi-hard pâte; uncooked, pressed*

## TOMME DE SAVOIE AU CUMIN

This cheese has a slightly viscous pâte containing seeds of cumin, which grows wild in the Savoie region. The cloth in which it is wrapped during pressing marks the rind. The cheese shown here has been ripened to perfection. Production of the cheese may be *fermier* or *artisanal*, with an affinage of three to four months.

♈ Condrieu

 Rhône-Alpes (74)

 Raw or pasteurized

---

*Rind of natural mould or washed rind*

ESSENTIAL FACTS

◯ 17–18 cm diameter,
   5–6 cm high
⚖ 2 kg
▭ 45%
✔ End of summer
   to winter

*Semi-hard pâte; uncooked, pressed*

## TOME ALPAGE DE LA VANOISE

The naturally red, mimosa-yellow, and violet-grey mould of this cheese is reminiscent of a meadow full of wild flowers. The variety of colours in the rind is said to be due to the high level of carotene in the milk produced by cows grazing on alpine meadows in the mountains of the Vanoise. This is a mild, full-flavoured *fermier* cheese made in summer in a *chalet*. Affinage takes two to three months.

♈ Crozes Hermitage

Rhône-Alpes (73)

Raw, whole

## TOMME GRASSE
## FERMIÈRE DES BAUGES

This is a *fermier* cheese from the Bauges mountains in the French Alps. The cheese shown has been made from whole milk and ripened for three months. It has a thick crust and a strong pâte. Affinage takes 40 days to three months.

♟ Hermitage

*Semi-hard pâte; uncooked, pressed*

*Rind forms naturally*

 Rhône-Alpes (73)

Raw, whole

ESSENTIAL FACTS

◒ 17 cm diameter, 5 cm high
⚖ 1–1.2 g
🌡 45%
✔ Best from summer to winter

## TOMME DU FAUCIGNY

The Faucigny region, where this *artisanal* cheese is made, lies on the edge of the Alps near the Swiss border. The Tomme du Faucigny has a reddish-brown rind covered with natural grey and white mould. The pâte, which is yellow when ripe, is full of small holes and sinks under finger pressure. It has a salty flavour. Affinage takes four to five months.

♟ Côtes du Jura

*Pâte is semi-hard; uncooked; pressed*

*Rind of natural mould*

 Rhône-Alpes (74)

Raw

ESSENTIAL FACTS

◒ 18–20 cm diameter, 5–6 cm high
⚖ 1.5 kg
🌡 40%
✔ All year

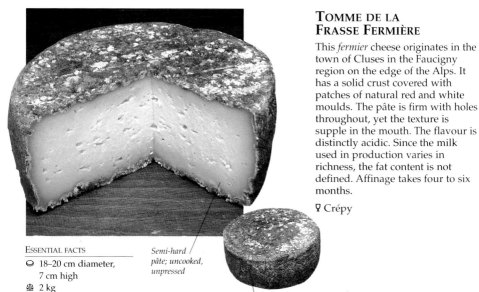

## TOMME DE LA FRASSE FERMIÈRE

This *fermier* cheese originates in the town of Cluses in the Faucigny region on the edge of the Alps. It has a solid crust covered with patches of natural red and white moulds. The pâte is firm with holes throughout, yet the texture is supple in the mouth. The flavour is distinctly acidic. Since the milk used in production varies in richness, the fat content is not defined. Affinage takes four to six months.

♥ Crépy

ESSENTIAL FACTS

◯ 18–20 cm diameter, 7 cm high
⚖ 2 kg
🌡 Not defined
✔ All year, especially summer to winter

*Semi-hard pâte; uncooked, unpressed*

*Natural rind*

Rhône-Alpes (74)

Raw

---

## TOMME GRISE DE SEYSSEL

*Semi-hard pâte; uncooked, pressed*

This *artisanal* cheese is produced in the town of Seyssel on the River Rhône. The cheese shown weighs 1.6 kg and is rather large for a Tomme. It is still young but already has a strong smell. The grey mould on the rind is called *poils de chat*, meaning cat's fur. During the affinage of two to six months, the cheese is rubbed by hand until the "fur" shortens to form the crust, which then hardens and thickens.

♥ St. Péray

ESSENTIAL FACTS

◯ 20 cm diameter, 6–7 cm high
⚖ 1.6 kg
🌡 40%
✔ All year

*Rind forms naturally during affinage*

Rhône-Alpes (74)

Raw

## TOMME FERMIÈRE DES LINDARETS

The village of Lindarets, where this *fermier* cheese is made, lies close to the Swiss border at an altitude of 1,500 m. The dry, brown, burnt-looking crust is broken by patches of white mould and has a rough, uneven surface due to a long affinage of six to eight months. The pâte, which is suffused with holes, is neither too dry nor too salty. The flavour opens as the cheese is chewed.

♈ Châteauneuf-du-Pape

*Semi-hard pâte; uncooked, pressed*

Rhône-Alpes (74)

Raw

*Rind of natural mould*

**ESSENTIAL FACTS**
- ⊖ 17–19 cm diameter, 6 cm high
- ⚖ 1.5 kg
- ▯ Not defined
- ✔ Spring to autumn

---

## TOMME AU MARC DE RAISIN

This *fermier* cheese is made by soaking a ripened tomme in *marc* for a month in an air-tight container. The heat caused by the fermentation heats the inside of the container, making the pâte tighten and become viscous. The taste of the *marc* permeates through to the heart of the cheese.

▢ *Marc* de Savoie

*Semi-hard pâte; uncooked, pressed*

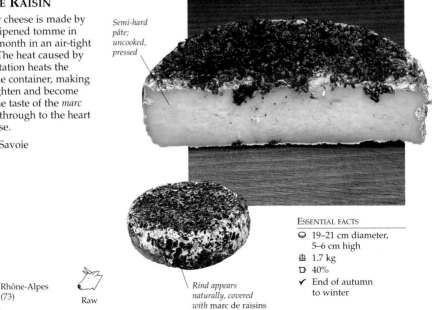

Rhône-Alpes (73)

Raw

*Rind appears naturally, covered with* marc de raisins

**ESSENTIAL FACTS**
- ⊖ 19–21 cm diameter, 5–6 cm high
- ⚖ 1.7 kg
- ▯ 40%
- ✔ End of autumn to winter

- ⊖ 18 cm diameter,
  5–8 cm high
- ⚖ 1.2–2 kg
- ⫧ 40% min.; 20 g per
  100 g cheese
- ✓ All year

*Rind of
natural mould*

*Semi-hard pâte;
uncooked, pressed*

## TOMME DE LULLIN

The village of Lullin, where this *coopérative* cheese is made, lies in the Alps at an altitude of 860 m. Tomme de Lullin is a Tomme Label Savoie (see p. 189) , which is a regional guarantee of quality granted by the Association Marque Collective Savoie. Strict guidelines control the place of production of the milk, as well as the quality of the rennet, the animal fodder, the size and weight of the cheese, and the period of affinage. This label, which is specific to the Savoie region, may be applied to hams, sausages, and fruit.

Tomme de Lullin has a soft, mild-flavoured pâte with small holes throughout. It feels thick on the tongue and melts in the mouth.

♀ Côtes du Rhône

## HOW TOMME DE LULLIN IS MADE

Some 15 farms share the same place of production and hire a *fromager* to produce both Abondance (p. 20) and Tomme from the milk of 200 cows. A Tomme of 1.5 kg needs 15 kg cow's milk, while the much larger Abondance of 9.5 kg requires 103 kg of milk.

### Coagulation
The morning milk is heated to 33°C and coagulated with rennet. The curd is cut, then mixed while being heated to 37°C. After 30 minutes, it changes into rubbery grains.

### Moulding
The curd is put into cloth-lined moulds. Once the whey has drained off, the "cheeses" are taken out of the moulds and turned. The cloths are removed and replaced with plastic net and red *casein* labels bearing the fat content, department number, and place of production. The cheeses are returned to the moulds.

Rhône-Alpes (74)

Raw

194

AFTER 48 HOURS
The cheese is still fresh and
shows no signs of mould.

SEVEN OR EIGHT DAYS LATER
The characteristic "cat's fur" mould
appears. This is brushed off.

AFTER A FURTHER 20 DAYS
The hairs of the "fur" are soft and
beginning to shorten and turn grey.

AFFINAGE OF FOUR WEEKS
After an affinage of four weeks,
the grey rind is starting to form.

### Pressing and salting

The moulds are stacked to create
gentle pressure on the cheeses and
enable drainage to continue.
About ten hours after coagulation,
the cheeses are taken out of their
moulds and soaked in brine for
24 hours.

### Affinage

Total affinage takes at least one-
and-a-half months. Once salted, the
cheeses are transferred to a cellar
at 90–95% humidity and 10–12°C.
Seven or eight days later, a mould
resembling cat's fur forms on the
cheeses. The mould is brushed.
Its texture is like fine powder and
its spores fill the air. This grey
mould, also called *tomme grise*, is
characteristic of the *tommes* of
Savoie. It tastes of the soil and is
the reason why the regions of
production and location of the

ripening cellars are specifically
defined. Cheeses from other
areas are brought to Savoie for
this greying process. After four
weeks, the cheese is given to
an *affineur* or a *fromager,* who
ripens it in a cellar.

MOULDING
Cloth-lined moulds
are filled with curds.

TURNING
The cheese is turned
quickly by hand

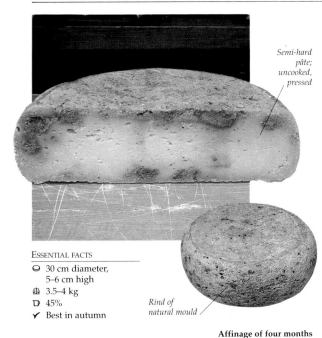

## TOME DE MÉNAGE / BOUDANE

*Semi-hard pâte; uncooked, pressed*

*De ménage* means "household", which is an exact description of this homemade *fermier* cheese. The cheese's local name, *boudane,* is simply the dialect word for *tome*. The cheese shown has had an affinage of four months and is very mature, with a smell of the cellar. Its pâte has a good, strong, fatty, consistency and is the colour of egg yolk. Affinage usually takes two to three months.

♀ St. Joseph

ESSENTIAL FACTS

- ⊖ 30 cm diameter, 5–6 cm high
- ⚖ 3.5–4 kg
- ⅅ 45%
- ✔ Best in autumn

*Rind of natural mould*

**Affinage of four months**

 Rhône-Alpes (73)

 Raw

## TOMME DU MONT CENIS

*Semi-hard pâte; uncooked, pressed*

This *fermier* cheese is produced in the area around Mont Cenis in the Alps, close to the Italian border. The pâte has small holes spread all over, and is moist, soft, and pleasantly sticky in the mouth. The taste of sweetness may be due to the alpine flowers on which the cows graze.

The cheese shown has the appearance of a typical alpine *tome*, with shades of grey, brown, red, and white mould. It was made in the month of September, just before the cows came down from the mountains at the end of the summer, making it one of the last *alpage* cheeses of the season. Affinage takes at least three months.

♀ Vinsobres

ESSENTIAL FACTS

- ⊖ 30 cm diameter, 5–6 cm high
- ⚖ 3.5–4 kg
- ⅅ 45%
- ✔ Best in autumn

*Rind of natural mould*

 Rhône-Alpes (73)

Raw

### TOMME DE THÔNES

This *fermier* cheese comes from the village of Thônes in the Aravis chain of mountains in the Alps. It has a hard, grey-brown crust covered with a white mould. The pâte is soft and yellow. Affinage takes at least six weeks.

♀ Vin de pays de l'Ardéche

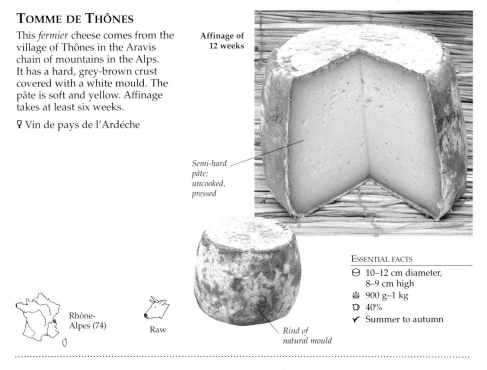

*Affinage of 12 weeks*

*Semi-hard pâte; uncooked, pressed*

*Rind of natural mould*

Rhône-Alpes (74)

Raw

ESSENTIAL FACTS

⊖ 10–12 cm diameter, 8–9 cm high
⚖ 900 g–1 kg
🝿 40%
✔ Summer to autumn

# Tomme de Chèvre, Savoie

### TOME DE CHÈVRE, BELLEVILLE

This mountain goat's-milk cheese is produced in the Vallée de Belleville in the Tarentaise region of Savoie. It is a pressed *fermier* cheese, with a thick, rubbery pâte riddled with holes. The cheese shown was made in September and kept in the cellar for 14 weeks, which is the usual period of affinage. It is at its best when bought and eaten in autumn.

♀ Condrieu, Château Grillet

*Semi-hard pâte; uncooked, pressed*

*Rind of natural mould*

Rhône-Alpes (73)

Raw

ESSENTIAL FACTS

⊖ 17 cm diameter, 7 cm high
⚖ 1.6–1.8 kg
🝿 45%
✔ All year; best in autumn

## TOMME DE CHÈVRE D'ALPAGE, MORZINE

*Semi-hard pâte; uncooked, pressed*

Morzine, where this *fermier* cheese is made, is a well-known ski resort in northern Savoie, some 10 km from the Swiss border. In summer, the region becomes a good grazing ground of alpine pastures and is well known for its cow's- and goat's-milk *tommes*.

The cheese shown is a *tomme d'alpage* made in an alpine chalet. It has a dry rind, covered with a grey to pale blue mould with red dots. When the cheese is young, the pâte has a light, flowery smell that becomes stronger as it matures. Affinage takes from two to 12 months.

♀ Vin de Savoie, Bourgogne Aligoté

### ESSENTIAL FACTS

- ◒ 19 cm diameter, 6–7 cm high
- ⊞ 1.8–2 kg
- ◻ 45%
- ✓ Best in autumn

*Rind of natural mould*

Rhône-Alpes (74)

Raw

---

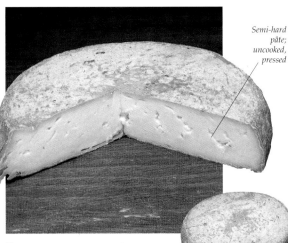

## TOMME DE CHÈVRE, VALLÉE DE MORZINE

*Semi-hard pâte; uncooked, pressed*

This is another *fermier* cheese produced from the milk of goats grazing in the alpine pastures of the Vallée de Morzine in northern Savoie. It has a moist and supple, reddish-brown rind and a heavy, cream-coloured pâte that sticks to the knife. The pâte melts in the mouth and has a surprisingly full aftertaste. Affinage takes between one and two months, during which time the cheese is washed.

♀ Graves *sec*

### ESSENTIAL FACTS

- ◒ 18–20 cm diameter, 4 cm high
- ⊞ 1–1.3 kg
- ◻ 45%
- ✓ Spring to autumn

*Washed, moist rind*

Rhône-Alpes (74)

Raw

## TOMME DE CHÈVRE, VALLÉE DE NOVEL

This *fermier* cheese comes from the area around Novel, a small village beside Lake Geneva, near the Swiss border. It is an attractive, moist cheese with a firm, mimosa-yellow pâte that slightly resists cutting. This cheese smells of the cellar and is very different from the goat's-milk cheeses of the Loire (p. 78). Affinage takes from four to five months.

❦ Vin de Savoie

*Soft pâte; uncooked, unpressed*

*Rind of natural mould*

Rhône-Alpes (74)

Raw

## TOMME DE COURCHEVEL

This *fermier* goat's-milk cheese is produced in mountain chalets in the area around the town of Courchevel in the Alps. In the winter, the area is a famous Olympic sports centre, but during the summer, the alpine slopes provide excellent grazing for herds of goats. The cheese shown has a hard crust and a soft pâte, with a rich flavour. Affinage usually takes around two months.

♈ Condrieu

*Semi-hard pâte; uncooked, pressed*

*Rind of natural mould*

Languedoc-Roussillon (48)

Raw

ESSENTIAL FACTS

◒ 20–25 cm diameter, 5–7 cm high
⚖ 1.5–2 kg
🍶 45%
✔ Summer to winter

*Semi-hard, grey-yellow pâte; uncooked, pressed*

## TOME MI-CHÈVRE DU LÈCHERON

This *fermier* cheese, which is named after a local mountain called the Lècheron, was made in a chalet in the Massif de la Vanoise. A decree of 1988 defines *mi-chèvre*, meaning half-goat, as a cheese containing 50% goat's milk. The other half, made up of cow's milk, softens the flavour. The cheese shown was washed with brine at the beginning of its affinage, but after four or five months the crust was quite dry.

♉ Crépy

ESSENTIAL FACTS

- ⊖ 20–24 cm diameter, 4–5 cm high
- ⚖ 2 kg
- ⋔ 45%
- ✓ Summer to autumn

*Washed, dry, white, brown, and orange rind*

**Affinage of four or five months**

Rhône-Alpes (73)

Raw

## TOMMETTE MI-CHÈVRE DES BAUGES

*Tommette* is a diminutive term, meaning a small *tomme*. The crust of this *fermier* cheese from the Massif des Bauges in Savoie is hard and dry, while the pâte is slightly moist, soft, and sticky. Affinage takes two to three months.

♉ Crépy

*Semi-hard pâte; uncooked, pressed*

ESSENTIAL FACTS

- ⊖ 10–11 cm diameter, 5 cm high
- ⚖ 400 g
- ⋔ 45%
- ✓ Best in autumn

*Rind of natural grey-brown mould*

Rhône-Alpes (73)

Raw

# Tome and Tomme

## TOMME D'ARLES

This *fermier* cheese was originally produced in the village of Montlaux in the Alpes d'Haute Provence, but it disappeared some time ago. Production was resumed in 1988 by two women who began to make it with the milk from their small herd of 60 ewes. Their cheese has a soft, white pâte, which is barely ripened and has a distinct flavour. Affinage is short, lasting only about ten days.

♀ Cassis, Palette

*Soft pâte; uncooked, unpressed*

*Rind of natural mould*

Provence-Alpes-Côte d'Azur (04)

Raw

ESSENTIAL FACTS
- ⊖ 8–9 cm diameter, 1.5 cm high
- ⊛ 90–110 g
- ↧ 50%
- ✓ End of winter to summer

## TOMME DE L'AVEYRON (PETITE)

This dry *fermier* cheese comes from the high plateaux of the Causse du Larzac in the department of Aveyron, from which it takes its name. The pâte is ivory-coloured, moist, and filled with small holes. It has a very slight acidity and a fairly strong flavour considering its low fat content of only 20%. It is an ideal choice for people who love cheese but who have to count calories. Affinage takes from one to three-and-a-half months.

❢ Cahors

*Soft pâte; uncooked, unpressed*

*Rind of natural mould*

Midi-Pyrénées (12)

Raw

ESSENTIAL FACTS
- ⊖ 12 cm diameter, 3 cm high
- ⊛ 310–350 g
- ↧ 20% or 40%
- ✓ Spring to autumn

*Soft pâte; uncooked, unpressed*

## TOME DE BANON

This *artisanal* cheese takes its name from the town of Banon in Provence. A blue and white, natural mould has just appeared on the golden rind of the cheese shown here. The sprig of savory on top is not merely decorative, but adds the scent of Provence. The pâte of the cheese is fine in texture, with a light smell of goat's milk and savory. Affinage lasts from five days to three weeks.

♈ Cassis

ESSENTIAL FACTS
- ⊖ 6 cm diameter, 2 cm high
- ⚖ 60–75g
- Ɗ 45%
- ✔ All year

*Rind of blue and white, natural mould*

Provence-Alpes-Côte d'Azur (04)

Raw

---

*Semi-hard pâte; uncooked, slightly pressed*

## TOMME DU BOUGNAT

A *bougnat* is a native of Auvergne. When one asks the cheesemaker where his cheese comes from, all he will say is, "From the mountains of Auvergne". The maker's name and location are commercial secrets.

The pale yellow pâte of this cheese tastes cool on the tongue, and has a concentrated flavour. Production is *artisanal,* with an affinage of two months.

❢ St. Pourçain.

ESSENTIAL FACTS
- ⊖ 30 cm diameter, 5 cm high
- ⚖ 4 kg
- Ɗ 45%
- ✔ All year

*Natural rind*

Auvergne

Raw

## TOMME CAPRA

This simple goat's cheese comes
from the village of St. Bardou in
the Drôme region. Its name comes
from the Italian word *capra*, which
means goat. The rind is thin and
the pâte is firm, even when fresh,
with a light flavour of goat's milk.
This *fermier* cheese is produced by
F. Pozin and has an affinage
of at least 12 days.

♈ St. Joseph

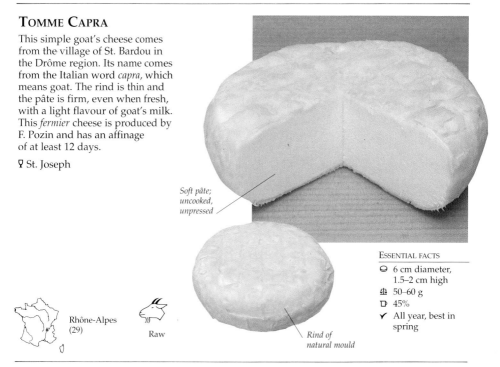

*Soft pâte;
uncooked,
unpressed*

*Rind of
natural mould*

ESSENTIAL FACTS
- 6 cm diameter,
  1.5–2 cm high
- 50–60 g
- 45%
- All year, best in
  spring

Rhône-Alpes
(29)

Raw

## TOMME DE CHÈVRE, PAYS NANTAIS

The Pays Nantais, from which this
medium-sized *artisanal* cheese takes
its name, lies at the mouth of the
River Loire, a region famous for its
white wine. The cheese shown has
a moist, orange rind. The pâte is
the colour of cream, with a fine
texture, and is firm with no
elasticity. The flavour is an unusual
combination of goat and wine.
Affinage takes three to six weeks,
during which time the cheese is
rubbed with a cloth soaked in
Muscadet wine.

♈ Muscadet sur Lie

*Semi-hard pâte;
uncooked,
pressed*

*Washed,
humid rind*

ESSENTIAL FACTS
- 20 cm diameter,
  3–4 cm high
- 1.5g
- 45%
- All year

Pays de la
Loire (44)

Raw

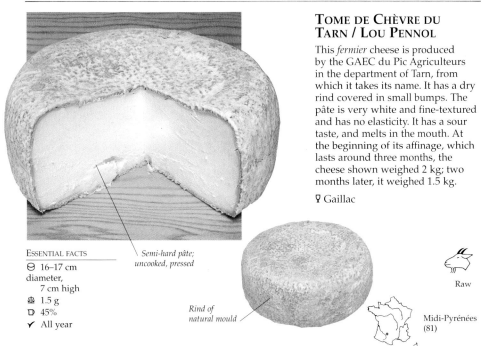

## TOME DE CHÈVRE DU TARN / LOU PENNOL

This *fermier* cheese is produced by the GAEC du Pic Agriculteurs in the department of Tarn, from which it takes its name. It has a dry rind covered in small bumps. The pâte is very white and fine-textured and has no elasticity. It has a sour taste, and melts in the mouth. At the beginning of its affinage, which lasts around three months, the cheese shown weighed 2 kg; two months later, it weighed 1.5 kg.

♀ Gaillac

ESSENTIAL FACTS
⊖ 16–17 cm diameter, 7 cm high
⚖ 1.5 g
ᗡ 45%
✔ All year

*Semi-hard pâte; uncooked, pressed*

*Rind of natural mould*

Raw

Midi-Pyrénées (81)

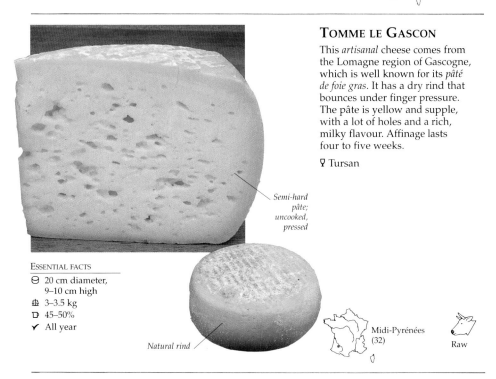

## TOMME LE GASCON

This *artisanal* cheese comes from the Lomagne region of Gascogne, which is well known for its *pâté de foie gras*. It has a dry rind that bounces under finger pressure. The pâte is yellow and supple, with a lot of holes and a rich, milky flavour. Affinage lasts four to five weeks.

♀ Tursan

*Semi-hard pâte; uncooked, pressed*

ESSENTIAL FACTS
⊖ 20 cm diameter, 9–10 cm high
⚖ 3–3.5 kg
ᗡ 45–50%
✔ All year

*Natural rind*

Midi-Pyrénées (32)

Raw

## TOMME DE HUIT LITRES

A couple, originally from Paris, makes this *fermier* cheese in the village of Puimichel in Provence. They raise 45 goats in the Alps of Provence and make several kinds of goat's cheese that are distinctive by their methods of production, flavour, and aroma, but alike in the superior quality of their milk. The Tomme de Huit Litres, which is made following an ancient method, has almost no smell and a light flavour of rich goat's milk. Affinage takes from two weeks to six months.

♀ Cassis

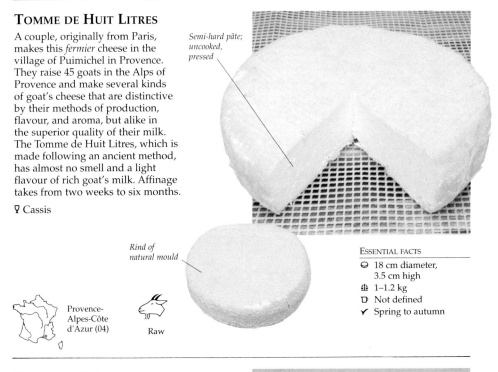

*Semi-hard pâte; uncooked, pressed*

*Rind of natural mould*

Provence-Alpes-Côte d'Azur (04)

Raw

ESSENTIAL FACTS

- ○ 18 cm diameter, 3.5 cm high
- ⚖ 1–1.2 kg
- ⊃ Not defined
- ✓ Spring to autumn

## TOMME DE MONTAGNE

The *fermier* cheese shown was made by couple of farmers who also make a fine Munster (p. 158) in the Vosges Mountains of eastern France. The rind is golden with red and white stains. The pâte is the colour of butter and firm, with a subtle flavour. Affinage takes two months, during which time the cheese is washed and brushed.

♀ Sylvaner (good vintage)

*Semi-hard pâte; uncooked, pressed*

*Moist, natural rind*

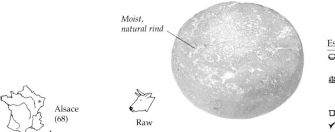

Alsace (68)

Raw

ESSENTIAL FACTS

- ○ 19–20 cm diameter, 7–8 cm high
- ⚖ 2.5 kg.– size and weight vary according to the quantity of milk produced each day
- ⊃ Not defined
- ✓ All year; best in autumn and winter

## TOMME DE ROMANS / ROMANS

*Soft pâte; uncooked, unpressed*

Some cheeses have continued to be produced in their region of origin, and are still known by their old names, while the milk used to produce them has changed with time. Romans is one such cheese. It used to be a *fermier* goat's-milk cheese, but now it is almost exclusively *industriel* or *artisanal*, made from pasteurized cow's milk. It smells slightly of the cellar in which it is matured. Affinage lasts for at least ten days.

❦ Crozes Hermitage, Cornas

*Rind of natural mould*

### ESSENTIAL FACTS
- ⊝ 8–9 cm diameter, 3.5 cm high
- ⚖ 200–300 g
- ◻ 45–50%
- ✔ All year

Pasteurized

Rhône-Alpes (26, 38)

## TOMME DE SÉRANON

*Soft pâte; uncooked, unpressed*

The town of Séranon lies at an altitude of 1,000 m just north of Grasse. The sea breezes blow in to the area and spread the scent of flowers. Even the cheeses produced here have a delicious, lingering aroma of flowers. Summer is the best season for Tomme de Séranon. The rind is thin and almost pink and the pâte is very supple and fragile. This is a *fermier* cheese with a short affinage of about two weeks.

❦ *Rosé* de Provence

### ESSENTIAL FACTS
- ⊝ 9 cm diameter, 4 cm high
- ⚖ 250–300 g
- ◻ 45%
- ✔ All year, best spring to summer

*Rind of natural mould*

Provence-Alpes-Côte d'Azur (06)

Raw

## TOMME DE VENDÉE

The pâte and rind of this large *artisanal* cheese from the Atlantic Coast indicate that the methods of production are different from those of the AOC goat's-milk cheeses of the Loire Valley. The taste of salt is quite strong, and the flavour is partly due to the careful affinage of one-and-a-half months.

*Semi-hard pâte; uncooked, pressed*

Ÿ Fiefs Vendéens *rosé*

Pays de la Loire (85)

Raw

*Rind of natural mould*

ESSENTIAL FACTS
- ☉ 20–22 cm diameter, 4 cm high
- ⚖ 1.7 kg
- 🗘 45%
- ✓ Spring to autumn

## TOMMETTE DE L'AVEYRON

This *fermier* cheese comes from the Causse du Larzac, which is the home of the famous Roquefort (p. 178). It is named after Aveyron, the department in which it is produced. This cheese is made with rich milk and has a dry rind and a white, grey, and reddish-brown mould. The pâte is firm and elastic under finger pressure. The cheese melts in the mouth and has a strong, salty taste. Affinage takes two to six weeks.

*Soft, yellow, or clear pâte; uncooked, slightly pressed*

❢ Gaillac, Cahors

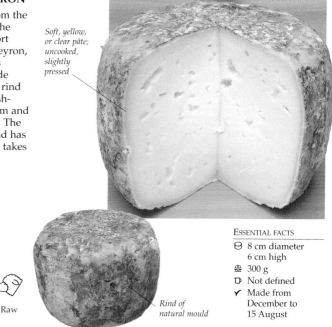

Midi-Pyrénées (12)

Raw

*Rind of natural mould*

ESSENTIAL FACTS
- ☉ 8 cm diameter 6 cm high
- ⚖ 300 g
- 🗘 Not defined
- ✓ Made from December to 15 August

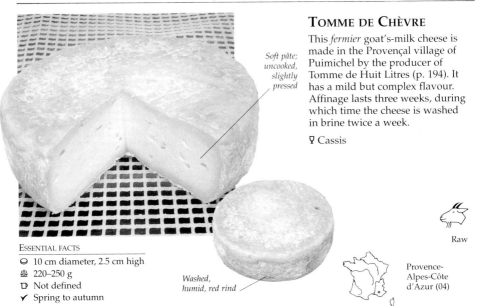

*Soft pâte; uncooked, slightly pressed*

*Washed, humid, red rind*

Raw

### TOMME DE CHÈVRE

This *fermier* goat's-milk cheese is made in the Provençal village of Puimichel by the producer of Tomme de Huit Litres (p. 194). It has a mild but complex flavour. Affinage lasts three weeks, during which time the cheese is washed in brine twice a week.

♈ Cassis

ESSENTIAL FACTS
- ⊖ 10 cm diameter, 2.5 cm high
- ⚖ 220–250 g
- ◻ Not defined
- ✓ Spring to autumn

Provence-Alpes-Côte d'Azur (04)

# Tomme de Chèvre, les Pyrénées

*Semi-hard pâte; uncooked, pressed*

*Natural rind, marked by the cloth; stamped with a heart*

### FROMAGE DE CHÈVRE FERMIER

Sheep's-milk cheeses have been produced in the Pyrénées for centuries, but goat's-milk cheeses like this one are rare. The curd of the goat's milk is wrapped in a cloth, drained, and lightly pressed to discard the whey. This ensures that the cheese will keep for longer. The ripened cheese is large, heavy, and solid, with a firm, white, dry, and compact pâte that occasionally splits. The flavour is rich. The maker's mark – a heart – is embossed on the rind. Affinage of this *fermier* cheese takes one-and-a-half months.

♈ Jurançon

ESSENTIAL FACTS
- ⊖ 15–18.5 cm diameter, 8 cm high
- ⚖ 2.3 kg
- ◻ 45%
- ✓ Summer to autumn

Midi-Pyrénées (65)

Raw

## TOMME DE CHÈVRE/ LOUBIÈRES / CABRIOULET

This *fermier* goat's-milk cheese is produced at the Col del Fach farm in Loubières, near the town of Foix in southern France. The cheese shown has had an affinage of five months and the surface seems as dry as stone. The pâte is yellow-grey, with holes, and has little elasticity. This is a strong cheese with a smell of mould and the cellar. It is salty but well balanced, with rich flavours. During the affinage of at least two months, the cheese is washed in brine.

♀ Limoux

*Semi-hard pâte; uncooked, pressed*

*Washed, moist rind*

Midi-Pyrénées (09)

Raw

ESSENTIAL FACTS

◷ 20–21 cm diameter, 5–6 cm high
⚖ 2–2.5 kg
🖪 Not defined
✔ All year except December and January

## TOME PAYS BASQUE

This *fermier* cheese is produced by the Basque shepherd who makes Ardi-Gasna (p. 44) near the town of St.-Jean-Pied-de Port, close to the Spanish border in southwest France. It is also ripened by the same *fromager*. The rind of the cheese shown here is dry and shows traces of the cloth used during pressing. The pâte is firm, with no elasticity, and breaks easily. Although it is dry, it contains a good balance of salt and fat and melts in the mouth to a sticky consistency. Affinage lasts for two months.

♀ Irouléguy

*Semi-hard pâte; uncooked, pressed*

*Natural rind*

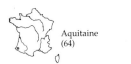

Aquitaine (64)

Raw

ESSENTIAL FACTS

◷ 12–13 cm diameter, 6–7 cm high
⚖ 1–1.2 kg
🖪 45%
✔ Summer, autumn, and winter

## TOMME DE CHÈVRE DE PAYS

*Semi-hard pâte; uncooked, pressed*

This *fermier* cheese is produced in Les Barronies in the department of Gascogne. It has a dry rind with a light brown and red mould showing traces of the cloth used in the production. The flavour has a balanced sweetness and no acidity. Affinage takes two months.

♈ Tursan

ESSENTIAL FACTS

- ◯ 19 cm diameter, 7–8 cm high
- ⚖ 2–2.2 kg
- ❒ 45%
- ✔ All year; best in autumn and winter

*Rind of natural mould*

Midi-Pyrénées (65)

Raw

---

## TRAPPE (VÉRITABLE)

The name of this *artisanal* cheese means "real Trappist" – it is made in the Trappist Abbaye de la Coudre close to the town of Laval in the province of Maine. It is a mild cheese with a slight smell of mould. Affinage lasts at least three weeks, during which time the cheese is washed in brine.

❢ Chinon

*Semi-hard, elastic pâte; uncooked, pressed*

ESSENTIAL FACTS

- ◯ 20 cm diameter, 4–5 cm high
- ⚖ 1.7 kg
- ❒ 40%
- ✔ All year

*Washed rind*

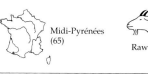

Pays de la Loire (53)

Pasteurized

## TRAPPE DE BELVAL

This *artisanal* cheese is produced in a convent called the Abbaye de Belval, in the province of Artois. The nuns orginally came from Laval and started to make the cheese in 1892. Every year, 40 nuns make around 40 tonnes. The wrapper of the cheese is tangerine-coloured, with six blue crosses and a picture of the abbey in dark blue. The cheese has a soft, pink rind the colour of coral. Its pâte is ivory, with a cool, elastic texture and a slight scent. Affinage takes a minimum of six weeks.

❦ Bordeaux, Médoc

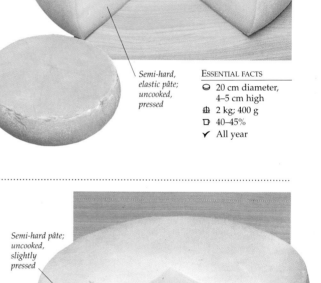

*Washed, pink, dry rind*

*Semi-hard, elastic pâte; uncooked, pressed*

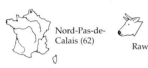

Nord-Pas-de-Calais (62)

Raw

ESSENTIAL FACTS
- ⊖ 20 cm diameter, 4–5 cm high
- ⚖ 2 kg; 400 g
- ⛉ 40–45%
- ✓ All year

---

## FROMAGE D'HESDIN

This *artisanal* cheese is named after the town of Hesdin, which lies just 20 km from the village where Trappe de Belval is made. The cheese was probably modelled on a similar monastery cheese. Production of Fromage d'Hesdin began around 1960. The smell is soft and light and the aftertaste is slightly sweet. Affinage takes two months, during which time the cheese is washed occasionally in white wine.

❦ Haut Médoc

*Semi-hard pâte; uncooked, slightly pressed*

Nord-Pas-de-Calais (62)

Raw

*Washed, red, humid rind*

ESSENTIAL FACTS
- ⊖ 12 cm diameter, 3–3.5 cm high
- ⚖ 400–450 g
- ⛉ 40–42%
- ✓ All year; best from spring to autumn

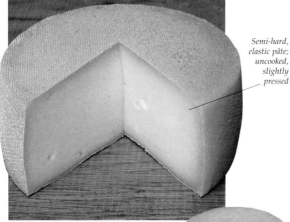

ESSENTIAL FACTS

◯ 9–10 cm diameter,
   3–4 cm high
⚖ 270–300 g;
   2 kg
🔽 45%
✓ All year

*Semi-hard, elastic pâte; uncooked, slightly pressed*

*Washed, slightly moist rind*

## TRAPPE ECHOURGNAC

Since 1868, Trappist nuns have been collecting milk from neighbouring farms to make and ripen this *artisanal* cheese in l'Abbaye d'Echourgnac, in Périgord. They use the same methods of production as for Port-du-Salut (p. 173) and succeed in producing 52 tonnes each year.

The rind of the cheese is very slightly moist and bounces under finger pressure. The flavour is balanced and simple. Affinage takes two months in the abbey cellars, plus a further month at the cheese shop.

🍷 Cahors

Aquitaine (24)

 Pasteurized

---

ESSENTIAL FACTS

◯ 8–9 cm diameter,
   2–2.5 cm high
⚖ 160 g; 300 g; 1.5 kg
🔽 45%
✓ All year

*Semi-hard pâte; uncooked, slightly pressed*

*Washed, pink, moist rind*

## TRAPPISTE DE CHAMBARAN

This *artisanal* cheese comes from the town of Roybon on the Plateau de Chambaran, in the province of the Dauphiné. It has a moist, pale pink rind and a mild flavour. Production, which is modelled on that of Reblochon (p. 175) and Port-du-Salut (p. 173), began in 1932. The milk is bought from neighbouring farms, then pasteurized. Around 80 tonnes of cheese are produced each year.

During the affinage, the cheeses are washed in brine over two weeks in the natural cellars of the abbey. Large cheeses need at least four weeks.

🍷 Côtes Rotie

Rhône-Alpes (38)

Pasteurized

# Triple Crème, Double Crème

*Triple crème* and *double crème* cheeses are popular because of their subtle, creamy flavour. They may be found in most French cheese shops and are often included on a cheese platter to add variety to a selection.

These cheeses are made by adding cream to the milk during production. *Triple crème* has a minimum fat content of 75%, whereas *double crème* contains between 60 and 75% fat. These cheeses generally have no rind at all, or a soft rind

of mould. The pâte is soft, sweet, and tastes pleasant; there may also be a slight sourness. The smell is faint. Since these cheeses do not have strong flavours, they are often used in the production other cheeses (p. 218). The length of affinage is usually short. The cheeses may be eaten fresh and go particularly well with a red wine such as Moulis, which is also known as Moulis-en-Médoc, the smallest of the communities of Haut-Médoc.

## LA BOUILLE

This *artisanal* cheese was first produced in Normandie at the end of the 19th century by "Monsieur Fromage". Fromage de Monsieur (p. 216) was also first made by the same man. It is possible that this cheese no longer exists today. Despite its high fat content, this *double crème* cheese is ripened for two months.

🍷 Médoc

ESSENTIAL FACTS
⊖ 8 cm diameter, 5–5.5 cm high
⚖ 220 g
🌡 60%
✔ Summer to winter

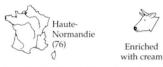

Haute-Normandie (76)

Enriched with cream

*Rind of white mould*

*Soft pâte; uncooked, unpressed*

## BOURSAULT

This *industriel* cheese has a mild flavour, reminiscent of Brie (p. 56), and a slight acidity. It was first made after World War II and was named after its creator and maker. It is a soft, creamy cheese with a slight smell of mould. Affinage lasts two months.

🍷 Bordeaux

ESSENTIAL FACTS
⊖ 8 cm diameter, 4 cm high
⚖ 200 g
🌡 70%
✔ All year

Ile-de-France (77)

Enriched with cream

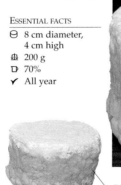

*Rind of very light, white mould*

*Soft pâte; uncooked, unpressed*

*Fresh pâte;
uncooked, unpressed*

*No rind*

## BOURSIN

ESSENTIAL FACTS

⊖ 8 cm
diameter,
4 cm high
⚖ 150 g
⊐ 70%
✓ All year

The picture on the near left shows a Boursin made with garlic and herbs; the one on the far left has been made with black pepper. Boursin is a soft, creamy, *industriel* cheese from Normandie with no affinage. It goes well with fresh bread and dry white wine.

🍷 Graves

Haute-Normandie (27)

Enriched with cream

---

*Soft pâte;
uncooked, unpressed*

*Rind of
white mould*

## BRILLAT-SAVARIN

ESSENTIAL FACTS

⊖ 12–13 cm
diameter,
3.5–4 cm high
⚖ 450–500 g
⊐ 75%
✓ All year

This cheese was created in the 1930s by Henri Androuët, father of French cheese expert Pierre Androuët. It was named after the renowned 18th-century French food writer Brillat-Savarin. This is an *industriel* cheese with an affinage of one to two weeks.

🍷 St. Emilion, Fronsac

Mainly Normandie

Enriched with cream

---

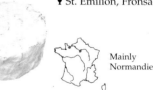

*Soft pâte;
uncooked, unpressed*

*Rind of
white mould*

## CAPRICE DES DIEUX

ESSENTIAL FACTS

⊘ 14 cm long,
6 cm wide,
3.5 cm high
⚖ 210 g
⊐ 60%
✓ All year

This *industriel* cheese from the Bassigny region of Haute-Marne was first produced commercially in 1956. Besides the cheese shown here, which weighs 210 g, there is a larger version weighing 310 g and a smaller version weighing 150 g. Affinage takes two weeks.

🍷 Coteaux Champenois

Champagne-Ardenne (52)

Enriched with cream

## CROUPET

The name of this cheese derives from a village in the Brie region of the Ile-de-France. It is produced in a small *industriel* dairy. Affinage takes one to two weeks.

❢ Bourgogne

ESSENTIAL FACTS
- ⊖ 11 cm diameter, 5 cm high
- ⚖ 450 g
- ⟲ 75%
- ✓ All year

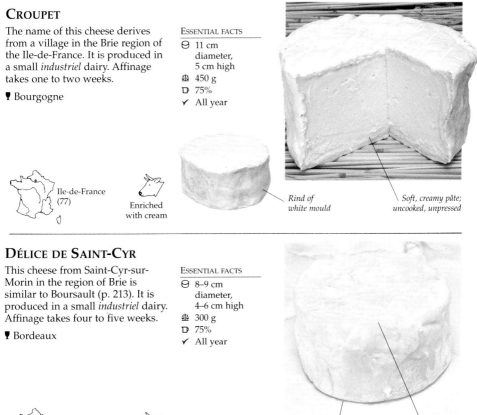

Ile-de-France (77)

Enriched with cream

Rind of white mould

Soft, creamy pâte; uncooked, unpressed

---

## DÉLICE DE SAINT-CYR

This cheese from Saint-Cyr-sur-Morin in the region of Brie is similar to Boursault (p. 213). It is produced in a small *industriel* dairy. Affinage takes four to five weeks.

❢ Bordeaux

ESSENTIAL FACTS
- ⊖ 8–9 cm diameter, 4–6 cm high
- ⚖ 300 g
- ⟲ 75%
- ✓ All year

Ile-de-France (77)

Enriched with cream

Rind of white mould

Soft pâte; uncooked, unpressed

---

## EXPLORATEUR

This *industriel* cheese has a slight smell of mould and a creamy texture and taste. Affinage takes two to three weeks. As well as the cheese shown here, there are also larger versions weighing 450 g and 1.6 kg that are usually sold pre-cut.

❢ Bordeaux

ESSENTIAL FACTS
- ⊖ 8 cm diameter, 6 cm high
- ⚖ 250 g
- ⟲ 75%
- ✓ All year

Ile-de-France (77)

Enriched with cream

Rind of white mould

Soft pâte; uncooked, unpressed

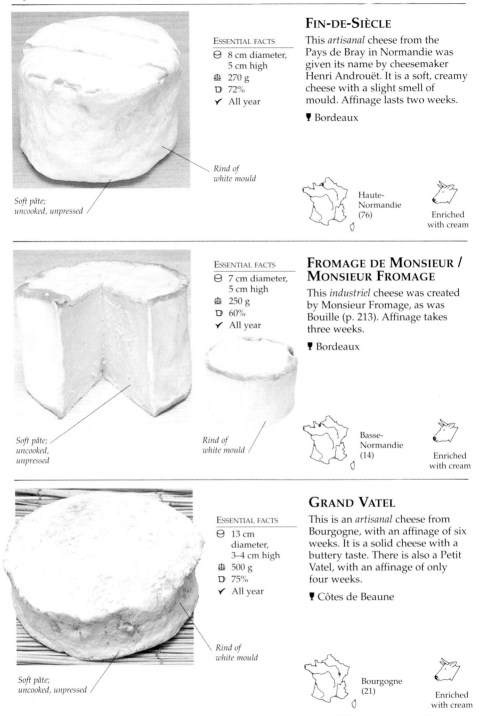

Soft pâte;
uncooked, unpressed

Rind of
white mould

## Fin-de-Siècle

This *artisanal* cheese from the
Pays de Bray in Normandie was
given its name by cheesemaker
Henri Androuët. It is a soft, creamy
cheese with a slight smell of
mould. Affinage lasts two weeks.

❢ Bordeaux

ESSENTIAL FACTS

⊖ 8 cm diameter,
5 cm high
⚖ 270 g
D 72%
✔ All year

Haute-
Normandie
(76)

Enriched
with cream

## Fromage de Monsieur / Monsieur Fromage

This *industriel* cheese was created
by Monsieur Fromage, as was
Bouille (p. 213). Affinage takes
three weeks.

❢ Bordeaux

ESSENTIAL FACTS

⊖ 7 cm diameter,
5 cm high
⚖ 250 g
D 60%
✔ All year

Soft pâte;
uncooked,
unpressed

Rind of
white mould

Basse-
Normandie
(14)

Enriched
with cream

## Grand Vatel

This is an *artisanal* cheese from
Bourgogne, with an affinage of six
weeks. It is a solid cheese with a
buttery taste. There is also a Petit
Vatel, with an affinage of only
four weeks.

❢ Côtes de Beaune

ESSENTIAL FACTS

⊖ 13 cm
diameter,
3–4 cm high
⚖ 500 g
D 75%
✔ All year

Rind of
white mould

Soft pâte;
uncooked, unpressed

Bourgogne
(21)

Enriched
with cream

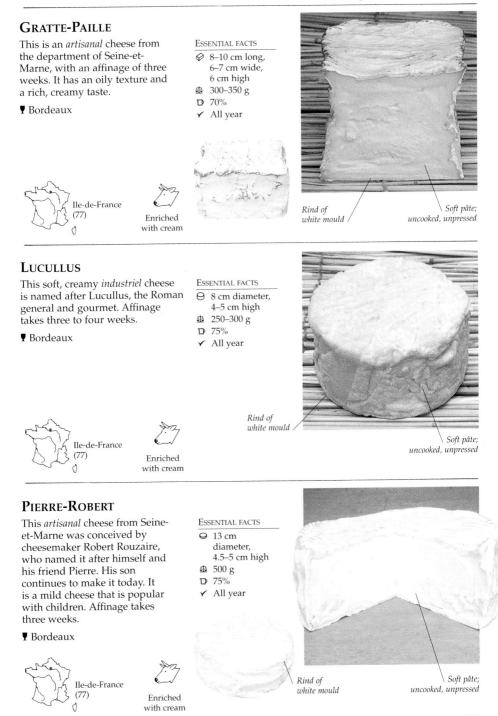

## GRATTE-PAILLE

This is an *artisanal* cheese from the department of Seine-et-Marne, with an affinage of three weeks. It has an oily texture and a rich, creamy taste.

❦ Bordeaux

ESSENTIAL FACTS

◈ 8–10 cm long,
  6–7 cm wide,
  6 cm high
⚖ 300–350 g
🌡 70%
✓ All year

Ile-de-France
(77)

Enriched
with cream

Rind of
white mould

Soft pâte;
uncooked, unpressed

## LUCULLUS

This soft, creamy *industriel* cheese is named after Lucullus, the Roman general and gourmet. Affinage takes three to four weeks.

❦ Bordeaux

ESSENTIAL FACTS

◗ 8 cm diameter,
  4–5 cm high
⚖ 250–300 g
🌡 75%
✓ All year

Ile-de-France
(77)

Enriched
with cream

Rind of
white mould

Soft pâte;
uncooked, unpressed

## PIERRE-ROBERT

This *artisanal* cheese from Seine-et-Marne was conceived by cheesemaker Robert Rouzaire, who named it after himself and his friend Pierre. His son continues to make it today. It is a mild cheese that is popular with children. Affinage takes three weeks.

❦ Bordeaux

ESSENTIAL FACTS

◗ 13 cm
  diameter,
  4.5–5 cm high
⚖ 500 g
🌡 75%
✓ All year

Ile-de-France
(77)

Enriched
with cream

Rind of
white mould

Soft pâte;
uncooked, unpressed

IMAGINATIVE CREATIONS
The cheeses shown on this page are all double crème and triple crème cheeses that have been decorated by the *fromager* with a variety of herbs and spices.

*Cannelle*, covered with cinnamon

*Gargantua à la feuille de sauge*, decorated with sage leaves

*Paprika*, covered with paprika

*Poivre*, covered with coarsely ground black pepper

*Dried grapes marinated in rum cover the cheese entirely*

*Soleil*, covered with raisins and sultanas

*Trois-Epis*, covered with cumin seeds

# Vache des Pyrénées

The Pyrénées are some 400 km long and extend over five French departments and 11 provinces. At the centre of this area, in the departments of Ariège and Haute-Garonne, the cheeses that used to be made from sheep's milk are today being made with cow's milk.

These cheeses are solid and quite large, with tough rinds that protect firm, fat, and fruity pâtes. They bear the names of their villages, although the local people simply call them *fromage de montagne*, meaning mountain cheese. They are nearly all *fermier* cheeses made from raw milk, and have small eyes, or holes, in the pâte. Affinage develops the full character of a mountain cheese. The cheese becomes meaty and retains none of the softness, mildness, and sweetness of milk. It should be matched with a fruity red wine.

## BAROUSSE

This cheese is named after the Vallée de Barousse de l'Ourse in the Pyrénées. Both Barousse and Esbareich (below) are produced by similar methods. This one looks homemade. The taste varies according to whether they are made with the milk of cows fed on spring and summer grass, or with milk from cows fed dry fodder in their sheds during winter. The cheese shown was made by the Sost family from the village of the same name, where they make five cheeses a day. It is a strong-smelling *fermier* cheese, with an affinage of at least one-and-a half months. It is washed, wiped, and turned every day for the first two weeks of its affinage.

❡ Madiran, Côtes du Frontonnais

*Semi-hard, elastic pâte, with many small holes; uncooked, pressed*

*Washed, pink-brown rind*

**Barousse**

## ESBAREICH

This cheese is the twin of Barousse. It is a *fermier* cheese from Esbareich, 2 km from Sost, with an affinage of two-and-a half months.

❡ Madiran, Côtes du Frontonnais

Midi-Pyrénées (65)

Raw

**Esbareich**

ESSENTIAL FACTS
⊖ 19 cm diameter, 7 cm high
⚖ 2 kg
↻ Not defined
✓ All year

ESSENTIAL FACTS
⊖ 19 cm diameter, 7.5 cm high
⚖ 2.5 kg
↻ Not defined
✓ All year

ESSENTIAL FACTS        *Natural rind*

- ⊖ 25–40 cm diameter,
  8–10 cm high
- ⚖ 3.5–6 kg
- 🌡 45–50%
- ✔ All year

## BETHMALE

This is the best-known of the traditional cow's-milk cheeses from the Pyrénées. It is named after the village where it is made, in the Couserans region of the Comté de Foix. Legend has it that it was favoured by King Louis VI, who passed through the area in the 12th century.

Bethmale is probably the mildest of all the cow's-milk cheeses of the Pyrénées. The cheese shown here has a semi-hard, uncooked, pressed pâte and smells of the cellar. Affinage takes two to three months, during which time the cheese is brushed and turned.

🍷 Collioure

Midi-Pyrénées (09)

Raw or pasteurized

## E BAMALOU

*Semi-hard pâte; uncooked, pressed*

This *artisanal* cheese is made in two sizes, large and small, in the town of Castillon-en-Couserans in Comté de Foix. It is probably the strongest of all the cow's-milk cheeses of the Pyrénées. The pâte is supple, greasy, and well wrapped in its solid rind, which is brownish with red spots. The taste and smell of this cheese blend well with a red wine with good tannin. Affinage takes about six weeks.

🍷 Châteauneuf-du-Pape, Cahors

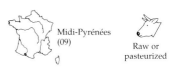

ESSENTIAL FACTS

- ⊖ 24–29 cm diameter,
  10 cm high (large)
- ⊖ 11–13 cm,
  7 cm high (small)
- ⚖ 6 kg (large)
  700–800 g (small)
- 🌡 50%
- ✔ All year

*Natural reddish-brown rind*

Midi-Pyrénées (09)

Raw, whole

## FROMAGE DE MONTAGNE

The tiny house of the two young cheesemakers who produce this *fermier* cheese lies at an altitude of 1,300 m in the Pyrénées in Poubeau, close to the town of Luchon. The crust of the cheese is less strong smelling than the pâte, and is orange and pinkish-white in colour, and soft and moist. The pâte is egg-yolk yellow and suffused with holes. It smells strong. The cheese shown here looks young but it is already four months old, which is about the right age for eating. Affinage takes at least three months, during which time the cheese is washed and turned regularly.

❦ Bergerac, Bordeaux, Fitou

*Elastic, semi-hard pâte; uncooked, slightly pressed*

Midi-Pyrénées (31)

Raw

*Supple, natural rind*

**ESSENTIAL FACTS**

- ⊖ 20–22 cm diameter, 8–9 cm high
- ⚖ 2.7 kg
- ▯ Not defined
- ✔ All year

## FROMAGE DE MONTAGNE DE LÈGE

This *fermier* cheese is produced by the Camille Cazaux farm in the village of Lège. It has a reddish-brown, sticky, and slightly moist rind, and a dense, yellow pâte, which is full of holes. This cheese may be eaten after an affinage of just three months, but true connoisseurs prefer to wait six months until it is completely mature.

❦ Madiran, Cahors, Fitou

*Semi-hard, elastic pâte; uncooked, pressed*

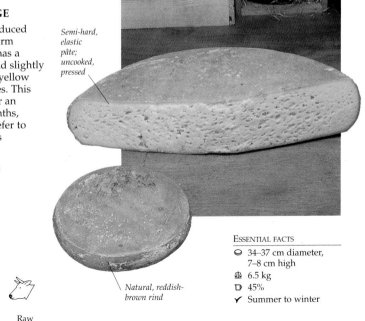

*Natural, reddish-brown rind*

Midi-Pyrénées (31)

Raw

**ESSENTIAL FACTS**

- ⊖ 34–37 cm diameter, 7–8 cm high
- ⚖ 6.5 kg
- ▯ 45%
- ✔ Summer to winter

221

## FROMAGE DE MONTAGNE, LE PIC DE LA CALABASSE

This *artisanal* cheese is made in the village of Saint-Lary at the foot of the 2,210-m Pic de la Calabasse mountain. Besides the large cheese shown here, there is also a smaller version. The cheese shown is ripe and has hints of white, grey, pink, and brown on the rind. The pâte is yellow and brown, and full of holes; it is firm but melts in the mouth. The smell of this sticky cheese is strong and fruity, with a trace of flowers. Affinage takes three months.

🍷 Corbières, Minervois, Fitou.

*Semi-hard, elastic pâte; uncooked, pressed*

*Natural rind, marked by cloth*

ESSENTIAL FACTS
- 😊 28–37 cm diameter, 7–8 cm high
- ⚖️ 6 kg
- 🗓 45%
- ✓ Best in spring

Midi-Pyrénées (09)

Raw

---

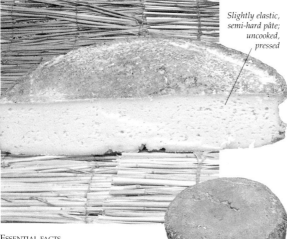

*Slightly elastic, semi-hard pâte; uncooked, pressed*

## FROMAGE DE MONTAGNE / LE ROGALLAIS

This *artisanal* cheese is made by the Fromagerie Coumes in Seix, in the Couserans region of Comté de Foix. It has a well-ripened, brown, or pinkish-brown rind, and a yellow to light brown pâte with "eyes" or holes in it. The pâte is thick and greasy and smells of the cellar and mould. The cheesemaker explains: "The eyes form during the affinage of one-and-a-half months and air the pâte. Their quality depends on how the whey is drained. The cellar is at 14°C with a humidity of 95%. This humidity and the board of oak on which the cheese matures cause the mould to form and the pâte to ferment to create the eyes."

🍷 Graves, Medoc

*Natural rind*

ESSENTIAL FACTS
- 😊 33 cm diameter, 5 cm high
- ⚖️ 4.5 kg; 2.5 kg
- 🗓 50%
- ✓ All year, especially spring to autumn

Midi-Pyrénées (09)

Raw

## Le Moulis

This is an *artisanal* cheese made by a long-established family business in Moulis in the province of Comté de Foix. Sixty tonnes are made each year, which amounts to some 17,000 cheeses.

Both young and mature Moulis have strong tastes. At first the pâte is straw-coloured, then it turns brown. Despite its many holes, it is moist, fatty, and melts softly in the mouth. The distinct taste of fermentation and decay stings the tongue. The cheese smells strong and is piquant when old. During affinage, it is washed in brine once every two days for the first two weeks, then brushed and turned for one to two months.

♀ Vin du Jura *sec*

*Semi-hard, elastic pâte; uncooked, slightly pressed*

**Young Moulis**

*Natural, dry, white, brown, and black mould marked by cloth*

**Moulis after an affinage of six months**

*Pâte darkens and becomes harder with age*

Essential facts

- ◉ 22–24 cm diameter
  7 cm high
- ⚖ 3.5 kg
- ⊡ 48%
- ✔ All year

Midi-Pyrénées (09)

Raw

223

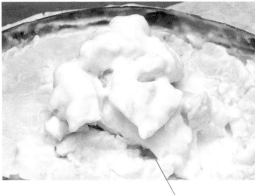

*Soft, cream-like pâte that smells of spruce wood; uncooked, unpressed*

Rhône-Alpes (74)

Raw

*Thin rind with natural white mould*

## Vacherin d'Abondance Fermier

This *fermier* cheese is made in Abondance in Savoie. The unusual feature of this cheese is the strip of spruce bark in which it is wrapped. The bark protects the exterior and its scent permeates the cheese. The pâte is fine-textured, with a mild, creamy, slightly salty flavour. Affinage lasts three weeks.

Locally, Vacherin d'Abondance fermier is eaten with *patates au barbot*, which means potatoes boiled in their skins in salt water.

🍷 Vin de Savoie, Marin

Essential Facts

- 13 cm diameter, 3 cm high
- 400–500 g
- Not defined (including wood covering)
- ✓ Winter and spring

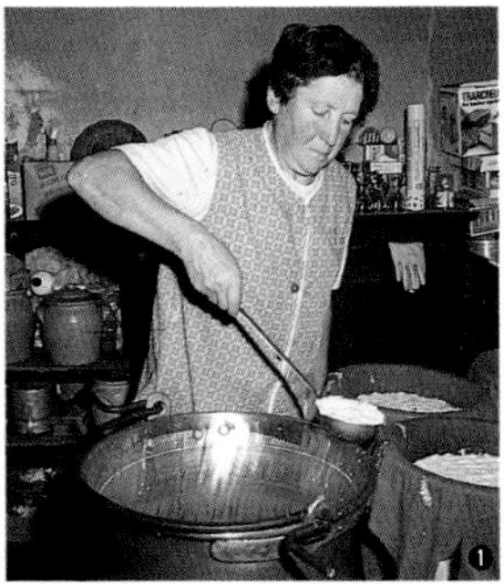


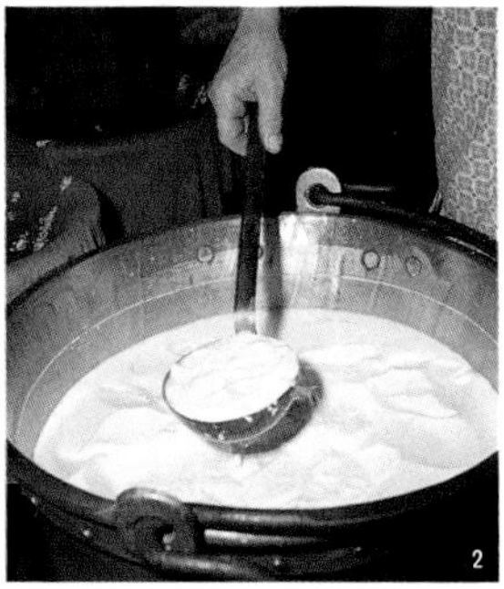


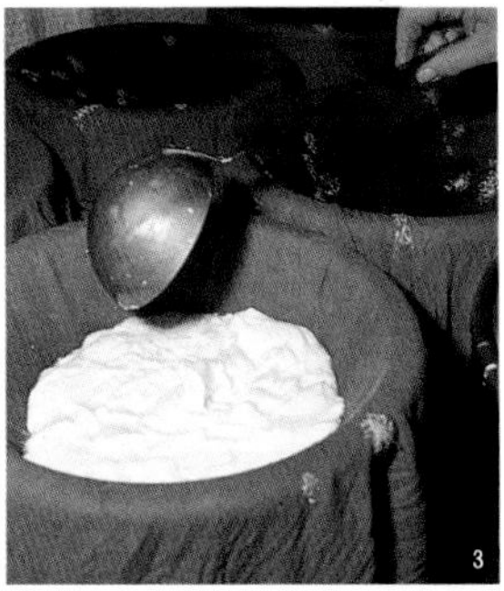


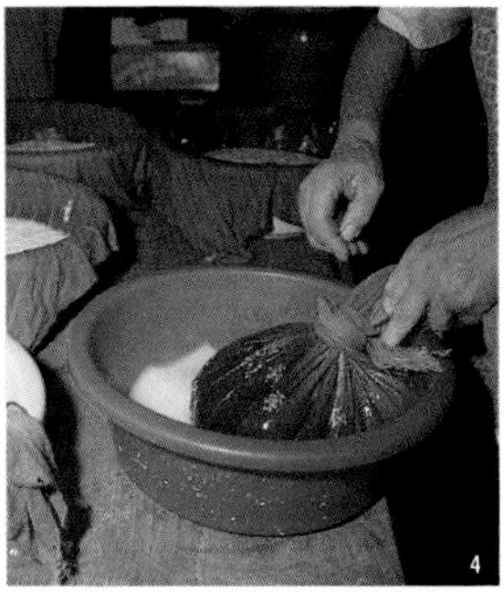


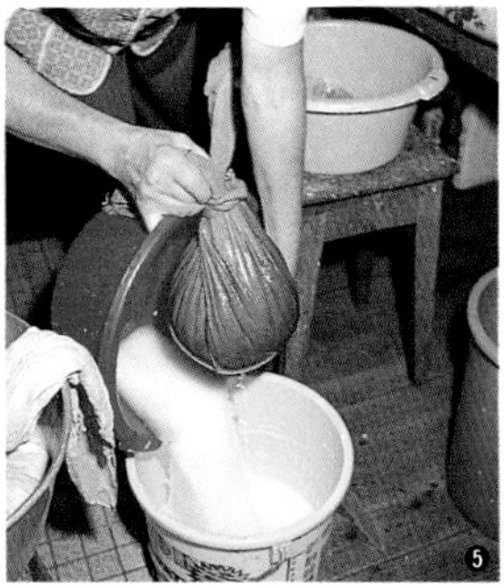


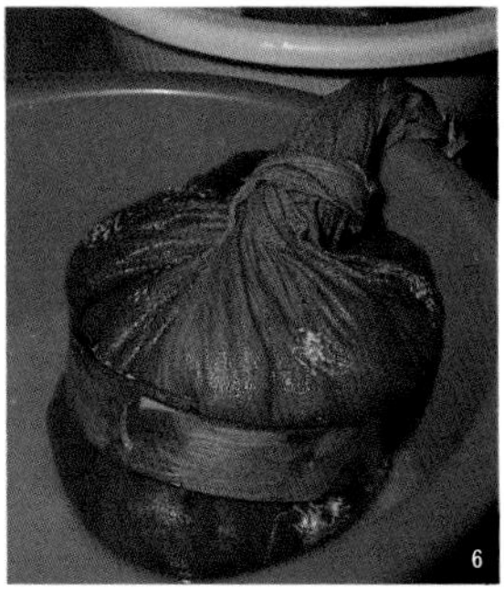


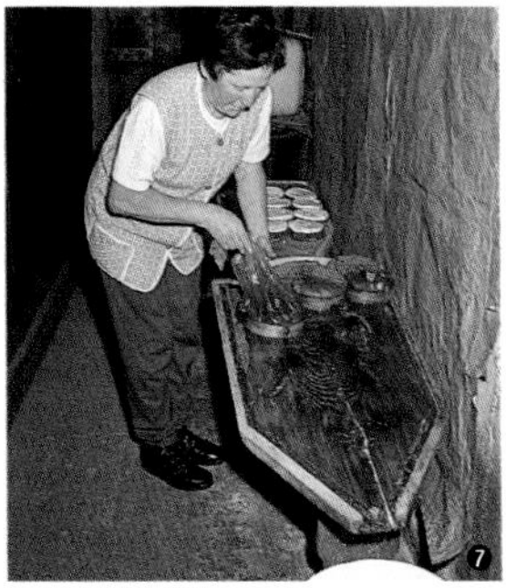


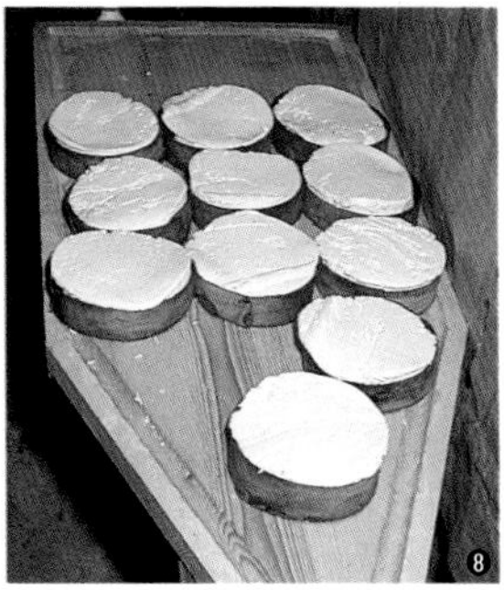


## How Vacherin d'Abondance is Made

Cheesemaker Célina Gagneux produces this cheese following traditional methods. The numbers below refer to the photographs.

**1.** At 6.30 a.m. the cows are milked and the milk is poured into a large copper bowl.
**2.** The rennet is mixed in with a ladle and coagulation begins. The mixture is left to rest for an hour at 12°C.
**3.** At 8 a.m. the curd is poured into 15 bowls lined with gauze.
**4.** The gauze is knotted around the curd to drain off the whey.
**5.** The whey is discarded and kept to extract the cream.
**6.** The balls of curd in cloth are bound with bands of spruce bark and left to rest for about three hours, then transferred to the draining board. At 3 p.m. drainage continues.
**7.** The cloth is removed.
**8.** The cheeses are laid on the draining board until the next morning. The whey continues to drain off while the cheeses remain sweet, light, and soft.

**9.** At 8 a.m. the following morning, the cheeses are moved to a cellar at a temperature of 12°C, and salted on one side only. After 48 hours, they are taken out of their bands, turned, and salted on the other side. The bands are put back and tightened as the cheeses ripen.

The cheeses are turned every morning for 15 to 20 days and the cloth covering the board is changed, leaving marks on the surfaces of the cheeses. About 15 to 20 days later, white mould appears on the surfaces. The rind is not yet formed, but a thin, creamy-white skin has appeared. The cheeses are ready for sale.

### The cheesemaking year

Célina Gagneux, who is the only person to produce this cheese in Abondance, learnt her technique from her mother-in-law soon after she got married over 30 years ago. Cheesemaking begins in December and goes on for 210 days of the year until July. With nine cows, which give 60 litres of milk every morning, she makes 15 cheeses. The evening milking is less productive and results in another 12 or 13 cheeses. Each cheese requires four litres of milk.

In July, the cows go up to the alpine pastures, where they join others in a herd of about 50. The summer milk is used to make the big Abondance cheeses (p. 120) in *chalets* in the mountains. The herdspeople and the cows return in early October and the cows calve. The female calves are kept and reared for three years before they themselves start to produce milk. Each cow can continue to produce milk for ten years.

ABONDANCE
The peaceful mountain town of Abondance lies on the river of the same name in the Alps close to the Swiss border.

## VACHERIN DES BAUGES

Two people make this *fermier* cheese in the Massif des Bauges in Savoie. According to a local cheesemaker, although it is generally better to allow the cheese to ripen fully, it can be eaten two weeks after the start of affinage, as long as it is wiped once every two days with water in which cream has been diluted. This is also done during the full affinage, which should ideally last a month. The cheese shown has been ripened for two weeks and includes patches of a bad grey mould that will impair the flavour.

🍷 Vin de Savoie, Arbois

*Soft, white pâte with a smell of spruce resin; uncooked, unpressed*

*Washed rind*

*Bad grey mould*

*Spruce band*

Rhône-Alpes (73)

Raw

ESSENTIAL FACTS
- ⊖ 21 cm diameter, 4–4.5 cm high
- ⚖ 1.4 kg in a band of spruce bark
- ⌷ Not defined
- ✔ Winter

---

## How to cut a cheese

The most important thing to bear in mind when cutting a cheese is to give everybody a chance to enjoy each part of the cheese, from the rind to the heart. The way a cheese is cut depends largely on its shape and size. The illustrations show typical cuts for some of the cheeses in this book.

**Valençay (p. 84)**          **Emmental (p. 132)**

**Camembert (p. 66)**          **Brie (p. 56)**          **Charolles (p. 92)**

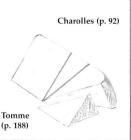

**Pont l'Évêque (p. 172)**     **Picodon (p. 170)**

**Epoisses (p. 133)**

**Tomme (p. 188)**

Band of hoop wood keeps cheese in shape and should not be removed, even when serving

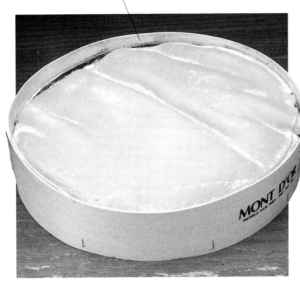

**Vacherin du Haut-Doubs as it is sold in wooden box**

Washed, wrinkled, yellow to light brown crust of natural mould

Soft, runny, white to ivory pâte; uncooked, very slightly pressed

# Vacherin du Haut-Doubs / Mont d'Or (AOC)

The Massif du Mont d'Or, which rises to a height of 1,463 m, lies near the French border with Switzerland. Although this winter cheese has been made on the French side for two centuries, for many years there was disagreement over its origins, with both the French and the Swiss maintaining that they were the first to make it. The controversy ended when the Swiss conceded to the French.

Mont d'Or is simply called Vacherin in the shops. It is sold and presented in a wooden box in which it continues to ripen. The cheese is bound by a band of spruce, the scent of which permeates the cheese and gives it a distinct and pleasant aroma. The spruce band also helps the cheese to keep its shape and should not be removed even when serving.

The surface of the cheese is moist and the rind golden and slightly reddish, with imprints of the cloth. The pale yellow pâte is creamy. It can be spread on bread or boiled potatoes.

The AOC permits both *artisanal* and *coopérative* production of this cheese. Affinage must take place within specified areas over three weeks at a maximum temperature of 15°C. After three weeks of ripening, the aroma of spruce is distinct. The cheese is cured on a board of spruce wood and turned and rubbed with a cloth soaked in brine.

❢ Beaujolais Nouveau, Côtes du Jura, ❢ Champagne

## Essential facts
- ◒ 12–30 cm diameter, 4–5 cm high
- ⚖ 500 g–1 kg in a band of spruce bark
- ⦂ 45 g min. per 100 g cheese
- Ꝺ 45% min., 20.25 g per 100 g cheese
- ✓ Best winter, autumn, and spring

Franche-Comté (25)

Raw

**Vacherin du Haut-Doubs
out of its wooden box**

*In the cheese shop, a piece
of marble is used to stop
the cheese from running*

## Winter cheesemaking

On the French side of the Massif du Mont d'Or, there are around 40 villages that lie above 800 m, spread from the source of the River Doubs to the Saut du Doubs. Between them they produce 1,700 tonnes of cheese every year. From 15 August until 31 March, milk from Montbéliard and Pie Rouge de l'Est cattle is gathered from farms in the mountains, and the cheese is made at the same 20 *fruitières* where Comté (p. 112) is produced in spring and summer. The AOC does not permit cows to be fed on silage or other fermented fodder, and the milk must be produced in the mountains at 700 m or higher.

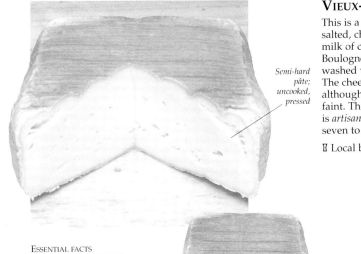

*Semi-hard pâte; uncooked, pressed*

*Washed, orange-red, moist rind*

## VIEUX-BOULOGNE

This is a new *pré-salé*, meaning pre-salted, cheese. It is made from the milk of cows raised by the sea near Boulogne. The rind, which is washed with beer, is moist and red. The cheese has a strong odour, although the smell of beer is quite faint. The pâte is elastic. Production is *artisanal*, with a long affinage of seven to nine weeks.

Ⅱ Local beer, Ⅴ Champagne

ESSENTIAL FACTS

◈ 11 cm square, 4 cm high
⚖ 300–500 g
🗓 45%
✓ All year

Nord-Pas-de-Calais (62)

Raw

---

## Processed cheese

Processed cheese was invented in around 1908 by the Swiss, who were looking for a way to use up surplus cheese. In 1911, it was made with Emmental and commercialized by the Swiss firm Gerber. At the same time, processed cheese was being developed in the United States.

The first European factory for the mass production of processed cheese was opened in 1917 in the Jura, France by the Graf brothers, and in 1921, the trademark for La Vache Qui Rit cheese was registered by Léon Bel. In 1953, a French decree laid down strict guidelines as to what exactly a processed

**BONJURA**
This is a type of canned processed cheese spread specially produced twice a year for the French Army. It keeps for a long time and is available in plain or ham flavour.

cheese should contain in terms of minimum fat and dry matter, and established a law, which was revised at the end of 1988.

Processed cheese has little to do with real cheese. One or several ripened cheeses are heated and mixed, then pasteurized at high temperature (130–140°C) after other dairy products, such as liquid or powdered milk, cream, butter, *casein*, whey, and seasoning, have been added. Processed cheese has the advantage of a long shelf life, although the flavour of the original cheeses alters during processing.

Some processed cheeses are made with several ripened cheeses of the same type, others with cheeses of different types. The most often used are Emmental and Cantal, but Saint-Paulin (p. 180) or Roquefort (p. 172) may be used to vary the taste. They are sometimes seasoned with pepper, herbs, ham, onions, mushrooms, or even seafood.

# Glossary

**AFFINAGE** The curing and maturing of cheeses.

**AFFINEUR** Specialist in the curing and maturing of cheeses.

**ALPAGE** Movement of animals and herdspeople high into the mountains for summer grazing.

**AOC** Appellation d'Origine Contrôlée. See p. 77

**À POINT** A cheese that is just at the right point of ripeness.

**ARTISANAL** Used to describe a cheese that is made by hand rather than by machine.

**BREBIS** The French word for a ewe, or a ewe's-milk cheese.

**BRINE** Very salty water.

**BRIQUE** A rectangular, brick-shaped cheese.

**BROUSSE** A cheese made from whey or skimmed milk.

**BÛCHE** A log-shaped cheese.

**BURON** A simple mountain dairy and cheese-store, with a sleeping space (Auvergne).

**CABANE** Mountain *chalet* where cheese is made in summer (Pyrénées and Corsica).

**CAILLÉ** Curd.

**CARRÉ** Adjective used to describe a square cheese.

**CASEIN** The main protein in milk, precipitated into curd by the use of **rennet**. It is used to make some edible cheese labels, which are embedded in the crust.

**CAUSSES** Limestone plateaux of the Massif Central.

**CAVE** Natural cave or cellar in which cheeses are ripened and stored until ready to eat.

**CENDRÉ** A cheese traditionally coated with ash from burned vine roots, but today usually covered with industrially powdered charcoal mixed with salt.

**CHEESE IRON** A small metal corer for removing a plug from the interior of a cheese to test aroma, flavour, and texture.

**CHÈVRE** A nanny goat, or a goat's-milk cheese.

**COAGULATION** The clotting of milk, usually by rennet.

**COMMUNE** The smallest unit of French local government.

**CURD** The coagulated fats and other solids produced from milk by natural ripening and renneting.

**DEPARTMENT** (French *département*) Modern administrative division of France, often disregarding old provincial boundaries.

**DRY MATTER** The remaining solids after all the water in a cheese has been eliminated.

**EAU-DE-VIE** Spirit, usually made from wine-pressings e.g. **marc**.

**FAT CONTENT** Degree of fatness of cheese, expressed as a percentage of fat in total **dry matter**.

**FERMIER** Adjective used to describe a farm-made cheese.

**FOURME** The old word for cheese derived from the form or mould in which it was made.

**FRAIS, FRAÎCHE** Fresh.

**FROMAGE** Cheese.

**FROMAGE BLANC** A fresh cheese that has been lightly drained.

**FROMAGE FORT** Strong preparation usually made in a pot from cheese leftovers with alcohol and herbs added.

**FROMAGE FRAIS** Cheese that has been salted, but sold unripened.

**FROMAGER** 1. Cheesemaker. 2. Wholesaler, or retailer of cheese.

**FROMAGERIE** Cheese-dairy. Also used by some cheese shops.

**GAEC** This stands for *Groupement Agricole pour l'Exploitation en Commun*, which is an agricultural association for common exploitation, that is a kind of cooperative.

**HALLE** Covered market.

**INDUSTRIEL** Indicates a large-scale, factory-style creamery with mechanized cheesemaking.

**LAIT** Milk.

**LAURIER** Bay leaf.

**MAÎTRE FROMAGER** Master cheesemaker, or cheese expert. Fewer than 100 are listed by the Guilde des Fromagers.

**MARC** Spirit made from distilled wine-pressings.

**MOELLEUX** Soft and velvety.

**MORGE Brine** enriched with scrapings from old cheeses, used to rub the surfaces of some cheeses during affinage.

**MOULD** 1. Wood, metal, or plastic container used in cheesemaking to shape the cheese. 2. Fungal species that form on the crust of cheeses or form veins within the pâte. Some moulds occur naturally, but many are artificially introduced.

**PÂTE** Everything that appears within the rind of a cheese.

**PAVÉ** A thick, square cheese, shaped like a paving stone.

**PAYS** Village, district, or province.

**PELLE** Round cutting-edged shovel used to handle curd (Brie).

**PERSILLÉ** Blue cheese.

**PETIT LAIT** Whey.

**RENNET** The enzyme derived from the fourth stomach of a calf or goat, used in cheesemaking to break down the solids in milk into digestible form, helping coagulation. Some plants can have the same effect as rennet.

**TOME, TOMME** 1. Small, round goat's-milk cheeses. 2. Larger pressed cheese of all types of milk.

**TRANSHUMANCE** The movement of flocks or herds from winter pasture or stabling to high mountain pastures in summer.

**VACHE** A cow, or a cheese that has been made with cow's-milk.

**WHEY** Residue of milk after most of the fats and other solids have been coagulated into the curd.

**VDN** *Vin doux naturel* – a naturally sparkling white wine.

# List of contributors
The authors wish to thank the following producers and *fromagers*

**ABBAYE DE LA JOIE NOTRE-DAME, 56800 Campénéac.**
The nuns at this convent produce chocolate as well as cheese.

**MME CAZAUX, 65250 La Barthe-de-Neste.**
Based in the region noted for Pyrenean cow's-milk cheeses, Mme Cazaux has a stall at the morning market.

**PIERRE ANDROUËT**
Formerly head of the Androuët cheese shop in Paris, M. Androuët is the author of several books, including *Le Brie*, *Le Livre d'Or du Fromage*, and *Le Guide du Fromage*.

**GILBERT CHEMIN**
**Crémerie du Couserans, 3 rue de la République, 09200 Saint-Girons.**
M. Chemin has a shop in the town, but also runs a mobile service to local villages.

**ROLAND BARTHELEMY**
**51 rue de Grenelle, 75007 Paris.**
One of the best young *fromagers* in Paris, M. Barthelemy supplies cheese to the Elysées Palace.

**EDOUARD CENERI**
**La Ferme Savoyarde, 22 rue Meynadier, 06400 Cannes.**
Known for his brie with truffles, M. Ceneri owns several ripening cellars.

**J. BLANC**
**Crémerie des Halles, 64500 St-Jean-de-Luz.**
With his daughter, M. Blanc runs a shop in the town market.

**BRIGITTE CORDIER AND FRANÇOISE FLEUTOT, 04230 Montlaux.**
These *fromagers* have successfully revived a legendary and once extinct *Tomme d'Arles*.

**DANIEL BOUJON, 7 rue Saint-Sébastien, 74200 Thonon-les-Bains.**
This second-generation *fromager* has saved the *Vacherin d'Abondance* from extinction.

**JACQUES AND JACQUELINE COULAUD, 24 rue Grenouillit, 43000 Le Puy.**
From their shop on the eastern edge of Auvergne, M. and Mme Coulaud offer a wide range of local cheeses.

**XAVIER BOURGON, XAVIER, 6 Place Victor-Hugo, 31000 Toulouse.**
M. Bourgon is the owner of *Xavier*, a high-class cheese shop that has become an institution in Toulouse.

**M. AND MME CLAUDE DUPIN, 41 rue Gambetta, 64500 Saint-Jean-de-Luz.**
The Dupin's shop on the Spanish border has an excellent selection of Basque cheeses.

**MICHEL BOURGUE, La Maison du Fromage, Les Halles Centrales, 84000 Avignon.**
This third-generation *fromager* sells an unforgettable *Brousse du Rove*.

**HENRI GRILLET, Crémerie du Gravier, 22 Cours Monthyon, 15000 Aurillac.**
M. Grillet runs his shop in the region of *Saint Nectaire*, *Cantal*, and *Salers* cheeses.

**M. AND MME CANTIN, 12 rue du Champ-de-Mars, 75007 Paris.**
A second-generation *fromager*, Mme Cantin is the founder of the Association Respect Traditionnel Fromage Français (ARTFF).

**M. AND MME JACQUES GUERIN, La Fromagerie, 18 rue Saint-Jean 79000 Niort.**
The Guerin's distinctive affinage produces unforgettable *Chabichous* and *Mothais*.

**Raymond Lecomte / Odette Jenny, 76 rue Saint-Louis-en-l'Ile, 75004 Paris.**
Although both owners have retired the shop is still open.

**A. Penen and family, Préchacq-Navarrenx, 64190 Navarrenx.**
These *fromagers* offer a unique cheese from their farm in Navarrenx.

**M. and Mme Jean-Pierre Le Lous, Marché des Grands-Hommes, 33000 Bordeaux.**
These *fromagers* can be found at the morning market in Bordeaux.

**Denis Provent, Laiterie des Halles, 2 Place de Genève, 73000 Chambéry.**
With his knowledge of the mountains, M. Provent, a third-generation *fromager,* travels on foot to small mountain villages.

**Michel Lepage, Conseils-Assistance-Fromagers, 3 Les Prés Claux, 04700 Oraison.**
M. Lepage advises on cheesemaking and also participates in reviving extinct cheeses.

**Jacques Vernier, La Fromagerie Boursault, 71 avenue du Général Leclerc, 75014 Paris.**
M. Vernier is well known in Paris for his excellent Beaufort.

**Gérard Loup and family, Les Provins, 04700 Puimichel.**
Preferring to make cheese rather than live in the city, M. Loup and his family left Paris to become *fromagers* in the country.

**Henry Voy, La Ferme Saint-Hubert 21 rue Vignon, 75008 Paris.**
M. Voy owns a restaurant adjoining his shop that specializes in cheese dishes.

**M. and Mme Marius Manetti, Col de San-Bastiano, 20111 Calcatoggio.**
M. Manetti is a member of the Chambre d'Agriculture Corse du Sud (Corsican Agricultural Chamber).

**François Durand, La Heronnière, 61120 Camembert.**
M. Durand, a second-generation *fromager,* is one of only two producers of Camembert *fermier.*

**Alain Martinet, Halle de Lyon, 102 Cours Lafayette, 69003 Lyon.**
This young *fromager* runs a stall in Lyon market, where *fromagers,* Mme. Richard and Mme. Maréchal can also be found.

**Jean-Pierre Moreau, Elevage Caprin de Bellevue 41400 Pontlevoy.**
M. Moreau is an expert producer of goat's-milk cheese. His Selles-sur-Cher is excellent.

**Philippe Olivier, 43-45 rue Thiers, 62200 Boulogne-sur-Mer.**
One of the best young *fromagers* in France, M. Olivier belongs to the "short affinage" generation of cheesemakers.

**Jean-Martin and Margot Kempf, 155 Ferme du Saesserlé, 68380 Breitenbach.**
The Kempfs produce and sell a very popular Munster cheese, which is matured in their own cellar.

**B. Antony,** 17 rue de la Montagne, 68480 Vieux Ferrette.
**R. Bousquet,** Halles Centrales, 11000 Carcassonne.
**Le Cagibi,** 17 allée d'Etigny, 31110 Luchon.
**Marechal,** Halle de Lyon, 102 Cours Lafayette, 69003 Lyon.
**E. Millat,** Halle Brauhauban, 65000 Tarbes.

**G. Paul,** 9 rue des Marseillais, 13100 Aix-en-Provence.
**Rfné and Renée Richard,** Halle de Lyon, 102 Cours Lafayette, 69003 Lyon.
**Batut** 22 rue Vieille-du-temple, 75004 Paris.
**Le Calendos,** 11 rue Colbert, 37000 Tours.
**Fromageries Bel,** 4 rue d'Anjou, 75008 Paris .

# List of producers, shops, and markets

The following numbered list of producers, shops, and markets works in conjunction with the index on pages 236–239.

Each cheese in the index is followed by a number in brackets and a page reference. The number in brackets refers to the number beside each producer, shop, and market listed here, and shows where the cheese was bought. The list, which is organized by region, (see map on p. 16–17) also serves as a quick-reference guide as to where good cheeses can be bought in France.

**ALSACE**
**1.** Margot and Jean-Martin Kempf, 155 Ferme du Saesserlé, 68380 **Breitenbach.**

**AQUITAINE**
**2.** A.–M. Garat, Halles de Biarritz, 64200 **Biarritz.**

**3.** Jean-Pierre Le Lous, Marché des Grands-Hommes, 33000 **Bordeaux.**

**4.** Daniel Casau, 6 rue de Bordeu, 64260 **Izeste.**

**5.** Etablissement Canonge, 64440 **Laruns.**

**6.** A. Penen, Préchacq-Navarrenx, 64190 **Navarrenx.**

**7.** Chez Roger, Halles de Pau, 64000 **Pau.**

**8.** J. Blanc, Crémerie des Halles, 64500 **Saint-Jean-de-Luz.**

**9.** Claude Dupin, 41 rue Gambetta, 64500 **Saint-Jean-de-Luz.**

**AUVERGNE**
**10.** Henri Grillet, Crémerie du Gravier, 22, Cours Monthyon, 15000 **Aurillac.**

**11.** Fromageries Morin, Bvd Pavatou, 15000 **Aurillac.**

**12.** La Maison du Bon Fromage, Marché Saint-Pierre, 63000 **Clermont-Ferrand.**

**13.** Marché d'**Egliseneuve d'Entraigues** (cheese stall).

**14.** Jacques Coulaud, 24 rue Grenouillit, 43000 **Le Puy.**

**15.** G.A.E.C. Louvradou, Margorce, 15140 **Saint-Rémy-de-Salers.**

**BOURGOGNE**
**16.** Tast Fromages, 23 rue Carnot, 21200 **Beaune.**

**17.** Marché de **Dijon** (cheese stall).

**CENTRE**
**18.** Halles Châtelet, 45000 **Orléans.**

**19.** Elevage Caprin de Bellevue, 41400 **Pontlevoy.**

**20.** Marché de **Sainte-Maure.**

**21.** Le Calendos, 11 rue Colbert, 37000 **Tours.**

**CORSE**
**22.** Marché d'**Ajaccio** (cheese stall).

**23.** Marché de **Bastia** (cheese stall).

**24.** Super Viva, 20224 **Calacuccia.**

**25.** Marius Manenti, Col de San Bastiano, 20111 **Calcatoggio.**

**26.** Auberge Chez Jacqueline, Pont-de-Castirla, **Corte.**

**27.** Domaine de Porette, 20250 **Corte.**

**28.** Coopérative A Pecurella, Route d'Afa, Appietto, 20167 **Mezavia.**

**29.** Paul Cianfarani (cheesemaker), 20190 **Sainte-Marie-Sicché.**

**30.** Supermarché Tomy, **Sartène.**

**ÎLE-DE-FRANCE AND PARIS**
**31.** Ferme Jehan de Brie, 15 Place du Marché, 77120 **Coulommiers.**

**32.** Ganot, Marché de **Meaux** (cheese stall).

**33.** Jacky Boussion, 8 rue Carnot, 77000 **Melun.**

**34.** Alleosse, 13 rue Poncelet, 75017 **Paris.**

**35.** Androuët, 41 rue d'Amsterdam, 75008 **Paris.**

**36.** Restaurant Ambassade d'Auvergne, 22 rue du Grenier Saint-Lazare, 75003 **Paris.**

**37.** Roland Barthélemy, 51 rue de Grenelle, 75007 **Paris.**

**38.** Batut, 22 rue Vieille-du-Temple, 75004 **Paris.**

**39.** Gisèle Cantin, 2 rue de Lourmel, 75015 **Paris.**

**40.** Marie-Anne Cantin, 12 rue du Champ-de-Mars, 75007 **Paris.**

**41.** Jean Carmès et fils, 24 rue de Lévis, 75017 **Paris.**

**42.** A. Dubois, 79 rue de Courcelles, 75017 **Paris.**

**43.** La Ferme Saint-Aubin, 76 rue Saint-Louis-en-l'Ile, 75004 **Paris.**

**44.** Fromagerie de Montmartre, 9 rue du Poteau, 75018 **Paris.**

45. Lecomte,
76 rue Saint-Louis-en-l'Ile,
75004 **Paris.**

46. La Maison du Bon Fromage,
35 rue du Marché Saint-Honoré,
75001 **Paris.**

47. Jacques Vernier,
La Fromagerie Boursault,
71 avenue du Général Leclerc,
75014 **Paris.**

48. Henry Voy,
La Ferme Saint-Hubert,
21 rue Vignon, 75008 **Paris.**

49. La Ferme (shop),
Société Brie le Provins (maker),
77160 **Provins.**

50 Société fromagère de la Brie,
19 Avénue du Grand Morin,
77169 **Saint-Siméon.**

**LANGUEDOC-ROUSSILLON**
51. R. Bousquet,
Halles Centrales,
11000 **Carcassonne.**

52. Fromagerie du Buron,
Le Polygone, Niveau Bas,
**Montpellier.**

**LORRAINE**
53. Marché d'**Epinal** (cheese stall).

54. Ferme Marchal,
La Chapelle des Vés,
88160 **Le Thillot.**

**MIDI-PYRÉNÉES**
55. Marché de Bagnères-de-Bigorre
(cheese stall),
65200 **Bagnères-de-Bigorre.**

56. Le Cagibi,
17 allée d'Etigny, 31110 **Luchon.**

57. G.A.E.C. de Poubeau,
31110 **Luchon.**

58. Fromagerie à Millau,
**Millau.**

59. Marché de Mirande,
32300 **Mirande** (cheese stall).

60. Marché de Montesquieu-
Volvestre (cheese stall),
31310 **Montesquieu-Volvestre.**

61. Marché de Montréjeau (cheese
stall), 31210 **Montréjeau.**

62. Fête des Fromages,
46500 **Rocamadour.**

63. Gabriel Coulet,
Le Papillon, Société des Caves,
12250 **Roquefort-sur-Soulzon.**

64. Cap del Mail,
Cierp-Gaud,
31440 **Saint-Béat.**

65. Gilbert Chemin,
Crémerie du Couserans,
3 rue de la République,
09200 **Saint-Girons.**

66. E. Millat,
Halle Brauhauban,
65000 **Tarbes.**

67. Xavier Bourgon,
6 Place Victor-Hugo,
31000 **Toulouse.**

**NORD-PAS-DE-CALAIS**
68. Marché d'**Arras** (cheese stall).

69. Philippe Olivier,
43-45 rue Thiers,
62200 **Boulogne-sur-Mer.**

70. Cave de l'Abbaye de Maroilles,
59550 **Maroilles.**

**NORMANDIE (HAUTE-)**
71. Marché de Rouen (cheese stall),
76000 **Rouen.**

**POITOU-CHARENTES**
72. Jacques Guérin,
La Fromagerie,
19 rue Saint-Jean,
79000 **Niort.**

**PROVENCE-ALPES-CÔTE-D'AZUR**
73. Gérard Paul,
9 rue des Marseillais,
13100 **Aix-en-Provence.**

74. Restaurant de Puyfond,
Lieu-dit-Rigoulon,
13100 **Aix-en-Provence.**

75. Michel Bourgue,
La Maison du Fromage,
Halles Centrales,
84000 **Avignon.**

76. Halles Centrales, **Avignon**
(cheese stall).

77. Fromagerie Ranc,
40 rue Bonneterie,
84000 **Avignon.**

78. Edouard Ceneri,
La Ferme Savoyarde,
22 rue Meynadier,
06400 **Cannes.**

79. Le Fromagerie,
5 rue de l'Oratoire,
06130 **Grasse.**

80. Laiterie du Col Bayard,
Laye,
05500 **St-Bonnet-en-Champsaur.**

81. Bataille,
18 rue Fontange,
13006 **Marseille.**

82. Brigitte Cordier
& Françoise Fleutot,
04230 **Montlaux.**

83. Gérard Loup,
Les Provins,
04700 **Puimichel.**

**RHÔNE-ALPES**
84. Raymond Gagneux,
Sur le Cret, Richebourg,
74360 **Abondance.**

85. Denis Provent,
Laiterie des Halles,
2 Place de Genève,
73000 **Chambéry.**

86. Maréchal,
Halle de Lyon,
102 Cours Lafayette,
69003 **Lyon.**

87. Alain Martinet,
Halles de Lyon,
102 Cours Lafayette,
69003 **Lyon.**

88. Renée & René Richard,
Halles de Lyon,
102 Cours Lafayette,
69003 **Lyon.**

89. Daniel Boujon,
7 rue Saint-Sébastien,
74200 **Thonon-les-Bains.**

# Index

# Bibliography

Androuët, Pierre, *Guide du Fromage*, Stock, Paris, 1971 (in French). English translation, Aidan Ellis, 1973; 2nd edition, Aidan Ellis, 1977; revised 1983.

Androuët, Pierre, *Le Livre d'Or du Fromage*, Atlas, Paris 1984

Androuët, Pierre, and Chabot, Yves, *Le Brie*, Presses du Village, Etrepillat, 1985

*Annuaire des Industries Laitières*, Comindus, Paris, 1991

*Atlas Routier France*, Michelin, London, 1989

Bon, Colette, *Les Fromages*, Hachette, Paris, 1979

Cart-Tanneur, Philippe, *Fromages et Vins de France*, Trame Way, Paris, 1989

Charron, G. *Les Productions Laitières*

Chast, Michel, and Voy, Henry, *Le Livre de l'Amateur de Fromages*, Robert Laffont, Paris, 1984

Clozier, René, *Géographie de la France*, Collection "Que sais-je?" Presses Universitaires de France, Paris, 1970

Courtine, Robert J., *Grand Livre de la France à Table*, Bordas, Paris, 1982

Courtine, Robert J., *Larousse des Fromages*, Librairie Larousse, Paris, 1987

Eck, André, *Fromages,* Technique et Documentation (Lavoisier), Paris, 1987

Evette, Jean-Luc, *La Fromagerie*, Presses Universitaires de France, Paris, 1975

Foubert, Jean-Marie, *Guide de la Route du Fromage*, Charles Corlet, Condé-sur-Noireu, 1987

Girard, Sylvie, *Fromages,* Editions Hermé, Paris, 1986

Le Jaouen, Jean-Claude, *La Fabrication du Fromage de Chèvre Fermier*, Itovic, Paris, 1982

*Journal Officiel de la République Française*

Le Liboux, Jean-Luc, *Nouveau Guide des Fromages de France*, Ouest-France, Rennes, 1984

*Michelin Guide de Tourisme*, Michelin, Paris

Montagne, Prosper, and Gottschalk, Docteur, *Larousse Gastronomique*, Librairie Larousse, Paris, 1938

*Petit Robert* (I, II), Dictionnaires Le Robert, Paris, 1989

Rance, Patrick, *The French Cheese Book*, Macmillan, London, 1989

Roc, Jean-Claude, *Le Buron de la Croix Blanche*, Editions Watel, Brioude, 1989

Stobbs, William, *Guide to the Cheeses of France*, Apple Press, London, 1984

Viard, Henry, *Fromages de France*, Dargaud, Paris, 1980

# Acknowledgments

**The authors would like to thank the following for their help in the preparation of this book:**

Snow Brand Milk Products Co. Ltd.;
Chesco., Ltd.;
Cheese & Wine Academy, Tokyo;
Maison du Fromage, Valençay;
Fermier S. A;
SOPEXA, Japon;
Katsunori Kobayashi; Yohko Namioka;
Katsushi Kitamura;
Syndicat de Fromages d'Appellation d'Origine;
Institut National des Appellations d'Origine;
Association Nationale des Appellations d'Origine Laitières Françaises;
Association Marque Collective Savoie;
I.N.R.A. (Corte) E. Casalta /I.N.R.A. (Aurillac);
Chambre d'Agriculture;
La Société Fromagère de la Brie;
Société des Caves et des Producteurs Réunis de Roquefort;
INSEE / SOPEXA;

Centre Interprofessionnel de Documentation et d'Information Laitières;
Coopérative A. Pecurella;
A. Franceschi, A. Vinciguerra, J.-E. La-Noir, Crédit Agricole, Corsica;
T. Basset, Paris / D. Pin, Rungis;
Collette and Catherine Faller, Domaine Weinbach;
GAEC Louvradou, Margorce, 15140 Saint-Rémy-de Salers;
Fromageries Manhés, Bvd. Pavatou, 15000 Aurillac;
BATUT, 22 rue Vieille-du-Temple, 75004 Paris;
François Durand, Heronnière, 61120 Camembert (p. 64–65);
Coopérative de Lullin, 74470 Bellevaux (p. 21, 195).

**Special thanks are extended to:**
Kikuko Inoue, Takayoshi Nakasone,
Kozue Tarumi, andReiko Mori.

**PAGE*One*** wishes to thank
Matthew Cook for design assistance;
Neil Kelly for DTP assistance.